First published in Grea
by Jay F Kay P

Deep Productions Ltd
34B Whitton Road
Hounslow
London
TW3 2DA

British Library Cataloguing-in
Publication Data
A catalogue record for this book is
Available from the British Library

ISBN 978-0956848918

Written by David Cann - edited by Sharon Mackellar

Contents

Foreword

Have you ever read a book or watched a programme that has captured your imagination like nothing before? Well that is exactly what happened to me in May 2011. A BBC documentary from 2010, *'Madness in the Fast Lane'*, came to my attention; it told the bizarre and truly mysterious story of Sabina and Ursula Eriksson. The Swedish twins ran on to the M6 motorway near Stoke-on-Trent and despite being hit by traffic, both twins survived. Sabina not only lived to tell the tale but tried to escape the scene, requiring six people to restrain her.

The intrigue continued as she received a startlingly short sentence, allowing her the freedom to "kill" a local man, Glenn Hollinshead, only three days later. From start to finish there were so many twists and turns it made most best sellers or TV dramas look like a children's story. To use the popular phrase 'you couldn't make it up.'

Determined to delve into this story further, I spent many days researching the incident and contacting other people who had worked on this. This is how I met David Cann. David had made progress on matters that I was about to pick up on, in fact his delving was so close to my own views that I knew I had to talk with him. After a number of long conversations we decided to join forces and work on this story; David as an author and myself on an investigative documentary.

David has what most of us would call a colourful past; but to me his work was meticulous and painstaking. His previous knowledge of criminal activities has also proved hugely beneficial in understanding aspects and workings of this case. His work on this case would be called obsessional by some, but take my word, that no matter what your views are on anything you may read here, do not doubt that David has examined and analysed this work to its limits.

In this book you will find analysis on the twins' backgrounds, their movements on the day, possible reasons how they could have ended up in this situation, further details on the incident, the anomalies in the justice process and two never heard before revelations which will PROVE this case hides much darker secrets, and was not simply the story that has been told so far.

All work has been undertaken with full support from the Hollinshead family. They have reopened old wounds to try and get an answer as to why they lost a much loved family member. This backing is a huge testament to David as it is the strength of his work that convinced them to get involved with us.

I speak for both David and I, by saying that whilst both of us were intrigued by this case, the injustice this family have received has always been a driving force.

Do we expect you to agree with everything we have said? No. Some ideas are our theories, but throughout this book you will find facts and figures to back all our ideas. After reading this book, I am convinced you will agree that sometimes things are not quite as they seem.

Sharon Mackellar.

A Cause for Concern

Following the murder of my brother Glenn Hollinshead, and the mysterious events that surround his demise, I would like to highlight a few things that concern me a great deal. I had a strange 'gut feeling' from my initial contact with the police to the end of the court case when Sabina Eriksson was imprisoned, that something was not quite right. This is from my perspective, an understatement. Hindsight is a wonderful thing and had I known at that time what I have since learnt [and what this book reveals], I would have been far more insistent that the police answer my questions at that time in a more concise and truthful way.

At all times it seemed to me that the police were to close rank. The word *evasive* is the easiest way to describe their whole demeanour. My experience with the Family Liaison Officer appointed to our family, was cold. He seemed very uneasy whenever the 'official' explanations he offered were questioned further and he was not going to deviate from his script. He was it seemed to me, uneasy when questioned about the logic of the police actions taken from the onset, starting from St Anne Police Station in Liverpool and their subsequent discovery on the M6 motorway.

The court trial of Sabina seemed equally staged. It seems that it was a foregone conclusion that it would not involve a jury, a fact that the police seems relieved about. That 'gut feeling' remains even to this day, as the family remained suspicious about the whole event, it seemed so staged. As a family, we had always thought that there must be more to the whole tragic affair that was portrayed by the circus of an investigation and consequent conviction of Sabina. Our family spent months

3

discussing the convenience of Sabina's medical condition, and the fact that we didn't get the closure we richly deserved from the British justice system.

Several months went by, when out of the blue I was contacted by David, whom was it seems was performing his own investigation into the affairs and actions of the Eriksson twins and it was no coincidence that our suspicions about the 'modus operandi' of the police in particular, was suspicious to both of us.

To say that I was delighted that the family were not alone in our thoughts came as a great relief. It wasn't just us, other people thought the same, and they had their own views and ideas as to what seems to be an obvious 'cover up'. As time progressed my brother Garry and I met up with David and Sharon in Staffordshire. By comparing notes at that time and subsequent months, we have it seems developed a completely different perspective about what we were told and what really is the true story behind the Eriksson twins.

Yes, there are grey areas that may never see the light of day, but from what we have all achieved together and the material gathered by David and Sharon, it seems a logical thing for us to conclude that the rabbit hole goes far deeper than we were led to believe by the police, the hospital and the lawyers. It seems therefore that the whole Eriksson investigation has been a tissue of lies, cover ups and deceit from the start. I feel more than justified now than ever, for thinking and believing that there really is more to the events and lives of the Eriksson twins than 7 million TV viewers were led to believe by the authorities and the media.

In conclusion, I'd like to say that without the help from David, Sharon, and their team - my family would have rolled over and accepted the outcome and got on with our lives. However, considering the evidence uncovered and learning more facts along the way, we now feel that we owe it to Glenn to take legal action and redress what is obviously a 'cover up' by all those involved including the police, the legal system and the health services from the start to the end.

Our thanks go to David and Sharon, since without them the truth would have remained hidden, even though it seems farfetched and incredulous.

It seems that the system is stacked against justice for all. But that is nothing new in Britain. Make of this fascinating book what you will, but bear in mind that it could happen to your family. The public demand fair treatment and justice for all.

Jon Hollinshead - 23rd September 2012.

We would like to offer our special thanks to: The Hollinshead family, Frank Booth, Peter Molloy and Melissa Dutton. And for the ongoing assistance the Staffordshire and Merseyside police forces, the Independent Police Complaints Commission, Stoke-on-Trent Coroner's Office and the University Hospital of North Staffordshire and all the other governmental departments we have contacted and who are still working on and addressing this matter, - we too offer our thanks.

The authors and Mackellar families and friends and all those who have helped in research and by giving their time, – you know who you are.

Introduction

On an ordinary day in May 2008, and completely out of the blue, *News Rooms* from around the globe relayed the shocking and disturbing images of two Swedish twin sisters on a UK motorway; as one threw herself under the wheels of a speeding articulated lorry and the other running directly into the path of a hurtling silver VW car.

I had been writing about another subject at the time and just happened to look up at my TV set to see the latest news headlines. My eyes soon became transfixed on the screen as my brain tried to register and workout what was being asked of it. It was almost like the time when the footage of a second aircraft was seen crashing and exploding into one of New York's Twin Towers on 9/11, back in 2001. I had to question myself – was this fictitious or real?

My stomach turned as soon as I realised what I was watching was genuine and real as I witnessed one of the twin sisters being churned by the wheels of this 40 ton truck, whilst the other was thrown into the air like a ragdoll.

I understood their injuries would have been horrific, and the one hit by the truck, I assumed must have certainly died. When to everyone's amazement this very same woman, Ursula Eriksson, soon recovered and started to scream obscenities at those trying to help her and her twin sister Sabina, - who too by now had regained consciousness and wanted to fight those wishing to assist her.

Though that was it, the news item ended and I heard no more on the matter.

Then as part of the BBC's *Motorway Cops* series, (also known as *Traffic Cops*), it was Mentorn Productions who first captured this extremely disturbing and shocking - yet remarkable film footage of the Eriksson twins sacrificially lunging themselves into the fast lane of the M6 motorway.

It was first shown on the 25th September 2008, titled; *Dicing with Death*. Then apart from this incredible footage, this was just part of an even more beyond belief story which couldn't be told at the time for legal reasons - and why for almost two years it laid in wait for the outcome of a court case that took over 16 months to conclude.

For what was to be the consequence of these sister's actions was an even more bizarre and spine chilling story of what was to take place over the next 72 hours, that left one of the sisters, Sabina, having an alleged chance encounter with two men she had just met in the street, then going back with them to one of the men's homes - when hours later she had been seen fleeing the murder scene where 54 year old Glenn Hollinshead had been stabbed to death.

This was then followed-up with another death defying act by Sabina as she jumped off a 25ft/30ft bridge-way and onto the A50 carriageway below in what appears to be another bid to kill herself, - and again in which she also remarkably survives. Sometime after this, she was charged with his murder.

Our own investigations have amazingly uncovered evidence that indicates the possibilities that more than one person was involved in the murder of Mr Hollinshead, and if this is the case, which we're convinced it was, then it suggests this person/s are still at large.

The evidence uncovered in this book has led the Hollinshead family contacting the Independent Police Complaints Commission (IPCC) and the Staffordshire Police force asking them to reinvestigate this case. In addition legal action is to be taken against various authoritative bodies and an inquiry is to be called for in the House of Commons.

The BBC's *Madness in the Fast Lane* documentary first aired on 10th August 2010, in which one preview that appeared on that same day in *The Guardian* newspaper, read: *'On no account miss this documentary. It opens with what is perhaps the most extraordinary footage I've ever seen on TV.'*

It was this programme that exposed that Sabina had been discharged from hospital just five hours after the M6 incident and whilst her twin Ursula was still being operated on in intensive care. Unfortunately, the film incorrectly portrays what happened in the previous hours and before their cameras were able to capture what occurred on the M6 motorway, and even then that account is not entirely accurate. Nevertheless, when it was first shown on BBC1 nearly 7 million viewers were glued to their TV screens. Since then a conservative estimate of around a further 20 million people have watched these films via the internet and on websites such as *YouTube* and worldwide.

Due to other commitments I ironically never saw either of these programmes, until February 2012 and when straight away I knew something major was amiss. When I say this I'm not really referring to the actual actions of these two sisters. I was more looking into what else had probably happened as the "official storyline" didn't ring true. Some of the people and witnesses involved in the documentary were far from convincing that they were telling the truth, though I couldn't quite put my finger on what was causing my unease.

There appeared to be too many inconsistencies and the accounts of what was alleged to have occurred were so contradictory that is was obvious something key was missing here. Through my own life experiences, I could quite clearly see that these two sisters seemed to have been treated beyond all exceptions. What I mean by this is that under "normal" circumstances, say had it been you or I in the place of these twins, then I can assure you we would've been treated completely differently.

So it was for these reasons alone I suspected and could see there was indeed something wrong, yet I didn't expect to find an even more sinister side to this story - and what I shall now reveal to you.

It wasn't until early 2012 that I first wrote about the Eriksson twins in various blogs, - though at the time little did I realise what I was soon to discover. I could instantly see there was a collective interest in the case as my blogs received thousands of hits straight away and many people contacted me in relation to them. Though there was one person in particular who seemed more determined and knowledgeable about the subject and demonstrated wanting to take further action in helping me investigate the matter, - that in a sense this is why we joined forces and Deep Productions was then formed by Sharon Mackellar and I.

It must be said, considering we were complete strangers not long ago, we didn't know how each other would go about our separate tasks. From the very beginning Sharon has been extremely tenacious in her work. She crucially and critically proofread and looked out for anything that could lead to legal repercussions over a course of eight drafts. Her editing skills have been a great asset. If she disagreed with my findings, which at times was the case, she would cross-out what I'd written and offer an alternative suggestion. She also spent relentless hours working on the Eriksson file, which led on to her investigating all the leads that were connected to them in the USA, Ireland, Norway and Sweden. Much of what doesn't appear in the book for we were unable to include them for either legal or ethical reasons or they ended proving negative or irrelevant, though you're not going to know that until you've investigated it.

She too, has written to, spoken to and interviewed many individuals and organisations connected to our investigation. Without her drive and enthusiasm in wanting to expose the truth and her love for journalism in general, then it's quite possible I would have never even written this book, so for this alone, I thank her.

We seem to agree that many of the things being presented to us, - certainly didn't add up and why we decided to revisit the original places and see the same people and eye witnesses who first appeared in the BBC *Madness in the Fast Lane* film in order to try and help set the record straight after our repeated requests to both the BBC and Mentorn Productions - to make a follow-up programme - were completely ignored.

Perhaps what we've been able to unearth is an indicator as to why they decided to pay no heed to us in the first place. These two sisters were in fact arrested under a 'special clause' in the 1983 Mental Health Act. Yet incredibly this vital piece of evidence was then

10

covered-up. It has never been seen or heard about by the millions of people who watched the film footage or know about this case. And it is here - for the very first time you'll be able to read and learn about what truly happened that fateful day on the M6 motorway and beyond.

Not only will we explain what really occurred, we'll provide the verbatim description of events by the witnesses and police officers involved, alongside a Youtube link where you can see for yourself this damning evidence and what should have been previously shown to all concerned, - especially the Hollinshead family - and arguably Sabina Eriksson herself.

In addition and equally as shocking and has never been exposed until now - is that there appears to have been a series of 'green lights' given to the Eriksson twins in the guise of a catalogue of errors.

Glenn's brother, Jon Hollinshead, points out and questions; *"Why were the sister's visit to St Anne Street police station in Liverpool, not mentioned in the BBC documentaries?"*

We have recently uncovered fresh evidence that answers and explains why this was the case - in which is revealed further on. I would like to explain in advance and ask you to excuse what may appear as repetition and dragging out what it is we wish to reveal, though due to the seriousness of this matter - we want to make sure the reader fully understands the injustice and cover-up that has taken place in this case and therefore at times it is unavoidable not to repeat what's already been said and as and when new evidence presented.

We've scrutinised what appears to have taken place surrounding these events of where and when the "green

11

lights" seem to have been given. We've re-examined the official timings of when the twins were allegedly meant to have left Ireland for the UK etc., for our own findings seem to totally contradict such a journey ever taking place on the actual day in question.

We further suspect that these twin sisters had been involved in criminal activities and had been under police surveillance for some time and prior to this senseless incident being caught on camera and the killing of Glenn Hollinshead being brought to the public's attention.

So following all this, it was among these reasons why I decided to write; *A Madness Shared by Two...* - alongside helping Sharon Mackellar making a proposed documentary film - which is a full and thorough investigation into the lives of these Swedish twin sisters and what led-up to the avoidable tragic slaying of an innocent man.

This book and proposed short film are critique re-examinations of the BBC *Madness in the Fast Lane* documentary that many members of the public felt cheated as it left more unanswered questions than it actually addressed and answered.

Our objective is to enlighten and expose for the first time in over four years what really took place those out of the ordinary days in May 2008, as well as beforehand and beyond.

At one time we were getting a bit worried that people might think we're getting too carried away with our "cover-up theory". Though the recent revelations on the 12th September 2012, that those in the most highest of positions - were too deeply involved in the Hillsborough tragedy cover-up and where in excess of a 160 police officers altered their statements so as to just fit the "official storyline", - helped and forced us to carry on.

It was then reported on the 22nd October 2012, that there were calls for the Hillsborough inquiry to look at claims police 'colluded' on statements from Orgreave miners' strike riots when 190 people were arrested during clashes in the 1984 *Battle of Orgreave* between police officers and picketers. South Yorkshire police are accused of using the very same phrases in dozens of witness statement. Barrister Mark George QC, claims there was 'widespread collusion', - since this revelation the National Union of Miners have called on the IPCC to investigate.

It gives us consolation to know that the majority of our readers will be able to see through all the lies and deceit, - and will not simply try and categorise us as "conspiracy theorist" without any merit.

We also expect the book and our findings will probably be ridiculed by those we are exposing and accusing of being involved in the cover-up.

So expect negative comments and reviews online and on social media forums as soon as the book is released. I know how these government departments work so expect them to have their trolls and shills out in full force to debase our findings.

If this occurs, which we are sure it will, then perhaps it is a good indicator - as in many respects it will prove we have upset those we accuse of the police cover-up and denying the Hollinshead family the justice the truly deserve.

What is worse and despicable - is that it not only involves the police, but the Chief Executive of the hospital concerned as well.

One of the very first things that soon became apparent was that this astonishing story has gone completely global. As a direct result of its international infamy, it has unfortunately created a tsunami of inconsistencies, rumours, discrepancies, falsehoods and conspiracy theories.

Some of the most outlandish and yet quite common suggestions are that the Eriksson twins were either programmed assassins, MK-Ultra victims or Super Strength Soldiers. Others believe they are clones, aliens, reptilian hybrids or must be consumed by some form of demonic possession.

Whereas many people have suggested that the twins were under the influence of drugs, whether with or without their knowledge, i.e. their drinks, food or even cigarettes were spiked or laced with a mind altering substance, - which is a possibility – and we look into these matters.

According to the police and the reports they claim there was no evidence of drugs found in their blood. Though we will reveal what really would have taken place in regards to the blood tests the twins were meant to have undergone and prove this wasn't really the case.

It must be said, - as basically these are among the main reasons why investigative journalist Sharon Mackellar and I, in the capacity of an "amateur criminologist" and professional writer - decided to join forces and take on the challenge to dissect this matter further than anyone else has done so to date.

The contents of this book is a direct result and culmination of an investigation which has sent us down a whole myriad of rabbit holes - that in turn led us onto a series of corridors and places bringing us directly into contact with many individuals, groups, organisations and authoritative bodies; that from the on start of our task we really had no idea would turn out to be the case.

In the following chapters we have fully examined all the points that have been raised and accrued from our investigations. We're pleased to say we've been able to shed so much more light on what really did happened to the Eriksson twins and Glenn Hollinshead.

Without coming across as too facetious, we can confidently say that no one else should be able to surpass what we have achieved in relation to this case. Unless of course the 'Court Bundle' [the police evidence], is revealed in its entirety by the Staffordshire police.

Perhaps one of the best things about our explorations, is that we have hopefully been able to put to bed the abundance of weird and wacky theories that have arisen due to the countless number of unanswered questions the aforementioned documentaries seemed to create.

I am able to understand many aspects of criminal law and the procedures involved, which is fortunate otherwise the legal bill to date would be in the region of many thousands of pounds had the Hollinshead family or ourselves had to employ the services of a solicitor and barrister.

In regards to this case I have worked as a representative in the capacity of a 'McKenzie Friend' for the Hollinshead family. I have had to contact all the legal teams and people involved in the trial, whether it was the defence or prosecution solicitors and barristers, they have all been approached, including the judges, the Crown Prosecution Service (CPS), the Independent Police Complaints Commission (IPCC), Merseyside Police, Staffordshire Police and their legal representatives, known as the Professional Standards Departments (PSDs), the University Hospital of North Staffordshire (UHNS), and the Stoke-on-Trent Coroner's office.

According to the Hollinshead brothers, they ended up viewing DC Short, the Police Family Liaison officer - as a *"Spy in the camp."* They said they were promised a copy of the 'Court Bundle', which is all the collated evidence of the case. The Hollinshead's state that Mr Christopher Hotten QC, acting for the Crown, said he couldn't see there being a problem and indicated that DC Short would arrange this for the family, - yet it never materialised.

They ask; *"Why hasn't it?"* I put this question to Mr Hotten QC, and he told me he couldn't help us if he wanted to as the Court Bundle had been returned to the CPS.

I contacted the CPS and they informed me that all the paperwork was the 'property' of the Staffordshire Police.

I then approached the Staffordshire Police's legal department and cited the Freedom of Information Act (FOIA), though they insisted the Hollinshead family would have to employ a solicitor to help them in the matter. This is one of the reasons why we decided to go to the IPCC.

Up to the time of writing, the IPCC have handed the complaints over to the relevant PSDs, and each of the police forces involved are looking into the complaints to see whether the matter will be 'recorded'.

Merseyside police force have since confirmed they have 'recorded the complaint', and told me they are looking into it. Also on the 31st August 2012, the Staffordshire police force have said they have not currently 'recorded' it. This may have resulted in the Hollinshead family going back to the IPCC and appeal for the case to be investigated by them.

We were worried this would be the case with the Merseyside police for before they agreed to 'record' the complaint, they wrote on the 25th July 2012 that stated: *'In the event that the issues raised are over twelve months old it will be classed as out of time and we may seek dispensation from the IPCC.'* Obviously it's well over twelve months and seeking dispensation in this instance, means they would be asking the IPCC to exempt them from the complaints procedure. The Hollinshead family would have needed to appeal to the IPCC to instigate their own investigation had the Merseyside Police force refused to 'record it'.

We have a copy of the film that clearly shows the edited out film footage that proves these two women were in fact first arrested as "Mental Patients" under a special clause in the 1983 Mental Health Act and hope that the new evidence and our investigation into this case will be of some help and assistance to the IPCC and the police. This is why we've furnished them with copies of our 10 page (A4) report into the findings of this matter for their consideration. Despite us mentioning this "new" evidence to the PSD of Staffordshire police, they have since replied on the 31st August 2012, - though their reply doesn't bode well for them - in which I'll also explain further on.

It wasn't until my recent intervention and when I telephoned DCI Dave Garrett of the Staffordshire police, enquiring; "Why hadn't Glenn's personal property been returned to the family after four years?" - Then I don't think it would ever have been. Though to be fair to DCI Garrett, he took immediate action and got the property returned in no time at all.

Then following on from his previous comments on this matter, [which are quoted further on], we decided to contact the Stoke-on-Trent MP, Rob Flello and hold him to the words he said back in 2009 - which was he was calling for inquiry into; '...why was Sabina Eriksson released from hospital so soon?'

So we are pleased to be able to announce that he has agreed to come-on-board and help the Hollinshead family by seeking an inquiry via the House of Parliament as he said he shall raise the matter in the House of Commons.

We have also discovered that when Sabina appeared at Fenton Magistrate Court, Stoke-on-Trent, just 36 hours later on the 19th May 2008, 'no' Pre-Sentence Report (PSR) was called for by the magistrate. Had the magistrate insisted on one, as is the normal standard procedure in such cases - and the same could be said about Sabina being released from the hospital far too early, - then it has to be debated that Glenn Hollinshead would in all probability still be alive today.

From the very start of our investigation we've had the full backing and cooperation of the Hollinshead family, with some of the brothers appearing in the proposed forthcoming documentary film: *A Madness Shared by Two.* Which is currently a working title. Alongside the other main and vital witnesses, such as Frank Booth, the next door neighbour whom Glenn tragically died in front of and whose own spectacular statements clearly conflicts that of the official storyline and what many have already seen or read in the media as being true.

We have also met and interviewed Peter Molloy, the man who went back to Glenn's home with Sabina, though sadly he was not willing to be filmed. Though he has greatly helped us in our stern line of questioning and we would like to take the opportunity to thank him for all his contributions. He has since supplied us with his own personal written account as to what happened that night and we will cover this matter further on.

In addition, we quote and show the brothers of Glenn, especially that of Jon Hollinshead, as he makes a scathing attack against those he blames to have allowed a "catalogue of errors" to have occurred which led on to the avoidable death of his brother. They predominately point the finger of blame at those higher up in the chain of command and the health authorities in general, whose own "experts" came to the joint conclusion that Sabina was fine, fit and well to be released from hospital and so soon after their assessment.

We could clearly see what had previously been reported about the coach journey and what allegedly happened at Keele services - had caused even more uncertainty and confusion with no definitive answers being found - until now that is – as we explore the possibilities that the twins were not in fact 'London bound' after all. The Hollinshead family can't understand as to why the attending police officers to Keele services responded the way they did. Though since this time we've now been able to uncover what really occurred that day.

In addition we can see and include the Staffordshire police's own annual report for 2009/10 - clearly contradicts the BBC's documentary version of events.

We deliberately decided not to interview or include the officials seen in the BBC *Madness in the Fast Lane* documentary, for we understood from the very start it would be very unlikely they would change their original stories.

Our analysis tends to expose that there appears to be a deliberate cover-up, guised as the already mentioned series of 'green lights' and catalogue of errors, that we can only assume would have been orchestrated from the wings by an indistinguishable group of individuals who work for the powers that be in cases and circumstances such as this. - Whereas "they" deliberately gave the Eriksson twins the 'green lights' and thus allowed the amazing chain of events to occur.

I have direct evidence and personal experience of how this system works. When at certain times and in some high profile cases, it is what they term; *'Not in the Public Interest'* or *'...for matters of National Security'*, - that assures specific practices are put into place and unorthodox procedures are carried out. This appears to have been one of those 'certain times' as our evidence seems to indicate, alongside and according to an anonymous informer, that if it's true, the twins were but a mere tiny cog in a huge complex machine that had them embroiled within any one of a number of police undercover operations.

If this was the case it could have involved billions of pounds worth of drugs and, or cutting agents [a mix that dilutes the original drugs] being smuggled to and from various countries and such places like the USA, South

America, Ireland and the mainland's of the UK, Sweden and Norway.

Further examination seems to indicate that the prosecution's case against Sabina was really weak. It wasn't until 10th June 2012 that we had the opportunity to study the pathologist reports about the cause of Glenn's demise. Incredibly, our findings blow the original version of events clean out of the water.

It seems to indicate more than one person was involved in Glenn's murder and that Sabina could be innocent. One of the doctors, Dr Shorrock, the same pathologist who also carried out a post-mortem report on Jean Charles de Menezes, the Brazilin young man shot by police at Stockwell Underground station following the 7th July 2005 London bombings - and Ian Tomlinson, the newsvendor who died following an assault by a police officer at a G20 protest in London in 2008.

We've carried out and conducted some of our own experiments to help prove our point and why we query the coroner's reports.

In addition, we probe into the timings as to when the emergency services first arrived at the crime scene following Glenn Hollinsheads' murder.

We've questioned; 'How was it possible for the paramedics to be yards from where Sabina was and arrive before the police did - as she allegedly fled the murder scene and at the very same time Frank Booth was alleged to be telephoning for an ambulance? Thankfully, we can announce we conclusively have cleared this matter up and contradicts the police version of events.

It is due to our own findings as to why we query and examine the prospects of fabricated evidence being suggested or used so as to try to strengthen the case against Sabina.

We looked into the reason why and when Ursula might have left or fled the USA and then went to Sabina's home in Ireland? And then why as a couple they seemed to have fled for their lives from there as opposed to having casually left for the British mainland? According to our findings we don't believe they parted Ireland that weekend in question, despite police evidence seeming to suggest they must of.

Apart from the possible connections to drug smuggling, it has been thought they could have been involved in some sort of religious cult, like that of "the Family"[1][2], now known as; The Family International (TFI), formed as the Children of God (COD). Though there's no evidence reflecting this other than at the time of the M6 incident Sabina was wearing a visor with *"Time to Believe,"* embroidered on it.

According to Peter Molloy, when they first encountered Sabina she was praying outside a church. Yet recent evidence has come to light that seems to put doubt on Peter's version of events and again we examine this further on.

The police reported she had become very religious whilst in prison. Ursula is a member of the *Sacred Heart Church*, where and according to them last year in April 2011, Ursula received the: *"RCIA Rites of Scrutiny prayed over her as she open herself to be illuminated and healed by Christ and delivered from emptiness, illusions and death-prone effects of evil."* Sabina's son, Simon, seems to have started a page: *"Were banned by the church"*, on

22

Facebook, it's among his likes and noted as a 'favourite' book. As he appears to be the only one who has liked it, we assume he started the page.

The Eriksson twins appeared very fit and athletic, which has since been backed up to have been the case by their elder brother Bjorn, whom we will discuss in *The Eriksson's* chapter. Their actions on the M6 motorway appears to put them into the realm of some type of Super Strength Soldier or Olympian. It seems the case that when they were younger they had some kind of sports training. The twins were raised in an area where there's a ski resort with 16 pistes and 20 kilometres (12 miles) of cross country ski trails, - so it very likely they are competent skiers.

In Sweden, National Service was mandatory up until 1st July 2010. This was of course for men only. In the Swedish Army, women serve together with the men. They sleep together in the same tents and even shower together - though not literally. So it's possible the twins had some form of military training. They could have even been taught the techniques of stuntman-ship, acrobatics, gymnastics or martial arts.

Yet despite all this it's their injuries or should I say lack of them that often tends to stump or bewilder most people who have seen the film. We couldn't understand or fathom out; *'How did these women manage to escape with such minimal injuries and damage done to their bodies?'* Hence why the already mentioned possibilities of them being some form of a *'Super Strength Soldier'* - were being freely touted. [3][4]

So it is because of these rather out-of-the-box submission of ideas - often construed as irrational thinking or logic - that we decided to probe into these matters as well and confront them head on and try our best to explain as to why so many people genuinely do believe there is something that doesn't quite add up when it comes to the Eriksson twins body's or injuries. Yet their injuries are explainable, though we know a certain group of people will not be willing to accept these reasons and this is why we have covered these subjects in more depth in the eBook, as this permits us to include another 22,000 plus words in the *Appendix*, and keep the printing costs down on the paperback.

We also don't want to hinder our own findings by blurring all these issues together, when they are clearly separate debates and problems.

It has also been suggested that the twins' actions must have been triggered-off by some sort of 'self-destruct' mode. That perhaps this was achieved due to hypnosis or a form of brainwashing - or its been thought that they may have had microchips implanted within their brains or other parts of their body and were either programmed or remotely controlled to react the way that they did. In the eBook we show actual examples of people who claim this has happened to them, one is by a female addressing an American board of inquiry.

The twins bizarre behaviour certainly does seem to suggest they could be victims of some kind of modern day Project MK-Ultra program which was the code name for a covert, illegal CIA human experimentation program run by the CIA in 1950s and 60s.[5] According to Peter Molloy who was with Glenn when they both took one of Sabina's cigarettes; he said that as soon as they put them to their mouths she snatched them away, claiming; *"They could be poisoned"*. This type of suggestion can be found in a 1955 MK-Ultra document.[6] We look into the possibilities that some of her cigarettes were laced in something like the drug PCP and explain what this is further on.

Though there's no 'real' hard evidence that backs-up these theories and why these topics are only mainly discussed in the *Appendix* section of the eBook, though we do briefly examine it in the paperback as well. As mentioned, the inclusion of drugs being used either knowingly or unknowingly by the twins cannot be ruled out, despite it being believed their blood tests proved negative, - we will explain this was probably not the case and were probably positive.

Many advocate that some of the film footage has been edited and 'staged'. Some have even gone as far as saying there are actors involved and that it never *"really happened"*. Others are convinced the film footage has been interfered with. In a sense they are right, but it's not how it might appear, nor was it done to deceive. We know crucial evidence was edited out of the documentary and yet again we cover these issues further on.

The "Official" Storyline

The following is the typical "official storyline" you'll find reported in the media and on the internet in general. It's quite systematic, non-personal and nondescript but there to give you a guideline and rough idea of what it is the media and general public believe to have occurred. Please understand this ensuing "official storyline" you are about to read is riddled with incorrect facts and inconsistencies and why we challenge various parts of the 'official storyline' and place it under scrutiny further on.

We will show you what really happened on those fateful days in question, as it appears that those we expose in this book are also controlling the Wikipedia page about this particular case as most of the information on that dedicated page is totally incorrect. "Someone" who controls the page ignores our messages - as we question; - Why are they supressing the truth and endlessly removing our new evidence; yet permit a useless book that has nothing more than Wikipedia information and that the old incorrect version of events to remain there since 2008? We have never received a reply and our entries are regularly removed.

It's widely thought that Ursula and Sabina Eriksson first departed from College Wood, Mallow, County Cork, Ireland, on the 16th May 2008, at 02:00am [1]. It's then said they were next seen in Liverpool at 08:30 on the 17th May 2008, when they entered St Anne Street police station to report Sabina's concerns over the safety of her two children.[5] Soon after the pair boarded a London bound National Express coach.[6] A police report stated, *"...that the twins suddenly disembarked the coach at Keele services, around 13:05pm, as they were not feeling well."* [4] However, the driver of the coach left them at

Keele services [7] after becoming suspicious of their behaviour.

He noticed the twins clinging tightly to their bags and did not let them re-board because they refused to let him search their bags for illegal items. The manager of the service station was informed, and also feeling suspicious of the pair, called the police. The officers arrived to talk to the twins, but left after deeming them to be harmless. The Eriksson twins began to walk down the central reservation of the M6 motorway, before attempting to cross the motorway, causing chaos to the traffic and Sabina picking up minor injuries in the attempt.

With the twins caught on CCTV cameras, highway agency officers soon arrived, followed by the police to investigate what they were doing on the M6 motorway. Along with the police officers, came a small television crew from Mentorn Productions, who so happened to be filming a series of the BBC's *Motorway Cops,* with WPC Cope and PC Finlayson from the police motorway division.

Paramedics also arrived at the scene to help treat the twins with their injuries. Prior to them arriving, we can see the Eriksson twins standing on the hard shoulder of the motorway. The two police officers start to speak with one the highway agency officers about the twins, when without warning, Ursula ran past the other highway agency officer who was standing in front of them, and into the side of an oncoming 40-ton lorry travelling at around 60–70 mph.[1][8] Sabina then followed her into the road and threw herself into the path of a speeding Volkswagen Polo car.[1] Both survived. Ursula in particular, was fortunate not to be killed instantly. Instead, she was immobilised as the lorry had crushed her ankles. Sabina spent fifteen minutes unconscious.[1]

27

The pair were treated by paramedics, however, both women resisted medical aid, and started fighting and screaming at the paramedics and police officers. Sabina shouted; *"They're going to steal your organs"* and *"I recognise you, – I know you're not real"*. [8]

Sabina then got to her feet, whereupon a WPC Cope, attempted to persuade her to stay on the ground and receive further medical attention. Sabina then struck the officer and jumped back over the central reservation running into the oncoming traffic on the other side of the motorway, though she's not hit again. Emergency workers and several members of the public caught and restrained her and then helped carry her to the awaiting ambulance. At which point she was sedated. Ursula was also taken to the University Hospital of North Staffordshire, where she stayed for several weeks. Sabina was soon released from hospital after only five hours and then into police custody. It can clearly been seen on the BBC documentary, that she was calm and less deranged at the police station. [8]

On the 19th May 2008, she was released from Fenton Magistrates court without a full psychiatric evaluation, having pleaded guilty to trespass on the motorway and assault on a police officer.[1] The court sentenced her to only one day in prison, but because she had been in police custody for over 36hrs, Sabina was released. At 19:00,[5] 54 year old Glenn Hollinshead, along with Peter Molloy were walking home from the public house they had been drinking in. Glenn had his dog with him, when on Christchurch Street, Fenton, Stoke-on-Trent, they spotted Sabina.[1] Hollinshead, was unemployed at the time, though had been a self-employed welder, qualified paramedic, and former RAF medic.[10][11] Peter was a friend of Glenn's. Its alleged Sabina appeared friendly, and stroked the dog [9] as the three of them struck up a conversation. According to Peter Molloy, although Sabina was friendly, she appeared to be behaving oddly, and this odd behaviour worried Molloy.[9] It's further alleged by Molloy, that Sabina asked the two men for directions to any nearby bed and breakfasts or hotels.[1] According to Mr Molloy, Glenn Hollinshead took pity upon her, and instead offered to take her back to his house at Duke Street, Fenton. Sabina accepted the offer and the three walked to the house, as Sabina told the men how she was trying to locate her hospitalised sister.

Peter Molloy said it was back at Glenn's house that her odd behaviour continued; most notably, she offered the men cigarettes, only to quickly snatch them out of their mouths as the men lit them, claiming the cigarettes to be poisoned.[9] She was also carrying multiple mobile phones, as well as a laptop. She appeared to be paranoid and constantly looked outside the windows; this behaviour caused Molloy to assume that she had run away from an abusive partner.[9] It's alleged shortly before midnight, Molloy left,[5] and Sabina stayed the night in Glenn Hollinshead's home.[1]

The next day, Glenn called his family to help to locate Sabina's sister Ursula in hospital.[7] At 19:40, Glenn Hollinshead came outside of the house to ask a neighbour Frank Booth for tea bags. After receiving the teabags, he returned inside.[12] One minute after returning inside, he staggered back outside to Frank Booth, and told him; *"I've been stabbed, she stabbed me"*, before collapsing to the ground.[1] Sabina had stabbed him five times,[6] and Hollinshead died from his injuries.[1] Sabina fled the premises[1] and the neighbour Frank Booth dialled 999.

It's alleged that Sabina ran out of the house with a hammer, periodically hitting herself over the head with it.[6] It's further alleged that a passing motorist, Joshua

29

Grattage,[5] saw this extraordinary behaviour and decided to give chase and tackle her, in an attempt to confiscate the hammer. It's said, that while wrestling with Grattage, Sabina took a roof tile out of her pocket and struck him on the back of the head with it, stunning him temporarily. By this time paramedics had noticed her and gave chase. The pursuit was ended at Heron Cross, when Sabina jumped from a 40 ft [it's since been proved to be around 25ft - 30ft] high bridge onto the A50.[1][6] Having broken her ankles in the fall and fractured her skull, she was taken to hospital.[11] On 6th June 2008, she was arrested while recovering at University Hospital of North Staffordshire,[5] and was later discharged from hospital on 11th September, at which point she was charged with murder, and remanded to Bronzefield prison.[5]

Garry Hollinshead, one of four brothers of the man [allegedly] killed by Sabina, was critical of the justice system, which he viewed as enabling Sabina to kill his brother. *"We don't hold her responsible, the same as we wouldn't blame a rabid dog for biting someone. She is ill and to a large degree, not responsible for her actions. But her mental disorder should have been recognised much earlier."*[13]

It's been reported the murder trial was scheduled for February 2009, [14][15] but was adjourned after the court encountered difficulties in obtaining her medical records from Sweden.[16] The trial was rescheduled to start on the 1st September 2009. Sabina Eriksson pleaded guilty to manslaughter with diminished responsibility on the 2nd September 2009.[5] It's alleged, that at no point during her interrogation or during the trial did she explain her actions, only replying "no comment" to extensive police questioning. Both the prosecution and defence claimed that Sabina was 'insane' at the time of the killing, although she was 'sane' at the time of her trial.[17]

The defence counsel in the trial claimed that Eriksson was a "secondary" sufferer of folie à deux - *"A Madness Shared by Two"*, influenced by the presence or perceived presence of her twin sister; the "primary sufferer". The court also heard, that she had suffered from a rare psychiatric disorder which made her hear voices, but could not interpret what they said,[6] as well as an alternative theory that she had suffered from acute polymorphic delusional disorder; Bouffée Délirante [18] – *"A Puff of Madness."*

The plea of manslaughter on the grounds of diminished responsibility was accepted at Nottingham Crown Court on the 2nd September 2010.[1][19][18][20] Sabina was sentenced to five years in prison.[8] Having already spent 439 days in custody before sentencing,[21] this left her first eligible for release in 2011. It's said that whilst in prison, she turned to Christianity.[22]

Justice Saunders concluded that Sabina had a "low" level of culpability for her actions. *"I understand that this sentence will seem entirely inadequate to the relatives of the deceased. However, I have sentenced on the basis that the reason for the killing was the mental illness and therefore the culpability of the defendant is low and therefore the sentence I have passed is designed to protect the public. It is not designed to reflect the grief the relatives have suffered or to measure the value of Mr Hollinshead's life. No sentence that I could pass could do that. It is a sentence which I hope fairly measures a truly tragic event."* [6] Justice Saunders also stated that Sabina was: *"suffering from delusions which she believed to be true and they dictated her behaviour. It is not one of those cases where the defendant could have done something to avoid the onset."* [23]

31

Don't forget much of what this "Wikipedia" official storyline states and the way it reads is actually incorrect and why we now hope to set the record straight.

The Eriksson's

We would like to point out that we have tried our utmost to correspond with the Eriksson twins. We have contacted them and other members of their family to try and arrange some kind of communication so as they too can explain their side of the story. They appear to have deliberately chosen to ignore us, though for what we are about to reveal it is perhaps understandable as to why they haven't replied.

Unfortunately, we have no real choice other than to write and explain what our research has yielded. We made a conscious decision not to contact their elderly mother, Yvonne, who lives in Gothenburg, purely because of her age and we don't wish to cause any emotional upset.

We have gathered our information from a variety of sources; some of it is openly known about and can be found in public records, others - such as various photographs etc. were discovered via internet searches and where some unknown person/s have uploaded them - whilst in other cases they were sent directly to us.

At times we have been in personal contact with several individuals who have claimed to have known or know someone else who came from where the twins lived or went to the same school as them and who wish to remain anonymous. Others have been bloggers who have written on the subject or left comments on internet forums where the subject has been widely discussed. *Flashback*; is a Swedish website that covers a variety of subjects and this "Eriksson case" was extensively discussed among people who claimed to know the twins or about the family. The original comments were in Swedish and have been translated into English for the discussion here; originals can be checked by referring to the links in the back of this book.

We know where Ursula lives and what church she is actively involved in and regularly attends in America. We will not disclose exactly where but it's in the region of King County, Washington, which is part of the Seattle metropolitan area in the USA.

We also know where Sabina is currently living in Norway. Sabina, in particular, seems to have connections in that country and bordering Sweden and has dwelled between the two countries for the most of her life.

We explained to the family that we had unearthed some vital information and that it's quite possible that Sabina had become a victim of a miscarriage of justice. We revealed to them that when they were first arrested it was under the mentioned 1983 Mental Health Act - and therefore it is very likely that Sabina could have a case against certain authorities for being released far too soon from hospital. We also divulged the astonishing information we found in the coroner's report that perhaps would have got Sabina acquitted - had it been made public at the time.

So we can only assume the reason why they haven't come back to us - is because they fully understand what they were involved in and as did the police; "technically" speaking - because Sabina is still "under licence" from her five year prison sentence and until June-July 2013 – we wonder if this in some way has prevented her from being able to communicate with anyone and because of this reason?

Though Glenn's murder took place in May 2008 Sabina wasn't charged with 'Murder' until June 2008.

She was in hospital until September 2008, so over three months had passed and it wasn't until 16 months later the murder-charge was reduced to 'Manslaughter.'

It's even possible that on here release Sabina could be living under some kind of "Witness Protection Programme", whereas she is being protected by the police. She may have been given an additional identity and safe address to live at. For what doesn't add up is that following our investigations - we have exposed a police cover-up and this new evidence could help prove Sabina may well be innocent, especially of murder.

We can see that Sabina was insisting on her "innocence" during her 16 months on remand. She "technically" has a legal challenge to be able to help clear her name - and our evidence would help her mitigating circumstances.

Like Sabina and Ursula Eriksson, [who often go under the surname Erixon], it so happens Sven-Göran Eriksson - famous for his role in football - was also born in the small town of Sunne in Värmland County, Sweden - though on the 5th February 1940 and as far as we know there's no relation between them. The twins, though not identical - were born on the 3rd November 1967 - and lived in Gräsmark, a few miles from Sunne, Värmland.

(For reasons of privacy we will not include the actual birth dates and door numbers etc. - of other members of the family as they are irrelevant to this case.)

They lived there with their mother Yvonne Adéle Olsson, born in 1937 and their older sister Mona, born in 1961 - alongside their brother Björn, born in 1964. Their father, Janne Sixten Eriksson, was born in 1922 and died when the twins were aged 22, in 1989, aged 67. At just

18 he apparently lost one of his arms during the Finnish Winter War between the Soviet Union and Finland, which constituted the eastern part of the Kingdom of Sweden. It began on 30th November 1939 and ended on 13th March 1940. Some local people have said and the Swedish Census shows, that in 1981 the above five members of the Eriksson family [excluding the father] were still living there together.

According to two neighbours, so we can only speculate, they believe the Eriksson's moved to Gothenburg in the early 1980's. Yvonne does indeed live in another Swedish town, Alelyckegatan, in the Gothenburg region and lives there alongside another - but different man also named "Björn". We won't mention his surname which is not the same as the twins. (In Swedish, Björn, translates as - 'Bear'). It's been alleged she was arrested in Sunne in the 1990's for shoplifting, [1] though again we can't substantiate this and can only go on these alleged "witnesses" words. [1] We've been informed that before Yvonne moved to her current address she lived at the Skepparegångens Women's Housing Accommodation, in Saturn Street, Gothenburg.[3] In their literature it states: *'...targets women who are homeless or in need of temporary accommodation. Our purpose is to provide a safe and drug-free living with a focus on treatment. Most women in the target group are abused,'* *'...the women...may have substance abuse, mental health and or social problems'.*

It is further alleged that their father drank quite heavily and that the mother may too have had a drink problem.[2] Social Services visited their home periodically and they apparently had goats roaming and living in the house.[4] They described the twins as rather "mouthy and rude" - and said they could be fairly wild in their behaviour, as could their brother Björn but who become more "normal" in adulthood.[5]

Though to be fair we can't really judge the twins by these comments as many children are rude and wild and soon settle down. However, it gives us an insight as to how they were viewed by others as these people are not the only ones making such claims. They thought Björn at that time became a 'foreman' and worked for a company in the Gothenburg area.[4] They said the father died in the same place he was born, Fager city, Grassland. He was unmarried and the twin's mother left him some years before his death. [2][4]

In 1983/84 the twins started at Stjerneskolan Upper Secondary School in Torsby, Gothenburg. On the annual school photograph of Sabina [see 'Photo Section'], it reads; *'Franvarande - Urusla Eriksson'*, which means *'Absent'* in English.[6] The photo was at first uploaded onto the internet by someone who stated they went to school with them. All the other pupil's faces have been blanked out. It was a mixed sex school. Sabina, probably about 17 years of age, looks well and rather attractive with boyish looks. Her hair is fair in colour and cut short. She's wearing jeans and a t-shirt covered in rips and holes, though it was a kind of 'punk' fashion so intentional and not a sign of depravation. According to this persons comments - whose recollections are rather vague because it was so long ago; the twins didn't socialise much and kept mostly to themselves. They had their own special fashion style and appearance.

We've seen other photographs of the twins when in their 20's. Sabina has spiky hair in one, though stylishly cut. Though they seem perfectly normal young women, trendy in their style of dress, probably into *New Romance* bands, like *Duran Duran* or *Kajagoogoo*, - who had a No1

37

hit with *'Too Shy'*, for their hair style was like that of Limahl's, the lead singer of that band during the 1980's or that of the female singer, Alison Moyett, (see 'Photo Section').

It seems as if Ursula didn't complete her schooling and left before Sabina. Again this can't be substantiated, however, we found a person on a Swedish forum saying they also went to the same school as the twins; who accuse them of always being strange and violent. They remember their friend being *"knocked down - by one of the sisters."* [3] Another person claims that during the late 90's, her sister would come across them in some nightclubs, and describes that people would do their best to avoid them.[3] Though again we cannot substantiate any of these hearsay comments because there could be a hidden agenda to help defame the twins by way of salacious rumours.

This is why we regret the Eriksson's not coming back to us for though they might not have wanted to have admitted certain things, they could have helped set the record straight by saying what is and isn't true about them.

The twins have often been described as 'blonde' Swedish sisters. Their hair is actually dyed blonde and their natural colour is light brown, perhaps when they were very young it was much fairer. They're approximately 5'- 7" in height, of medium build, but athletically so. Even though you can see they are related they could easily pass as sisters as opposed to twins for there are clear facial differences. It's also been claimed on the internet that Sabina's nose is more flat looking due to an accident she had as a child, breaking it on the back of Ursula. Though we doubt this to be true and think its people taking the micky at the shape of Sabina's nose. Both have piercing dark blue eyes. Arguably Sabina's are more vacant than Ursula's that look vibrant and full of life, particularly in their recent photographs of 2011/12.

According to another person whom wishes to remain anonymous; it was around 1999-2000, when his girlfriend was the manager of the *Explorer Bar* at Gardermoen Airport in Norway.[5] He said Sabina was working there and according to his girlfriend Sabina was a good person with a boy-like appearance. But as soon as someone happened to ask her about her personal life she would allegedly turn on them and became "crazy". She apparently didn't like talking about her siblings or children. According to them; *"The other sister* [Ursula] *was completely "normal", but incredibly easily manipulated by the sister."*[5] Which is quite odd for the psychiatrists believed it was Ursula that had a dominating influence and effect over Sabina.

The above comments were made and appeared on the internet around the same time Simon (Sabina's son), who we wouldn't have personally mentioned until we saw how vocal and public he has been about this case and how significant his own comments were – that we reveal further on; had been living in the USA with his aunt Ursula.)

Dating back to as early as the year 2000, records show Ursula was living at two properties in Santa Barbara County, California, USA. Simon went to schools in that area. In addition, Sabina and Ursula can be traced living together at the same address in Goleta, Southern Santa Barbara County, in May 2007. That's exactly one year before the M6 motorway incident and the death of Glenn Hollinshead took place. Yet the public have been led to believe that it was only Ursula who was living in the USA and that Sabina had been living in Ireland for some years prior to Glenn Hollinsheads' murder.

Sharon uncovered some interesting information; that according to a close relative of the Eriksson's, Ursula then aged 31, [affectionately known as Utt-Utt] and using the surnames Erixon and Eriksson, was living in the USA. This would have been around 1998. She appears to have had a boyfriend out there - who we won't name - and according to the source worked as a waitress for some time. Also aged 31 and in 1998, Sabina along with Simon and a partner, who again we will not name - were living in Bergsjön, a district in eastern Gothenburg, Sweden. She was also working in Norway around this same period of time. Their brother Björn, was at this time in 1995 aged 34 and working as a fisherman in Norway. There's a younger male though again we won't name him as we are not certain of his blood-connection, though it's quite possible he is Björn's son. Even later in 2006-7 Simon at times refers to his uncle Björn - on social forums - as being a fisherman and that he bought a boat around that same period of time.

Gräsmark, where the twins were born and raised, appears to be a very nice rural area surrounded in woodland and countryside and near to Lake Rottnen. Gräsmark is located 20km north-west of Sunne. In 2008 it was reported there were around 1,200 people living there. In such a small populated area the twins must have been known or seen about 'town' by almost everyone who lived there. My secondary school had nearly as many pupils than the population of this churched village, where you'll find a shop, library, restaurant and a petrol station alongside the local school. The cultural buildings at the folklore museum - display the Finnish immigration and influences on that region. Unless their original "house" has been replaced, the home the Eriksson's lived in appears to not be of the brick and mortar kind you'd typically find in the UK as they are more like your archetypal wooden Swish chalet though not of the grand style and design you could imagine them to be - for these are more like what could be regarded as holiday chalets.

Apart from the police indicting this possibility when they told the Hollinshead family that Sabina's "partner" in Ireland is a "traveller" - which we cover further on - as it's not too clear as to why or where the gossip originated from but there seems to be a lot of reference to the sisters coming from a gypsy or traveller type of family,[1][2] other than the area where their house was situated could be described as a kind of trailer park area. What I mean by this is that it seems as if a clearing was made within a wooded area just off the main road and that inside this clearing a group of homes were erected. It's something like a *Centre Parks* area though much smaller and this is full time residential settlement - as opposed to being a purpose built area for holidaying.

Perhaps it's also because it's said Sabina was at one time seen living in a caravan on the KronoCamping Åby site near Gothenburg, Mölndal, [3][4] that has a large section for caravans, both static and mobile; though apart from these it also has chalets and areas for camping, with a clubhouse and other amenities – that again seems to be a very nice place according to the photographs and *Google's* satellite views. Perhaps out of season the area could be pretty bleak and not the kind of place you'd want to stay for a holiday. Again it has been alleged – that Sabina was seen with a group of "druggies" and alcoholics and stayed there for over a year or more. It's further alleged that some people recognised and saw Ursula there at this camp soon after her release from hospital in September 2008. It seems she was there convalescing and still in a wheelchair. Perhaps their family has (had) a caravan on this site like many people do on similar holiday camp sites in the UK and other parts

41

of the world. Simon also mentions that he too had bought a caravan which seems to indicate that living or travelling in a trailer is not so out of ordinary for this family.

According to the 'official' storyline and the Staffordshire police, Sabina and her "partner" lived on some kind of 'Travellers camp' at College Wood, Mallow, Cork, Ireland. We've tried to exactly locate where this was and found a travellers site there but not connected to Sabina or her partner. Sharon contacted the editor of the *Vale Star,* a local newspaper and made some enquiries. Here's his reply: *"I understand they sometimes frequented the Lodge pub near their estate, but apart from that I wasn't aware of them until YouTube footage on a UK motorway when one of them ran into traffic. Sorry I can't be of more help, they seemed to lead a low-key life when in Mallow."*

So he didn't even know of them until at least September 2009, almost 15 months after the M6 incident. College Wood, is not an estate as we know it but a small 'new town' development of private housing located at the Cork city side of Mallow, across the road from the Mallow golf course. Started in the mid 2000's, the majority were completed in 2007. It's in the heart of surrounding countryside with a few well established farms and houses that were there prior to *Flemings Homes* building four main areas of over 200 houses within the vicinity [see Photo Section]. It's far from the kind of place you'd find "travellers" though they could have been on vacant land as and when before they built on a particular section or in a field somewhere. It has since been proven the alleged partner of Sabina was living in one of the new houses on this new housing estate in College Wood.

Simon Leo Eriksson [and Erixon], is Sabina's son. Born in 1989, he's presently aged around 23. He appears to have gone to live in the USA, around the later part of 1999 or early 2000. He attended an elementary school in Oakland, California, and went on to a High School in Goleta, California, west of Santa Barbara. As mentioned we would have kept his name and details anonymous though following Sabina's conviction for the manslaughter of Glenn Hollinshead in September 2009; he has since come forward and often declared himself as being her son. He has defended her on various occasions: *"Sabina Eriksson" is not a murderer, she's raising two children and she is, and will always be a caring and loving mother. - Mother, not murderer...self-defence? I'm speechless, the media? Yeah...they have to have someone to write about...some story, fiction or nonfiction."* - *"Write about me, Simon Eriksson from Norway."*

He wrote quite a few other comments, much in the same vain following his mother's five year prison sentence that evoked a lot of criticism on many online forums and websites in general. It's his comments of; *"...loving mother, not murderer...self-defence?"* that led us down the road to examine his claims. Some of his other comments even indicate that Sabina may have known Glenn beforehand in some kind of way and we discuss this matter further on.

The below comment was made by Simon to Peter Molloy, the fellow seen in the BBC Madness in the Fast Lane film going back to Glenn's home with Sabina. It appeared on a social forum, they both used 'usernames' that are not their real names however, Simon signs off using his real name. You'll see that he is asking 'Peter', though Simon doesn't know that's who it is he is talking to. The following has been edited to shorten it. I also added Peter's name in brackets: *"Hey, Sabina's son here.*

You're not the only one up at night. I am sorry for your loss. But I'm also confident in stating that my mother wouldn't kill a fly. I strongly believe that she is being set up, because there isn't any doubt in my mind that she is innocent of killing Mr Hollingshead, unless of course, she was fighting for her own life. Which neither one of us can be sure of, the only thing I'm 100% positive of is that Sabina Eriksson is a good mother, no, she's more than that she's the best...- ...she works hard every day for one thing and one thing only, and that's her children, she's a honest and well caring person, has no criminal record, and has always been against drugs, the only drug I've seen her use is a beer or two in the weekend... has anyone of you internet geeks considered that she might have BEEN (Simon's capitals) *drugged? But hey, "Truth Freedom"* (that's Peter Molloy) *where did you meet Sabina? - And do you know what her relation to Mr Hollingshead was? - Simon Eriksson."* [6a]

Let's not forget that Simon had not lived with Sabina for at least 6 or 7 years whilst he was in the USA. These are the 'missing years' in Sabina's life and as said before something probably prompted her to handover her son to Ursula. Besides Glenn's murder, Simon must of questioned and see that both his mother's and aunt's surreal and bizarre behaviour and their 'suicide bid' was far from normal, though he does state; *"...she might have been drugged."* And like I say, that's possible. This is why we examine these probabilities further on. We must also appreciate that had his mother become embroiled in any kind of 'drug dealing' or was somehow connected to that kind of world or with someone within it, then I would assume it's very unlikely she would have told her son such a thing. At the very same time Simon was making these comments he was very much into smoking cannabis and talked openly about drugs in general on his own *MySpace* pages.[7] He talks to his friends about growing

44

and selling it and as I mention elsewhere, Simon own behaviour and comments sound quite odd and just days after the M6 incident Simon reports to have lost two or three phones within days from each other. He set up a special *Facebook* page dedicated to his lost phone numbers.

I quote some of the kind of conversations he was having at the end of this chapter. He also mentions 'going back' to Kileen, Texas, a town in the USA, which is quite significant and will explain further on.[11] It's almost as if he is trying to distance any suggestion Sabina might have been involved in drugs and of course in his situation this is understandable for these comments were being made whilst his mother was still on remand and in between court appearances, - so he would have to tread carefully with what he said.

Though quite rightly and as a son, he felt he had to defend his mother who was on a murder charge; but then again - he seems convinced his mother is innocent and being set-up and we tend to agree with him.

We have often wondered if Sabina had known Glenn and had they met before? It's almost as if Simon had perhaps heard about Glenn previously. Had he known his mother was in contact with an Englishman? His question; *"...and do you know what her relation to Mr. Hollingshead was?"* In another comment on *The Sentinel* newspapers website following an article about the court case, Simon said; *"...I never got to meet 'the man' Mr Hollinshead."* Again, it almost sounds as if he's talking in reference - that he has 'heard' or 'knew' about Glenn though obviously hadn't got to meet him. It's as though he's asking *"Truth Freedom"*, [Peter Molloy], who had made the previously mentioned comment saying he had met Sabina and in which Simon was replying to. Peter had said he knew Glenn and that Simon might have thought;

'well if this person knows Glenn and met my mother, then perhaps he knows about them knowing each other?' We put this question to Peter and he replied; 'that as far as he was aware, he didn't think Glenn knew Sabina prior to his encounter with her.' Though his answer wasn't an absolute 'no', it was more like; 'not that I was aware of' kind of response even though he had been convinced it was a chance encounter. Though since we have been able to put our new evidence to him that seems to prove Glenn did indeed encounter Sabina much earlier than Peter has led us to believe; Peter has conceded that Glenn must have known her [or met her] prior to "their" encounter some hours later in the street.

This is why we cannot rule out the fact that Glenn may have known certain people who also knew Sabina. And that due to what then happened to her, she might have been told to contact Glenn and for reasons explained further on. The Hollinshead family know nothing about Sabina and don't believe Glenn knew her beforehand. Though 54 year old Glenn led his own life. He obviously kept many things to himself. It's not out of the question he could of known people connected to her. He was a well-travelled man and knew some "heavy's" connected to the underworld and around different parts of the world. Like Sabina's brother Björn, Glenn too bought a boat and at one time had it moored in a marina down in Brighton's fashionably seafront area.

It's also interesting to note that on some of Simon's social network pages and in discussion with his friends in the USA, he refers to the M6 incident as a "car accident" that his mother and aunt were involved in. [11] It appears it was in 2007 when he left America and it's possible he returned to Norway with Sabina at the same time. He was at one time, in spring of 2008 talking about some of his friends coming from the US to stay with him for a holiday in Norway. Though he then states that his "step father" isn't so up on the idea and they couldn't stay at his home. Who is he referring to? "Stepfather", it doesn't sound like her alleged "partner" in Ireland, made clearer further on. Then some weeks later he tells them he has purchased the mentioned caravan and was hoping to move it down to the beach area, and that it would be okay for them to stay there with him. Though it then appears and because of what Sabina and Ursula did on the M6 motorway, that it scuppered his plans - for he then announced he had to return to Sweden and; *'be with the family'*.

We've only included the following out of a matter of interest and for reasons to help us understand a timeline as to where Sabina might have been prior to the 2008 incidents. For in our opinion we have been falsely misled into thinking she had been living in Ireland since at least the mid 2000's.

Sabina Erixon and Simon Leo Erixon are listed among the many people who participated in a public outreach program by filling out internet forms available in late 1997 and mid 1998 as part of NASA's Stardust robotic space probe that was launched on February 1999 to study the asteroid *5535 Annefrank* - and collect samples from the coma [stardust] of comet *Wild 2*. Stardust was launched carrying two sets of identical pairs of microchips that were engraved with over a million people's names suggesting this application was probably filled out online by Ursula in the USA sometime between 1997 and 1998. As mentioned above we know that around 1999-2000 Sabina worked at the *Explorer Bar* at Gardermoen Airport in Norway. It seems to be around this period of time that Simon then went to the USA and lived with Ursula - between the years 2000 and 2006 and what I've called before as the 'missing years' in regards to trying to place where Sabina was during this period of time. We have wondered; what perhaps was the catharsis - if of course there ever was - that may have caused Sabina to hand over Simon to Ursula and for him to go a live with her in the USA whilst Sabina remained working in Norway?

Did Sabina have some kind of mental illness or breakdown? Though perhaps something like that has nothing to do with it whatsoever. Sabina's partner, who I mention in the next chapter; appears to be an African-American, who was probably in the military. This kind of lifestyle can be disruptive to children and it is possible Sabina didn't want to disrupt Simons' schooling and thought it better off him living with Ursula –if of course this was the case to begin with.

Magnus Hellberg, a journalist working for one of Sweden's national newspapers, the *Expressen*, [8][9] wrote about this case on the 27th September 2008, and not long after Ursula had been released from hospital in the UK and then transferred to Sweden for further medical treatment. It was published in Swedish and has been translated from the original source. [8][9] They claim to have spoken to her older brother, Björn Eriksson. The translation doesn't seem to read accurately, the grammar is not precise. However, we can get the gist of what's been said. In another previous article in the *Expressen*, Magnus Hellberg states Björn had said: *"It was my nephew called and told me she was in hospital in England."* We presume this was Simon.

In the main article I am referring to, the quote is as follows: 'But according to their few years older brother of the sisters, who are from western Sweden, were being chased by madmen and forced to flee into the highway.' - *"They took rather a truck in the snout than to be gang-raped"*, he said. *"I had also run if I was girl."*

48

I've already explained elsewhere about the implausible possibilities about a 'gang of men' wishing to have wanted to chase the twins at Keele services with the sole intention of raping them at a very busy junction and service station area on the M6 motorway with CCTV all over the place. We have recently obtained evidence which is revealed further on, that proves the twins were already fleeing a "gang of men" and had been involved in a serious "argument" with her "partner", and why they first went to the police in Liverpool to report their serious accusations and allegations.

Maybe the above translation or what Björn was trying to say is not totally correct? For he too must have now known what it was about and why the sisters first went to St Anne Street police station to report their concerns that Saturday morning on the 17th May 2008.

Was he trying to explain that he was aware the twins were being "pursued" by a 'third party' - a group or gang of men?

As what we've recently discovered seems to add weight and some merit to what he was trying to convey. His reference to being 'gang-raped' and the following sentence; '...chased by madmen and forced to flee', could well turn out to have some kind of connection and reference to what had happened between her and her "partner" the previous day, [again this will be explained further on], and why it's said they first fled Ireland.

Perhaps something untoward did happen somewhere; again with drink and drugs involved - anything is possible.

The *Expressen* article goes on: 'One of the twin sisters are thus now incarcerated in England, on suspicion of murder. The other is back in Sweden. Her brother has been in touch and met her several times.' The following quotes are from Björn: *"She's in a wheelchair. She will surely be good eventually, but it will take time."* 'Not talking to her sister. The sister who remains in England has not got her brother to talk to. She had several internal bleeding and other injuries and broken bones.' *"I do not know exactly, but she had some form of spinal crimes and lies in gypsum rock."* 'He has not been told what his sister is charged with.' *"What I have with me is that she is suspected of having killed another person."* 'How would you describe your sisters?' *"Two sports maniacs. They have always been involved in sports and dance. They have always been overactive and so they cannot move anymore."* [8][9] I contacted Magnus Hellberg, at the *Expressen*,[9][10] back in May 2012, in relation to the "interviews" he had with Björn. I explained that we had uncovered some vital information that really alters the dynamics of this case. I never received a reply, though hopefully they will pick up on where they left it and report our findings soon. The same goes with our media in general, for without them covering such a story then without doubt it will be a challenge to get this information out to the masses and for them to know the truth.

It's difficult to work out Sabina's actual release date from prison. For was she a "remanded" prisoner for the remainder of the time she was in hospital or did her remand time start on the day she was discharged in September 2008? It's these dates that will determine the date her licence expires - sometime in 2013. It's feasible, which is explained throughout parts of the book, that Sabina could have made a "deal" with the police and that she's still under a "gagging order" for a set period of time; for as indicated we suspect the twins were in one way or another involved in some form of drug smuggling or something closely connected to such an criminal activity like that of money laundering or dealing in 'cutting agents'. Or perhaps some other major crime as someone has suggested, such as another murder which took place in Gothenburg, Sweden in October 2005. It's even possible they are part of some government experiment involving unscrupulous secret-service agencies.

Whilst Simon lived in the USA, it appears he made two particular close friends who he went to High School with. We know their names but there's no need for us to quote them. It appears Simon left America around 2007 and was arranging for these two friends to come and stay with him in Norway. Let's not forget they are young lads, around 17 to 18 years of age so a lot of young men this age - and when miles apart dream-up and fantasise about making crazy plans and schemes. It doesn't make them bad people. In fact what I can make of Simon, he appears to have grown into a nice young man who is happy in a relationship with his new girlfriend.

The following comments were made previous to the M6 incident, perhaps around 2007 for we can only see the approximate 'year' it was supposed to be posted. There is no month or day date, that's how it works on *MySpace*, - after some years have gone-by it just notes the year. So it was around this time he first mentions the town Kileen: *"...good hearing from you D. I'll be Terrorising the streets of Kileen in Noo Time!"* [11]

"Nah it's not at all like Ursula's tea..., P it's like weed-tea or hash tea, its fucking daank. I think the concept comes from Amsterdam.... dude your still down to go there right? How's it been like in Kileen's little town?" [11]

51

This is part of a comment made from a friend of Simon's in the USA, to their other friend: *"Oh Yea and Bro, we're gonna have so much Bud its Sick! I'm gonna try and get some seeds from SoCal ya know and plant them over there! Seriously when Simon was telling me about making $100 in like 20 mins, I was like what we're growing...lol But it has to be good though 2!"* [11]

The 17th May of each year is the *National Day* - Norwegian Constitution Day and is an official national holiday. It's like that of *Thanks Giving* day in the USA where family members try to get together and enjoy the holiday with each other. You will see that we think the twin sisters made a major mistake by boarding the wrong coach in Liverpool and that there was a possibility they were heading for Newcastle-upon-Tyne though accidently ended up heading towards Newcastle-under-Lyme instead. I will fully explain throughout the book how this could have been the case.

Had Sabina and Ursula wanted to get the ferry to Norway from Newcastle-upon-Tyne (see Photo Section), then it's possible they could have made it back home for a surprise visit that same weekend. Here's a comment made by Simon just prior to the M6 motorway dash: *"ALOOOT of shit has been going down, the 17th of this month is the national party day in Norway, well it's actually like the flag-day or some shit, but it's just another excuse to get pudekcuff :)"* [11]

The following comment was made around September 2008, four months after the M6 incident and when the twins were released from hospital. Sabina was sent to Bronzefield Prison whilst it was arranged for Ursula to be returned to Sweden: *"I'm back in Sweden, my aunt is getting a hospital transfer thingy so she's coming to*

52

Sweden on Friday... - but damn that's soo fucking crazy about getting chased down, fuck Kileen, you gotta bolt outta there bro, come be a professional stoner here in good ol Europe." [11]

This following appears to have been made around 2009; *"I've got a place in Sweden were we can hang, a trailer in Oslo, a place in Fredrikstad, and my uncle has a Sail Boat were we can chill ... "Oh and tell em, were gonna be selling on the side... man were gonna have it made by the summer..." - "We got a VW Hippy bus, a Bedford camping truck, a moped, and a car... so far..."* [11]

Sabina's "Mystery" Partner

The Eriksson twins were in mid-journey from wherever it was they really originated from and before turning up at St Anne's Street police station in Liverpool - when Sabina first reported her concerns about; "her children's safety." Though that's all the public have ever known; we have never heard what 'her concerns' were, - until now that is. We emphasise "her children" as Simon seems to suggest she's the 'stepmother' of her "partners" children. Simon acknowledges them on his social network sites as his; 'two crazy younger brothers', aged one and six years old and not long before the M6 incident in 2008. It seems to suggest they have 'other mother's'. We know there is a younger male in the family, though as said we're not sure if he's a cousin or sibling, though it's likely he is the son of Björn. Then again he also mentions having two mothers, though is probably talking about his stepmother, via his father's side and partner. It appears as if Ursula has no children.

We emphasise Sabina's "partner", because what has been described of him by the police really doesn't fit the kind of person you'd expect to find living among an Irish travellers site in Southern Ireland. According to Jon Hollinshead, both police officers; Chris Short and Neil Baxter of Staffordshire police, told him that the Sabina's "partner" was a big black man. They described him; '...as a big-black-bloke covered in gold jewellery'. In a sense they tried to paint a watered down picture of the partner as a kind of combination of *Mr T,* come Marlon Brando's *'Godfather'* type of character.

They referred to the 'two children' as being a young girl and boy. Perhaps there's 'step-children' on both sides of Simon's parents and their respected partners? Though if there is Simon has not mentioned them in the six years he maintained his social network forums and pages. He talks openly and freely about his mother, stepfather, aunt and 'stepbrothers', but doesn't mention a stepsister. He names many various places all over Sweden and Norway where he has both worked and lived, including members of his family who have done the same. When he has spoken of his stepfather, he states he works all the time and is a 'really early riser'. He even mentions having relatives in the USA, meaning Ursula - and that they know people in the UK. Yet not once in all this time and hundreds upon hundreds of comments over this six year period does he ever once mention Ireland. And this is another reason we find it hard to believe Sabina was living there for the time period we've been led to believe it was. She might have temporarily lived there or even been taken there for some unknown reason, ["kidnapped", this is not an exaggeration as you'll soon see what was meant to have really occurred in Ireland.] Apart from Merseyside police recently confirming the address in Ireland and an officer from the Garda police reluctantly telling me in September 2012, that Sabina briefly returned to Ireland after her release from prison; this still doesn't mean she was 'settled' and living there and especially not dating back to 2006-7 as has often been quoted in the media and by the police.

In the early days of Sabina's trial and when she was still on remand in Bronzefield prison, the Hollinshead family were informed by the family liaison officer DC Chris Short - that the police had been to College Wood, Mallow, County Cork in Ireland to interview the alleged "partner". Jon Hollinshead also said that following the return of Glenn's mobile telephone, the police officer, DC Neil Baxter who returned the phone to him at his home on the 7th June 2012; said Sabina's "partner" had gone to Stoke-on-Trent and made a statement to the police back in 2008. Following the M6 incident, in the BBC *Madness in the Fast Lane* film, we see PC Elliott from the Central Motorway Police Group, supposedly telephoning the "partner", and family of Sabina. PC Elliott claimed that the "partner" said he had: *'...no idea she had even left the country'*. Though surely the partner's response should have been more likely: *"You're the second police force to contact me today in regards to Sabina."* It was further alleged by DC Short back in 2008 and then reconfirmed by DC Neil Baxter on that same day he returned Glenn's mobile phone to Jon, that Sabina and Ursula were recorded on CCTV inside St Anne's Street police station, Liverpool, reporting they were "concerned" about the "children's safety". Though what has just recently been told to us by the Merseyside Police in October 2012 and what I soon reveal - is what the twins really reported to the police, as it was a far more serious complaint than we were first led to believe it was. In fact it's shocking to find out this matter has never been revealed before. For some odd reason their visit to that police station in Liverpool wasn't even mentioned in the original BBC film.

DC Baxter went on to say; *'...that the police in Liverpool contacted the Garda in Ireland who in turn checked out the "children", and confirmed they were okay'*. At this stage over 36hrs had gone-by since their alleged departure from Cork. Though before we received this recent news from Merseyside police, we were questioning; 'Who did the Garda talk to?' Was it Sabina's son, Simon, who the police also claimed was over there in Ireland? For that's who Jon Hollinshead thought the police officer was referring to. Or was he meaning one of the younger children were present? According to our findings Simon appears to have been in Norway and had to return to Sweden following hearing the news of what happened to his mother and aunt on the M6. Around that time he was hoping to have already returned to America and this is when he announced on one of his social networks, that; '...*he had to go home to his family, for his mother and aunt had been involved in a car accident in England'*.

Like I say, certain things have since been confirmed by Merseyside police who say it was the "partner" the "Garda" spoke to. Which totally contradicts what was said and portrayed in the *Madness in the Fast Lane* film by PC Richard Elliott allegedly proclaiming that her "partner" had *'no idea'* Sabina and Ursula had even left "Ireland", - and that was at least 48hrs since the sisters had allegedly fled from there.

Two days had passed, yet we're expected to believe that the "partner" had *'no idea'* they were gone. For PC Elliott to say this happened seems a rather odd thing to say. For the police go on and state in the same documentary that Sabina's Swedish family were also surprised to hear that was the case. Surely most people would have noticed their partner and the mother of their children, alongside her twin sister and 'aunty Ursula', had gone missing and would have notified the police.

So are these claims a complete fabrication or is it a major gaffe that has occurred here?

Astonishingly, Merseyside's version of events seems to prove this so called 'telephone conversation' between PC Elliott and the "partner" was probably fabricated. We also tend to side with Sabina's family at their surprise to hear that her "partner" 'had *'no idea'* she was even gone. Was this embellishment of the facts used, which we'll prove further on, to help cover-up the fact they were probably under police "Obbo".

The term *"Obbo"* is a slang word for suspected criminals being under 'police observation'. For those who don't know too much about how common such police operations are and to help the reader understand the possible connection between the Eriksson's; then perhaps you should read the *"Obbo's"* & *Drug Dealers* and *Supergrasses'* chapters first. Though in order to help keep fluidity in the storyline I have placed such chapters in the *"Appendix"*. I give an explanation as to what kind of predicament these twins likely found themselves in.

Then there's the way we've been led to believe Sabina behaved following her release from police custody and Fenton Magistrates Court, which also doesn't add up. For why didn't she contact the Garda in Ireland to try and arrange something with her "partner" as soon as possible? Being as "concerned" about her children as she was portrayed to be as the 'real' reason she was meant to have been concerned in the first place reveals why was it her partner wasn't prompted into action? Why didn't 'he' arrange to come and meet her with the children or for her to go and meet him? More incriminating and you'll see in the next chapter, is why the Staffordshire police didn't take over from what it is the Merseyside police had said they did which was help resolve her problems with her children and "partner" in Ireland - especially when they must have learnt what really happened at St Anne Street police station, which we'll get to in a minute.

According to Jon Hollinshead, another odd and abstract part of this painted picture was when DC Short commented about Sabina's "partner": *"...he's not the kind of bloke you'd wish to approach he's a very intimidating traveller."* He added; *"...he's a man the locals go to see to sort any trouble out they might have."* As I've already suggested - by giving the impression that the man was some kind of "Godfather" gangster like figure among the travelling community, the Hollinshead family can't help wondering why DC Chris Short would say such a thing to them. Was it to warn them off? Were they concerned that Glenn's four brothers might have wished to take the law into their own hands and go and visit the "partner" in Ireland? We doubt that was the reason, besides they don't blame the "partner" - or Sabina. And since we showed our evidence to Jon, he has been able to move on as since Glenn's murder he had felt embittered towards Sabina, though he now says he has forgiven her. So was this a tactic to prevent the family or anyone else from prying into who this "partner" really was/is or what really happened in Ireland? Knowing full well the family would tell others inquiring into the matter and like they told us. Is it possible they hoped they'd be scared-off and stop their investigating? In this case the term "intimidating traveller", was meaning the partner lived on an Irish traveller's site, which College Wood certainly isn't and they couldn't be more off the mark if they tried.

What really happened in Liverpool!

Again, the Hollinshead family cannot understand why they weren't told the following information by Staffordshire police back in 2008. Here we have the very same words that have been extracted from the statement made by Det. Constable Gaskell, from the Merseyside Police. It was sent to us on the 2nd October 2012 by Merseyside's PSD. It was first prepared for the Crown Court in 2009, for they had been 'warned' to attend court, then de-warned due to Sabina's guilty plea, so this statement was never heard in court.

At approximately 08:40hrs on Saturday 17th May 2008, Det. Constable Gaskell was on duty at St Anne Street CID, when they were informed by Enquiry Officer 9709 McKetterick that Sabina and Ursula Eriksson were at the front office and that Sabina had informed him that her "partner" Michael Dossou had 'kidnapped' her two children in County Court, Ireland, the previous evening at their home address [we won't print the door number], The Crescent, College Wood, County Cork, ROI. Sabina had felt frightened and left the children with Dossou who is the children's father. Sabina with her sister Ursula had left County Cork and travelled to Liverpool and attended St Anne Police Station and informed them of their concerns.

Det. Constable Gaskell spoke with the twin sisters in the presence of Enquiry Officer 9709 McKetterick, Gaskell said they would contact the Garda police in Cork and request that they visit Dossou and check on the welfare of the children.

Det. Constable Gaskell then telephoned the Garda Head Quarters and was put through to Mallow Police station and spoke to Garda Officer Patrick Dennohy, they explained the situation to him. Constable Dennohy stated he would conduct a check to see if the children were okay and will contact Det. Constable Gaskell when done so.

Det. Constable Gaskell then created a Police log from Merseyside Altaris System log number 0805170509 and input the enquiries that they had done on the log.

At around 11:00hrs, Det. Constable Gaskell received a call from Constable Dennohy who informed them they had attended the home address and spoke with Dossou. He had informed the officer that he had an argument with Sabina the previous day over money and he was shocked to hear that she had gone to England. Dennohy said he would do a follow up visit over the weekend and pass it over to the social services on the coming Monday.

Constable Dennohy requested that the details of himself and his colleague a Constable James Carroll, be passed over to the Eriksson twins, so that when they returned home, they could contact them for assistance if they felt fear.

Det. Constable Gaskell then relayed this message to Enquiry Officer 9709 McKetterick, informing him to tell the Eriksson twins to return home to Ireland and the local police will assist them. The contact details were given to the sisters.

It was Det. Constable Gaskells' understanding that the twins would have returned to Ireland that day to collect the children with the assistance of the Garda Police. Det. Constable Gaskell then made a full update and requested the log be closed as Merseyside police could not conduct any further checks. These were now being carried out by

Garda police and any offences disclosed would be investigated by them.

Det. Constable Gaskell said: *"No offences had been disclosed to me whilst dealing with the sisters. They had left the children with the father who had no idea that they had come to England. They had not reported any incidents to the Garda Police. The Garda police had seen the children safe and well and were conducting a follow up visit before transferring to social services."*

On Thursday the 22nd May 2008, Det. Constable Gaskell came on duty and had a message to contact Detective Constable Neil Baxter from Staffordshire Police. They rang and spoke to each other, with Constable Baxter disclosing there had been a major incident within his forces area involving the twin sisters.

On Friday the 23rd May 2008, Det. Constable Gaskell requested that the CCTV from the front office be downloaded for viewing. That was the first time they had seen it as they said they had no reason to view it prior to their conversation with Det. Constable Baxter.

On Tuesday the 27th May 2008 Detective Constable Baxter attended St Anne Street Police Station and Det. Constable Gaskell handed over the CCTV footage to him. No copy was made, as Merseyside Police said it wasn't their investigation.

"Kidnapped!"

Can you believe she reported her children had been kidnapped! Yet this major and highly significant piece of information and evidence had been suppressed for over four years and until now!

I have since spoken to Constable Dennohy and his Superintendent Patrick McCarthy at Mallow Garda Station, Mallow, Co. Cork, Republic of Ireland, via telephone and after writing to them. They currently will not agree to discuss the case. Constable Dennohy has said he is prepared to give a statement though needs permission first. He doesn't seem to appear to fully agree with Det. Constable Gaskell's statement. It as if he wanted to tell me; there is 'another story' and 'version of events', though refused to answer my questions.

This not only confirms the Staffordshire police knew about what had happened in Liverpool by the 22nd May 2008, but they had actually collected the CCTV footage on the 27th May 2008.

So what really happened that day? This seems to suggest that it couldn't have been the "partner" the "police" spoke to for as we know he allegedly proclaimed to PC Richard Elliott; that he had 'no idea' Sabina and Ursula had even left "Ireland."

So we can only currently assume the police at Liverpool or was it the Garda in Ireland - did not do what was proclaimed or they did - and it was PC Richard Elliott who didn't do what is said he did in the documentary?

In addition, according to Paul Hollinshead, Ursula was meant to have 'freaked-out' when a man with a bright yellow [or orange], High-Viz fluorescent jacket walked into the reception area of the police station - who apparently wasn't a 'police officer' but builder of some kind. Ursula seemed to take one look at this 'stranger' and then jumped up onto the counter and reacted as if she was in fear. I raise and examine the significance of these "High-Viz" "fluorescent" colours and uniforms and the possible affects these kinds of items can have on someone who may have been hypnotised; to act as "trigger" and we look more into that much further on.

As far as we can tell, Dossou, seems to be an African name, quite common in Gambia for instance. We've done due diligence and searches on Michael Dossou, and can corroborate he appears to be the same Michael Victor Dossou, who was living in Kileen, Texas, around 2006/7/8. He appeared to live with his own family at an address in Georgia for 23 years.[a] It seems he also lived with his parents for around 7 years at another address, though later on it was just him living there alone. In the old home there appears to be his siblings too.[b] He is also registered at these addresses with a woman named Rebekah.[c][j] His next address shows him living with another woman named Katherine. She also lived at the original family home [a], and we believe she was his wife, for we've found a marriage taking place between them, (nee Katherine Nienaber) [d]. We can also find them living together in further addresses in the Georgia area. [e][f][g][h][i] There's a Michael Victor Dossou from the same place, Georgia, aged 38 years, - when back in 2009, was arrested on an alleged; "Simple Battery" charge; which was processed on the 2/12/2010.

We don't know what the outcome was and if of course that information is correct. Though it is here in Simon's comments that we've already mentioned that we seem to find the confirming link that tends to indicate we are looking at the 'same' Michael Dossou. We can now find him living in Kileen,[k][l] the very same place Simon has been mentioning. There are army units and bases in Kileen, the main employer of that region. How and when Sabina first met Dossou, who knows - other than it's possible he was in the army and met Sabina whilst she was in the USA with Ursula and Simon or perhaps elsewhere and before.

The "Ferry" Crossing

Like most things within this case even the "official" storyline doesn't add up. The following seems to indicate that the twins were already here in the UK and that they didn't leave Ireland the day before on the 16th May 2008. For if they did then they must have arrived with others and were not alone as believed.

They may have visited Ireland sometime before, though probably arrived in Liverpool some days prior to the M6 incident, for we understand that among their possessions were packets of *Duty Free* cigarettes. Though being on a ferry port they're regularly available for sale in and around the Liverpool dock area and in the pubs and clubs in general. Then again it's the timings that don't really add up if we are to believe what happened in St Anne Street police station and that Det. Constable Gaskell did speak to Constable Dennohy and that he in turn went to the home in Mallow to see that the "partner" and children were safe and well. For as we know he was meant to have said they had a row the night before, so it appears she was must have been in Ireland at that time for that "row" to have occurred. Something is not quite right about what we're being led to believe took place between Sabina and her "partner", or are they talking about the evening before?

So let's examine their alleged journey and route via Cork to Liverpool; starting with their supposed departure from College Wood, Mallow, County Cork, Ireland, on Friday the 16th May at 2am. [1] They then apparently turn up at St Anne Street Police Station, Liverpool, to report concerns over the kidnapping of Sabina's children at 8:40am on the 17th May.

65

That's 36½ hours later! For arguments sake and according to the 'official storyline' of events, it means the twins had plenty of time to arrange whatever way they wanted to arrive in the UK from Southern Ireland.

It's very unlikely they arrived in Liverpool via airplane and for various reasons. Being that the *John Lennon* airport is about 9 miles away from St Anne Street police station and that Admiral Street Police Station is the nearest, about 3½ miles away then they would have surely gone to that police station. Besides, there's a dedicated police section at the airport. Also passport control is much tighter than the ferry ports.

It was reported by the BBC's, *Madness in a Fast Lane* documentary [2] that they only had one passport between them, which has recently been confirmed to us by the police that it was Ursula's, as it was found in Sabina's possession after she jumped off the bridge-way above the A50. It has been questioned; 'How did Sabina [and Ursula] travel to the UK unhindered?' Firstly, all citizens of the EU, in which Sweden, Ireland and the UK are, don't require a passport. Though technically it would be better if you had one, just in case you were stopped and checked by the border agencies, which could cause a delay, though that's all, as you're free to travel without one if you have valid ID, such as a drivers licence or National Identity Card (NIC) issued by your own country.

If they did come from County Cork they must have departed from Dublin to Liverpool for that's the only Southern Irish port that could take you to Liverpool from the Ireland. You could go to the North of Ireland and to Belfast where you can board a *Stena Line* ferry as a foot passenger and to Liverpool, though this would take even longer, as it's further away from Cork and ultimately London. That ferry journey take around 8hrs. *Stena Line;*

have their *Superfast VIII*, that takes 2:15hrs, though as far as we can see this wasn't operating in May 2008. You can get a direct ferry from Cork, to Swansea in Wales. It's a much longer crossing, almost three times the sea distance than that of Dublin to Holyhead, the favourable route for people wanting to go to London, and the South of England in general.

We know they couldn't have taken this route from Dublin if they were not in a motor vehicle, for none of the ferry companies that operate this route, permit foot passengers.[3] If they got the *National Express* coach from Cork and we are to believe their destination was London, [4] then they would have gone via the mentioned Holyhead in Wales. It takes only about 3 ½ hours [according to weather] from Dublin to Holyhead via ferry, and it's a lot less mileage to London. A ferry from Dublin to Liverpool takes anything from 7 to 8 hours, according to the weather.

So it is for these reasons, in addition to what we believe and have been told, that we can't see why the twin sisters would leave Dublin to Liverpool if they were London bound. And if they did then they didn't arrive alone. They would have had to book a crossing as passengers in a vehicle, and the only person who can do that is the owner/driver of that vehicle, for you have to supply the registration number and pay for the number of passengers in advance.

And to quell any suggestions that they could have hung around Dublin ferry port and got someone to let them become passengers in their car, it resolutely cannot be permitted for you have to pay in advance and there's always a ships log recording exactly how many passengers are on board, if you're not recorded then how would they know how many passengers were on board following an accident? Their tickets would have to show the number of passengers in the car, you cannot simply drive onto a ferry without pre-booking it. Especially considering the terrorist problems between the IRA and the UK. "They" know exactly who leaves Eire and who then re-enters! Unless of course the sisters knew these "other people" [if they exist], who they could have been travelling with and they've deliberately chosen to remain silent for their own reasons.

Though we must question this; why didn't or hasn't anyone come forward and soon or long after the M6 motorway event and telling the world about their infamous passengers?

Over four years have gone-by and thousands of comments, blogs and questions have been put forward and raised; yet not one single person on the planet has ever come forward confirming they saw the twins travelling from Cork to Dublin, then the ferry trip from Dublin to Liverpool or the ferry ports themselves and the many other places these twin sisters would have had to have roamed around in these 36½ hours.

The way they were dressed, their clothing seemed rather old fashioned. Sabina's jeans looked way too small for her, though perhaps this is a sign that confirms they had to flee whatever place they did and just grabbed the first things that came to hand. It's most odd that these two dyed blond haired twins; one with a black cap, the other with a red visor with; *"Time to Believe"* emblazoned on it, wearing a bright lime-yellow puffer-jacket and the other in a full length red cardigan style coat and in a pair of jeans inches too short for her, went totally unnoticed, under the radar so to speak. Yet how can this be possible in our 24/7 CCTV world?

Unless of course they didn't make that ferry journey at all on that day.

This makes more sense and seems to solve the problem as this could be the reason why no one could have come forward to declare such a thing.

In addition, not only do we question that the twins didn't arrive in Bootle, Liverpool, where the port area is - via Dublin on the weekend of the 17th May 2008 – we do not believe they were London bound at all. Granted they may have been on a London bound coach, but as suggested before and explained now this was probably due to the fact they missed the first Newcastle-under-Lyme coach that departed Liverpool at 09:00am; for they were still at St Anne Street police station, and had to get the 11:30am one later on.

Let's not forget that these coaches have at least several ports of call where many people embark and disembark, so they're not all "London bound" passengers. Yet there's even another spanner we have to throw into the works because here's something else that cannot be overlooked. We don't know how familiar Sabina and Ursula were with the routes in the UK, Ireland and Norwegian region. Newcastle-under-Lyme is in the Borough of Newcastle and not to be confused with Newcastle-upon-Tyne in the North-East part of the country, (which can be seen on the map in the Photo Section, with its routes pointing towards Gothenburg and Kristiansand, in which we know the twins are connected to both places). For this midlands town near Keele Services is 'Newcastle-under-Lyme.' Locals from both of these separate places refer to them as "Newcastle", - and both drop their 'distinct' locations. I've made some serious travelling errors over the years and have headed towards the wrong destination on more than one occasion.

I once ended up in Korea and not Thailand as I mistakenly thought Seoul was in Thailand. Even though I knew it wasn't my lazy mind thought it knew I was heading towards the right region without looking at a world map when booking my flight reservation; these places are 2,700 miles apart! I should have simply looked at a map to remind myself, but foolishly didn't. It's surprisingly quite common among regular business travellers, take this gentleman; Goltsch, an electrical engineer who lives in West Caldwell, in the USA. He flew into Memphis one afternoon, rented a car and asked the agent how to get to Powell, Tennessee. *"We looked up the town,"* says Goltsch, recalling the incident that happened about a decade ago; *"We were both shocked when we found it was nearly 400 miles away."* [4]

It's possible the twins made the same kind of mishap. Imagine, there they were at Norton Street, Coach Station in Liverpool. They then enquired in their Swedish accent and asked some local *Liverpudlian*, who speaks in a broad *"Scouse"* accent and dialect; *"Hi, do you know which coach is for Newcastle?"* They could have said; *'Newcastle-upon-Tyne,* or *under Lyme'.* When the *"Scouser"* (a term for people originating in Liverpool or their accent/dialect), pauses for a moment and thought he heard; *'Newcastle-under-Lyme',* and then points and directs them to the wrong coach. It's even possible they made this error with the coach-driver at Liverpool and when the twins first boarded, they simply might have misunderstood each other. There's no real evidence that shows the twins were 100% heading towards Newcastle-under-Lyme, any more than there is evidence showing they were heading towards London. It was proposed to us that the twins were likely heading towards that area though it has never been substantiated, but then again neither has the London bound story by the police.

We think it's important to take into consideration the possibilities that they could of have been heading back towards Norway or Sweden via Newcastle-upon-Tyne as like I've mentioned before they were travelling on the 17th May 2008, the National Day in Norway. This would be more logical reason as to why they would take the longer route from Dublin to Liverpool and not Holyhead had they been London bound.

This doesn't change our position; the fact about the ferry crossing times or that foot-passengers are not permitted on that route from Dublin to Liverpool speak for themselves and that's why we find it very unlikely they came from Ireland the time the "official storyline" states they did. As mentioned; it was suggested to me by someone who couldn't substantiate what they said and considering what I've just explained about possible mix-up with the two "Newcastle's", that the twins were probably heading for a 'traveller's camp' known as the *Linehouse's gypsy and Traveller site*, or a house or property nearby Newcastle-under-Lyme. [5][6] But this version of events could be disinformation and came about because the police had already mentioned the "partner" being of the "traveller" type to the Hollinshead family. Though there's also an abundant of comments on the internet, making such references to them being 'traveller types'.

We're still looking at the scenario that they were involved in some kind of "illegal" activity like that of *Operation Happy Fish* and were still under police 'Obbo', though then found themselves stranded at Keele services due to a stupid error. That's what may have led to the confusion as to why they headed northwards up the M6 motorway. They were probably getting instructions from those they knew, via their mobile telephones, who were telling them about the shortcut into Newcastle-under-Lyme. They would have had to get another coach back from there [or Stoke-on-Trent] to Liverpool, then another one to Newcastle-Upon-Tyne, if of course this was their route and destination. For as I state and you'll see in the next chapter; Keele Services isn't a scheduled stop for National Express coaches and particularly those two routes involved so they wouldn't have been able to have got another coach from there anyway. And like what else has been highlighted whatever the case may be, these facts do not affect or alter the rest of the storyline and outcome.

The Coach Journey: – Why on the M6?

So following on from what I'm saying; we need to appreciate that it really does appear that the twins ended up mistakenly getting on the 11:30am Stoke-on-Trent to London coach and not the 11:30am Newcastle-under-Lyme coach that also departed from Norton Street, Liverpool at the very same time.

There are three different versions of events as to why the coach pulled into Keele services. Firstly; it's said that the twins were causing trouble and reported 'feeling ill'. Secondly; it was due to a routine driver change. Then thirdly; it was because the driver wanted to get them off the coach for they were acting suspicious and wouldn't let them back on because they wouldn't allow him to check their luggage. We go with the first option which is that the twins may well have caused some trouble complaining they were on the wrong coach. This might not have worked on the driver as after all what could he do? It wasn't his fault they boarded the wrong coach, though the twins may not have seen it that way so 'pretended' they were feeling unwell instead. This was probably a ploy to make the driver pull into Keele Services for as we now know the 11:30am Stoke-on-Trent to London coach is not scheduled to stop there.

It would have gone straight past Keele Services and onto Stoke-on-Trent's Hanley Bus Station instead. By making the driver pull into Keele Services would have been far easier for them to get to Newcastle-under-Lyme [or to head back to Liverpool, if Newcastle-upon-Tyne was indeed their destination], which lay's behind Keele Services.

73

The other 'official storyline' is that Keele Services was a scheduled stop to switch over drivers; though this is not true despite Det. Supt Garrett saying that Sabina Eriksson was only in Staffordshire on the 17th May 2008, because; *"The coach they were on only stopped at Keele Services to change drivers." "The two sisters got off the coach even though it wasn't a scheduled 'comfort-break' stop."*[1]

Though as we know he was right about it not being a scheduled stop, though how is it the police don't seem to know the actual facts in this case? Due to it not being a scheduled stop means the coach doesn't normally pull into the service station at all. According to *National Express* it wouldn't have even stopped there for a 'driver change' for this is done at the said Hanley Bus Station, Stoke-on-Trent just a few miles past Keele Services. And as you'll see, if it doesn't happen there then it takes place at Norton Canes Services M6 Toll, for that's where it stops for 20 minute scheduled break or and a scheduled driver change.

So it was totally incorrect for Det. Supt Garrett to make this very important statement. If anything these comments seem to back-up our theory that the twins 'intended' to get off at Keele Services all along as they didn't want to carry on southwards after realising their mistake, - if of course this was the case. It's possible they got on the Stoke-on-Trent to London coach because they either mistakenly did so or as I say, because they just missed the 11:30am Newcastle-under-Lyme coach and that they were on their way to that area and not Newcastle-upon-Tyne! I guess we will never know their precise original destination, though of what we do know then it doesn't seem to suggest they were on their way to London at all.

According to the BBC's *Madness on the Motorway* documentary, the following was said, the wording is verbatim:

Det. Sup. Dave Mellor: *"Sabina was a woman who lived in Ireland with her partner and two children, with no convictions or any evidence that she suffered from psychological or mental problems. Sabina has a twin sister Ursula. Ursula lived in America and during 2008 visited Sabina in country Cork in Ireland".*

Narrator Michael Usher: *"Sabina's partner told police the sister became inseparable, and then disappeared. A day later, the sisters turn up in Liverpool. Witnesses see them on a National Express coach bound for London. But they never make it that far".*

Let's examine what the 'official story' states, for it's said in the BBC documentary that the driver allegedly wanted them to put their luggage into the undercarriage section of the coach. Though when the twins refused, he then allegedly asked to inspect their bags; but again the twins refused, - so he apparently drove off without them. Though as said that is inconsistent even the Staffordshire police force's Annual Report 2009/10 that states: *'When the coach stopped for a 'driver change' at Keele services the sisters left the coach.'* Though we now know this 'driver change' story is totally untrue. You'll see in the *"Obbo's"* and *Drug Dealers* chapter, where it states; 1.3kg of cocaine [1] 'with an estimated street value of up to £150,000', that's just 3.30lbs in weight, a bag of sugar weighs just 2lb. So these twins could easily have been carrying these kinds of quantities and it's not surprising they wouldn't want to place their bags in the underbelly of the coach. We really don't believe this scenario even occurred that way at all for their small bags come under the category of being 'hand luggage' anyway. It's almost as if 'someone' is trying to 'sell' us the idea this is what happened and was the reason they ended up in that area.

The comments made in the documentary by Det. Sup. Dave Mellor, Det. Supt Garrett and PC Richard Elliott, have been questioned by the Hollinshead family. They want to know: Why did these officers say what they did when our evidence totally contradicts this?

Sharon Mackellar contacted *National Express*. She asked them various questions and requested to speak to the actual coach driver. However, they preferred to supply a company statement, which read: *"On May 17, 2008, there were two passengers whose behaviour led to them not being permitted to re-board their coach. Because we were concerned for their welfare and public protection, the relevant police authority as well as the station manager, were quickly informed".*

We know the station manager was Melissa Dutton who funnily enough left working at Keele Services soon after this M6 incident. According to Melissa, she left because she didn't really get on with her 'boss'. Sharon first contacted National Express on the 7th June 2012, though didn't get a reply. So she contacted them again on the 14th June 2012. I wrote to Melissa Dutton on the 11th June 2012, wanting to interview her. Rosalyn Golds, the media manager of National Express then replied with the above statement to Sharon at 15:35 on the 18th June 2012, when coincidently, 52 minutes later, Melissa then contacted me. Is it possible that someone from National Express may have not long before spoken to Melissa and prior her contacting me? Yet why would they? How and why would they still have her contact details? I have nothing to substantiate this and can only assume it's yet another coincidence, however, it's suspicious as hell.

National Express's own guidelines permit hand luggage sized bags the same the twins were carrying on board the coach; so no driver would have insisted they would have to place them in the under-section of the coach. Also, if it was a Health and Safety issue; *"...we were concerned for their welfare and public protection."* Then why on earth would they let them re-board the next National Express coach?

Because something is said as part of a script on a documentary film it doesn't necessarily mean the information they received was correct. So they will therefore only report according to what they have been told. We know they couldn't have come from Dublin to Liverpool by ferry as foot passengers. For sure they were in Liverpool, [according to the police], but why didn't the police or the BBC documentary mention the fact that they were in Liverpool at 08:40am on the morning of the 17th May 2008[4] reporting Sabina's children had been kidnapped?

As noted before, the way the twins both wore their visor and cap seems to indicate they were trying to keep their heads down and not be facially recognised. The claim by the narrator; *"Witnesses see them"*, seems to be unsubstantiated [unless they meant Melissa and the driver as being the witnesses], as not one witness has ever come forward in over four years and claimed they were either on the coach, ferry, or any other place. Not that it matters in relation to the coach for we suppose it could be said there's no dispute they were on it as they must have come from Liverpool somehow. Though it would help clear-up the matter about their journey from Cork to Liverpool if anyone could confirm they saw them on the ferry and of course the coach. Don't forget that all these places and areas where the twins allegedly were, are saturated in CCTV cameras.

I mention the following for it demonstrates how the police normally react to a terrorist alert and especially if they think a bomb is involved. Like in the Eriksson case, the *Megabus* "fake-cigarette' incident on the M6 motorway on the 5th July 2012, there are also three different versions of events about what had happened on that coach. It was widely reported that an "unknown passenger" called 999 and claimed they see smoke coming out of someone's luggage. Then it was said an "unknown passenger" contacted the driver to call the police about this smoking 'bag'.

However, here's the truth; the first driver David Myerscough knew about this drama was when 'he' was called by his control room in Birmingham and told to pull onto the hard shoulder at the M6 toll plaza near Lichfield, Staffs.[2] Apparently, he was asked to step in at the last minute to cover for another driver who had called in sick, so no "unknown passengers" did any of the previously claimed. It seems to suggest the police knew in advance the bus was to be stopped. They closed the road in both directions between junctions 3 and 4 at Weeford Park Plaza, near Lichfield and for several hours after the 'alleged' emergency call was received at 8.20am. Aerial footage from the scene revealed passengers, including women and children, having to sit within a square enclosure at regular distances from each other surrounded by armed uniformed officers. Several other cordoned-off areas could be seen with bright yellow tents erected on the other side of the toll plaza. More armed police officers were spotted by some passengers hiding in the trees and bushes. At least eight fire engines and a dozen police vehicles were at the scene, with sniffer dogs examining the abandoned coach. Coincidently *Megabus* coach service is owned by *Stagecoach,* who in turn are franchisees of *National Express*.

Det. Sup. Dave Mellor: *"The reason for their visit to the UK, remain unclear, we still don't truly understand why these sisters chose to catch that bus for London. Sabina in particular never gave us any indication during any of the interviews that might have helped us to understand the true reason why her, and her sister were visiting London."*

Yet again, it's almost as if someone wants to convince us of this storyline, i.e. Ireland to London - and that's it. It could be said that Det. Sup Dave Mellor's comment: *"...we still don't truly understand why these sisters chose to catch that bus for London,"* has a ring of truth about it, because "they" couldn't perhaps understand why they boarded it at all and could also clearly see it was the twins intention to get off at Keele Services and head northwards as opposed to southwards to London. If they were 'under Obbo' - "they" would have wanted to divert the viewer's attention from any other areas of interest. We have to consider that had they been 'under Obbo' and were so whilst still in Liverpool then their error of judgement of not going to Newcastle-upon-Tyne, if that was of course their originally intended journey; would have perplexed those doing the "Obbo" and following them. Though they could hardly now intervene and tell the twins they had boarded the wrong coach and would have just had to follow them.

Surely these officers knew their own Staffordshire police force had sent one of their officers, D.C Neil Baxter to Liverpool to collect the CCTV footage on the 27th May 2008; a week after Glenn's murder. According to Jon Hollinshead this same detective told him that he also went and collected a copy of the documentary film from Mentorn Productions, in London. Det. Sup Dave Mellor made that interview for the documentary long after the

79

M6 motorway incident. By saying what he did; *"The reason for their visit to the UK, remain unclear,"* really makes no sense at all.

Melissa Dutton, the retail manager at Keele services, said: *"The coach driver explains there were two girls on his coach acting very suspiciously. They wouldn't let him take the bags off them to go into the coach. So his reaction was, there must be something in the bags that shouldn't be there. He wasn't willing to let them back on the coach again, so could I deal with it. I went over and found them wandering around. They were carrying their bags very close to their chests, as if everything they owned in the world was in there. They were having this conversation about something, almost as if they were plotting something. We are told to look out for suspicious behaviour, my main concern there was a 'bomb in the bag'. They just walked right around to the back of the building, alarm bells rang, you know, what are these girls going to do? They became aware I was watching them, and that's the point I phoned the police."*

But nor do her version of events tally-up with what National Express told Sharon; *"...because we were concerned for their welfare and public protection, the relevant police authority as well as the station manager, were quickly informed"*. So why didn't the relevant police authorities arrive before Melissa had to telephone them? She had told me that at least 45 minutes had passed before she decided to call the police. Why do her versions of events completely contradict those of the police; not forgetting they are stating it was a driver change? Had the girls made such an error as getting onto the wrong coach, then it's very likely the driver wasn't going to allow them back on the coach for the twins most probably harassed him to stop in the first place. Had they wanted to go to Newcastle-under-Lyme, which is only about two miles from Keele Services, they probably expected him to take them there not understanding that it doesn't work like that and that the driver's next stop would have been Hanley Bus Station in Stoke-on-Trent. His best alternative would be to get rid of them at Keele Services if they weren't prepared to stay on until Stoke-on-Trent. And if they had said they felt sick as claimed, then the last thing he'd want is a passenger to vomit on the coach which if that had have happened, then technically he'd have to take the coach out of service and until it was properly cleaned. So a quick pulling off the M6 and into Keele Services would be a lot more convenient for him to do and would only take a couple of minutes to do so. Melissa then reconfirmed that as soon as they got off the coach they went over to the North side of the services.

Narrator Michael Usher: *"Officers turn up and speak to the sisters."*

Melissa Dutton: *"The police said to me these girls are going to find their way back to London, we've done our bit. They just left them there, with a phone number to contact the coach company, to come and collect them with the next coach..."* - *"to find their way back to London."* Does that suggest that they may have originated from there? Had they a return ticket from London to Liverpool on them?

Not forgetting what Melissa said; *"...out of the three police officers who attended the scene, not one of them bothered searching the twins' luggage."* This rather strange reaction by these police officers appears to have been the same kind of reaction the police gave in Liverpool. Not forgetting that were they under "Obbo" - we would hardly be in possession of a police statement where it said something along the lines: *"...following a 'name-check', I was then informed the twin sisters were under police observation. "* So there obviously has to be another version of events to help cover-up what really does happen on such occasions.

So like those officers at Liverpool, the police officers at Keele services and following a 'name-check'; they were probably instructed 'not to search' the girl's luggage and let them continue unhindered and on their journey. Or they simply failed miserably in their duty of care towards the public. For how could they fail not to check the twin's luggage when reacting to such an emergency call? I raised these points with the police - wanting to know: Why weren't the twins searched? The Staffordshire police confirmed on the 31st August 2012: *"The officers who were dispatched to the scene were sent to a suspicious incident. On speaking to the two, they were satisfied that they could continue on their journey. Nothing has come to light since that time which indicates that the officers were wrong in their judgement. "*

Wow! *"Nothing has come to light since that time..."* The comment seems to be completely ignoring the fact that only minutes after their failure to carry-out the most basic of searches on the twins they threw themselves into the oncoming traffic on the M6 motorway and Sabina then went on to allegedly kill a man! So was this kind of comment just another misjudgement? Again, we only have to recall how the Staffordshire Police reacted to the described *Megabus* "terror alert" on the 5th July 2012.[5] Perhaps you could understand such a reaction had it been reported they suspected a 'passenger carrying a bomb', just as Melissa Dutton had. Though that 2012 M6 incident was just about the alleged smoking of an e-cigarette!

The twins coach journey ended at Keele Services around 13:00pm. They had been there for 2:20mins, before being spotted on the central reservation of the M6 at 15:20pm. Firstly, we can rule out the misconception that the twins ran down onto the motorway because they were being chased by a 'gang of rapists', for it's hardly a place or time of day that such a thing would occur at such a busy service station, unless of course "the rapists" deliberately wanted to get caught. Plus the twins would have simply gone to where all the shops were and seen Melissa or some other member of staff, who in turn would have called the police. We've also seen how the twins can handle themselves, so I don't think "the rapists" would have stood much chance in trying to achieve their objective on the roadside, in some bushes or inside a motor vehicle of some kind. Though clearly, something was going on there. We now know about the reported 'kidnapping', so we cannot help wondering whether that had anything to do with the way they reacted. Had they contacted someone to come and meet them there? Was that "someone" running late or got lost? Assuming they were 'under Obbo, had they noticed the twins being followed? Had the twins got fed-up waiting and confused the short cut behind Keele Services with that of the other short cut via Three Mile Lane, approximately 600 or so yards away?

(You can see from the maps in the 'Photo Section', that on both sides of the service areas there are small slip roads that lead directly onto Three Mile Lane. But these are hidden from ground level they are not obvious exits or entrances as they lay way back on the very edge of the Keele Services property line. It's as if the twins knew there was a shortcut to Newcastle-under-Lyme, but couldn't find those 'hidden' exits so ended going the longer and dangerous way instead.)

Is it possible they thought they'd head down the M6 and towards Three Mile Lane? In many countries around the world, it's fairly common for people to walk along the motorways and often use the central reservations, as arguably it is safer than the hard shoulders. At least they're surrounded by the barriers. The surrounding parts of Keele Services is huge and wooded in areas and why you can't easily see those exits in which the locals regularly use at the rear of Keele Services. They are a favourite route among students from the local *Keele University*, they use these short cuts to get provisions late at night, though there is certainly no need to go onto the M6 motorway. It's possible the twins misunderstood this short-cut and began to walk back down to the motorway from the Keele Services area heading northwards, then walked about 600 yards to where you can see the Three Mile Lane crossing over the M6, and how you get to Newcastle-under-Lyme.

The twins were spotted by Birmingham Central on CCTV 6516 251/6B J15-16, and were approximately halfway between Keele Services and the Three Mile Lane crossing, that's a bridge-way that the twin sisters would have had to have climbed up the embankment to have gained access to the B road. Though if they walked a few hundred yards past and under Three Mile Lane, they could have then walked up the slip road that comes off the M6 and towards the town that way. You can see the bridge-way on the BBC documentary, it's in the distance behind from where the helicopter ambulance comes from. You can also see where the twins ran out, particularly where Sabina jumped the central reservation after assaulting PC Cope. It was exactly where the motorway 'Location Sign': M6 B 251.9 was positioned. That's how we were able to work out exactly where and how far they were on the M6.

Birmingham Central noticed them and notified the *Executive Highway Agency*, who sent two of its officers towards the twins. On approaching them the girls noticed the officers, and that's when it appears they panicked and decided to get away.

On their first encounter with the traffic, Ursula can be seen dodging the cars. And a closer look at the film shows that Sabina didn't in fact throw herself into the oncoming traffic that's believed by millions, but it appears she slipped up on her own long red coat and for a brief second got clipped, perhaps even caught up with the wing mirror of the red vehicle seen in the footage. She was of course lucky that she didn't sustain any serious, if any injuries on that occasion. You can see further on in the film, and moments before she is surrounded by the six people who grab hold of her, that Sabina can't manoeuvre properly and nearly trips up on her long coat, so slips it off and let's it fall to the ground.

Going back to their fear of being "kidnapped", this may have been the reason they panicked and decided to jump over the central reservation and onto the other side of the motorway, when the Highway Agency officers arrived. It's probably why Ursula was shouting out; "Help! Call the police..., you are not the police," for it's almost as if they thought they were about to be kidnapped by this group of "people" dressed up in bright 'high-viz' florescent uniforms.

It could be said that had the twins had drugs on them, then they would have been discovered by the police. But we know the police didn't search them. We know Sabina had a large wedge of cash in her hand when she later on encountered Glenn and Peter Molloy, around 50hrs later. There could have been a lot more cash inside their bags or on their person and probably why they were holding them so tightly to begin with.

Let's consider the following which is a common procedure and practice by the police: 1.3 kilos were found on the 9th January 2011, it was discovered hidden in the base of a flower vase by UK Border Agency [UKBA] officers and the police in Belfast let that women travel-on with the drugs in her possession and whilst 'under Obbo. The police and UKBA often do this type of thing. They followed her to an address hoping she would have led them onto "bigger fish", such as those who must have funded this "courier" to begin with.[9] And the same sort of thing would have happened to Sabina, especially if she was already 'under Obbo' and due to her being released so soon from hospital seems to confirm that was indeed the case.

At Keele Services, there are the dustbins, bushes, flowers, trolley bins and an array of places they could have temporarily hidden something the size of a bag of sugar or less and this could well have been the case. I suppose we can assume had they had any drugs on them, then it's likely the drugs were concealed in some sort of professional way as in the nonrelated, cases I highlight below and elsewhere: *"...hidden in a false base in the vase which had been filled with expanding foam"*.[6] So drugs might not have been discovered, though let's say they could have been and if this was the case they wouldn't have been found until the police had the opportunity to fully examine their property, which was after the M6 mad dash incident. Which in this case and in Sabina's situation, she didn't end back into police custody until her release from hospital around 21:00pm that same evening. We know Ursula remained in hospital. They only briefly rummaged through the twins property on the hard shoulder of the M6, so they wouldn't have discovered anything professionally concealed. Had they found any drugs, then it wouldn't have been mentioned by the police if they/she was 'under Obbo for such a thing in the first place and the above example how the police normally deal with such cases would have probably been put into action.

We know it was around 15.20pm when the police were called to the M6 motorway about the twins, and that 2hrs 20mins had passed, which is quite a long time before they ventured onto the central reservation. We know it's very likely that the twins or those they might have been meeting, if of course they were, soon realised or understood they too were being observed by undercover police, or their other related agency agents. Had they pulled into the services and waited about, observing the cars and people in the vicinity? Did they see the twins being observed, and thought it's too dangerous to make contact with the twins, so aborted their plans to meet them?

Then reflecting on their reports at the Liverpool police station about Sabina's children being kidnapped, this vitally important information cannot be disregarded as it seems to show how serious this matter really was and from the very onset.

Even though it appears the Eriksson twins were directly 'under Obbo', as a duo they were probably but a small cog in a series of linked police operations that the "police", and no doubt other related agencies had been observing as they built upon a sequence of events and evidence. The data they were compiling would hopefully lead them directly to the other members of the gang and ultimately "Mr Big".

So as we end this chapter; "The Coach Journey:-Why on the M6?", another fact about the Liverpool-Newcastle-under-Lyme to the South Coast coach route is that it normally takes 1hr 40mins to arrive at Newcastle-under-Lyme. The Liverpool-via Stoke-on-Trent to London coach, takes 1hr 35mins to get to Stoke-on-Trent. We know Keele Services is not an official break or driver change location and it goes straight past Keele Services then onto Stoke-on-Trent, Hanley Bus Station and either changes drivers there or at Norton Canes Services M6 Toll - where as I said it takes a 20 minute scheduled break, [or and a driver change], this is the standard route since it was built in 2004. So now finding themselves "stranded" at Keele Services and like I've mentioned before; this could be the logical reason they then decided to walk down the central reservation in a northern direction towards Newcastle-under-Lyme.

As just pointed out, the only obvious reason they may have decided to walk down to the central reservation of the M6, was because they probably realised they weren't being met or collected after all, - if of course they were in the first place. This is why we believe they couldn't have made that journey from Dublin to Liverpool on the day in question and nor were they London bound the way we have been led to believe.

Cover-up - "Arrested" Under the 1983 Mental Health Act

Is this simply a case of negligence or is it a series of circumstances that led onto and permitted a deliberate act of dereliction of duty and care to then arise.

Let us remind ourselves, that on the 10th August 2010, [the 10th September 2010 in Scotland], the BBC's *Madness in the Fast Lane* film was first aired on TV. This documentary film carried on from where the news media had left it back in May 2008. It clearly showed two deranged women running into the oncoming traffic on the M6 motorway, in what can only be conceivably described as a suicide bid. Both had been sedated before being taken away. Ursula was airlifted to hospital and Sabina went by road in an ambulance. Yet as we know Sabina was then remarkably discharged from the University Hospital of North Staffordshire [UHNS] after only five hours. Then within around 48 hours after that M6 incident she had appeared at Fenton Magistrate Court, despite 'endangering the lives of many other people', she was only charged for 'trespassing onto a motorway.' The 'assault' charge was dropped.

Though saying that, this is not what the public have always been led to believe, however, in his reply to Rob Flello MP, on the 24th September 2012, Jeremy Wright MP, acting as the Parliamentary Under-Secretary of State for Justice, seems to indicate Sabina was only charged with 'trespass onto the motorway' and not the 'assault charge' for striking PC Cope. That means the charge must have been dropped within less than 36hrs. For Mr Wright doesn't mention it, and only refers to the 'trespass charge'. Perhaps this makes it more understandable as to why Sabina only received 24hrs imprisonment and because she'd already been in police custody for longer than this period she was immediately released.

To date, Ursula has never been charged with anything. We know it was very soon after this court appearance that Sabina went on to allegedly kill Glenn Hollinshead and before throwing herself off a bridge-way and onto the A50 road below breaking both her ankles and fracturing her skull. The very same injuries it's said Ursula had sustained on the M6 motorway.

You'll now read for the first time what truly happened that day on the motorway and that this crucial evidence and information was deliberately covered-up and hidden from the Hollinshead family and the public for all this time.

These women were clearly viewed as being "mentally disturbed", which was certainly a fair assumption. At Sabina's Crown Court trial hearing in September 2009, two forensic psychiatrists had examined her and came up with an astounding diagnosis of; '...an induced delusional disorder', termed; folie à deux = '*a madness shared by two*', and an 'acute polymorphic psychotic disorder', termed; bouffée délirante = '*a puff of madness*'. These diagnoses are within them self an admission that the twins were indeed categorised at the precise time they ran onto the M6 motorway, (and following the death of Glenn Hollinshead in Sabina's case), as being 'insane', 'mentally ill', and as such this kind of condition was recognised by the arresting officer, PC Finlayson, who in turn then implemented that 'special clause' in 1983 Mental Health Act at the time of their "arrest".

Technically, this isn't an "arrest" as we know it and why this clause is used as an alternative measure. The twins actions of wanting to kill themselves that way, clearly displayed to PC Finlayson that they appeared to be suffering from some kind of 'mental health condition' this was then seconded by his superior on the hard shoulder of the M6. They could obviously see what millions of viewers also did, along with those two psychiatrists quoted above that these twins were indeed "mentally ill", and needed to be taken to a secure place of safety. Perhaps they are/were suffering from another "mental illness" or a long term condition such as Schizophrenia, though the Folie à deux and Bouffée délirante diagnosis seem far too convenient. Why aren't other defence teams pulling this 'puff of madness' clause out of the hat as and when a person has lost the plot and done something equally as mad or disturbing?

Their sudden change of composure whilst on the hard shoulder of the motorway almost seems as if "something" triggered them off. There they were both standing and smoking the cigarettes each had in their hands, about which we discuss the significance of further on, when slowly and casually and without a word said between them, they telepathically seem to understand one another. Ursula then places her bag onto the ground then dashes out into the oncoming traffic. When instantaneously and without so much of a glance at her sister, Sabina went on to do exactly the same thing.

When we first informed the Hollinshead family what we had discovered and then showed them the evidence that these women were in fact "arrested" under the 1983 Mental Health Act, they were completely flabbergasted. They obviously felt betrayed and deceived by those involved. They questioned: *'So what went wrong with the system?'* Though much more worrying and a concern to them was why was there a need to cover-up such a thing in the first place?

Currently it appears that certain members of the UHNS and the police had colluded with each other for this to have happened. In addition members of the judiciary, solicitors and barristers, including the magistrate at Fenton Magistrates Court and of course the judges at the Crown Courts following Sabina's hearings, must have known there was something amiss here. Someone out of all those professionals involved in these types of cases, should have questioned and tackled these anomalies as and when they must have presented themselves.

The Hollinshead family can clearly see this abysmal case was fraught with so many errors from start to end, that they now feel its paramount this is addressed so as nothing like this can ever be permitted to happen again. So much so were the concerns as to why Sabina was released so prematurely from the A&E department that immediately following the outcome of her trial for the manslaughter of Glenn Hollinshead at Nottingham Crown Court on the 1st and 2nd September 2009, Stoke-on-Trent MP, Rob Flello, said; *"I think there needs to be an inquiry into what happened. It is a tragedy for everyone. Where things have been done wrong they need to be put right so that they don't happen again."*

Glenn's brother, Garry Hollinshead, said: *"I do question the criminal justice system for allowing somebody like this to be let out when she is capable of committing such a crime. - Her mental condition should have been properly assessed after what she did on the motorway and the experiences the police had. - Her mental disorder should have been picked up prior to her being let out in to the community."*

Paul Hollinshead also said: *"...is convinced this 'Puff of madness' diagnosis is very, very convenient for the state, and since Sabina is to be released in April 2011, she is not going to be closely watched/monitored after her discharge".*

Jon Hollinshead asks: *"Why did the hospital not keep her in hospital for observation over night as they do with all head injuries? What was the rush to get her processed by the police? Why was she ejected from court with no fixed abode, no money etc., like a piece of dirt cast out onto the general (unsuspecting) public in Fenton?"*

The Guardian's journalist, John Crace, wrote after the airing of the *Madness in the Fast Lane* documentary on the 11th August 2010; *"...if I was a relative of Glenn Hollinshead, the man who was stabbed to death, I'd want to know why Sabina had been released without being offered serious psychiatric help."*

It seems that it wasn't just the Hollinshead family that were deliberately misled and misinformed, but so were the public in general. They too were led to believe the police had no other alternative other than to process Sabina through the usual means of charging criminals. Yet the following will embarrassingly confirm that this wasn't the case and that someone along the way must have intervened and prevented this course of action from taking place.

Our emergency services do indeed have such procedures and practices in place. We currently do and did have back then in 2008 such government safeguards that are there to help prevent the very thing it's said Sabina Eriksson allegedly went on and committed. It's the already mentioned 'special clause' known as: *'Section 136 of the Mental Health Act 1983 - Police Power to Remove to a Place of Safety'.*[1]

There are occasions when the police may act if they believe that someone is suffering from a mental illness and is in need of immediate treatment or care. Trained for such events, PC Finlayson rightly so implemented and quoted Section 136 whilst Sabina and Ursula were still on the hard shoulder of the M6 motorway and, when they were being sedated by the doctors and paramedics at the scene. These powers are for when such occasions arise. They're clearly set out in Section 136 of the 1983 Mental Health Act. This gives the police the authority to take a person from a public place to a *"Place of Safety"*, either for their own protection or for the protection of others, so that their immediate needs can be properly assessed and appropriately dealt with. [1]

The 1983 Mental Health Act applies to people in England and Wales. It covers the reception, care and treatment of mentally disordered persons, the management of their property and other related matters. In particular, it provides the legislation by which people diagnosed with a mental disorder can be detained in hospital or police custody and have their disorder assessed, or even treated against their wishes, unofficially known as "sectioning". [3]

According to the 'Act', a 'place of safety' could be a hospital or a police station. A police station should only be used in exceptional circumstances, such as a serious threat of violence or danger to people providing care or support. A person may be transferred from one place of safety to another before assessment.[2] Taking someone to a place of safety will allow that person to be assessed by a doctor and interviewed by an Approved Mental Health Professional [AMHP][2], who are specially trained in both mental health - and the law relating to it. They are appointed by local authorities to interview people and assess their well-being.[2] The maximum time someone can be detained is 72 hours. By then, any necessary arrangements for the person's treatment and care should have been made. [3]

What seems to have been overlooked among all the chaos and confusion created by Ursula and Sabina, is that the paramedics refused to take them in that condition and this is why a sedative was used on both the Eriksson twins. Only minutes before Sabina rose back to her feet after being unconscious on the motorway for several minutes, striking PC Tracey Cope and knocking her to the ground as she jumped over the central reservation in a bid to escape the police. She clearly didn't believe they were the police and it then took six people to eventually get her pinned down and strapped up securely. This procedure was edited out of the original BBC documentary, but is clearly seen in the 'leaked' version [3] of the footage; and following the release of this book we have now uploaded it on *Youtube*, titled: *The "Edited-Out" Evidence from the BBC Madness in the Fast Lane Documentary.* [3b]

The following words are the actual transcript verbatim from the above footage and just quoted leaked version of the; *Madness in the Fast Lane* documentary which millions have never seen nor heard before. The camera shot is of an inspector on the scene standing next to PC Paul Finlayson. Sabina has just been sedated on the ground in front of them;

Narrator: *"Now the woman is safely restrained, PC Finlayson updates his senior officer."*

PC Finlayson: *"This one, has gone over the bonnet of that car, she's then got up, punched Tracey and gone over there."*
Inspector: *"This one, - is she arrest note..."* - [Meaning has she been 'notified' of arrest].

95

PC Finlayson: *"Well, 136 and she is..."*

Police Inspector: *"Well she needs to be, but, but if nothing else being on the carriageway, and err, for her safety"* [3b][4]

(Note: 11:00 minutes into the 'leaked unedited version' of the film and onwards, or just watch the 27 second video we uploaded onto *Youtube*, covering that above conversation only.)

Here we can clearly see and hear PC Finlayson reply; *"Well 136 and she is..."*, meaning that in this instance she will be treated under Section 136 of the 1983 Mental Health Act, under the section: - *Police Power to Remove to a Place of Safety*, and that his superior clearly agreed with his analysis.

This is because; "Arrests" under English law fall into two general categories; 'with' and 'without' a warrant and then into more specific subcategories. Regardless of what power a person is arrested under, they must be informed: [4] *"...that they are under arrest,"* [as soon as is practicable after the arrest], and: *"...of the ground for the arrest,"* [at the time of, or as soon as is practicable after, the arrest], otherwise the arrest is unlawful.[5] The "Warning of Arrest", which in the United Kingdom; a person must be told that he/she is under arrest, [6] and; *"...told in simple, non-technical language that he/she could understand, the essential legal and factual grounds for his/her arrest".*[7]

A person must be 'cautioned' when being arrested or subject to a criminal prosecution procedure, unless this is impractical due to the behaviour of the arrestee i.e. violence, drunkenness or under sedation. The caution required in England and Wales states; *"You do not have to say anything, but it may harm your defence if you do not mention when questioned something which you later rely on in court. Anything you do say may be given in evidence".* [8][9] Deviation from this accepted form is permitted, provided that the same information is conveyed.

In the case of the Eriksson twins and due to them having to be sedated, they were of course 'not' informed of their arrests. Nor could a 'warning of arrest' be issued. However, there are exceptions to the rule when dealing with members of the public suspected with having some kind of 'mental health' problem and why the 1983 Mental Health Act [9] exists and includes such sections. This is why PC Paul Finlayson and his superior were content with exercising Section 136 in the circumstances of the sedated and unconscious Eriksson twins. Upon arrival at the place of safety, the police will hand their completed Section136 documentation; a Form 434 that goes to the 'Bleep Holder' or nurse in charge. (The white top copy should be retained by police officer/s). Then there is a set format and procedure to follow, making sure all the documentation is completed correctly and that the attending AMHPs etc. are informed and that the patient is properly cared for. An assessment of the patient's mental condition and state of mind then takes place as soon as appropriate.

I wanted to know what kind of training was available for frontline police officers on Section 136 procedures and especially in May 2008. An internet search brought me to a website called: *What do they know?* It's dedicated to Freedom of Information Act [FOIA] requests. I noticed that on the 6th November 2011, a person named Hannah Wilson made a FOIA request to Staffordshire Police. [10]

On the 5th December 2011, Mr N. Jones on behalf of the Staffordshire Police force replied: ref No FOI 2938.

Hannah raised six questions though in order to save time and space we will only refer to question No 6. The question raised refers to the periods between 01/11/2006 and 31/10/2011 under Section 136 of the 1983 Mental Health Act. The question and reply was;

Q. 6. *"What training is provided to frontline officers with regards to identifying mental health illness?"*

Reply: *"With regards to question 6, I can confirm that all new Police officers and PCSO staff receive training with regards to dealing with and identification of Mental Health issues. Input from local partner agencies is vital to this training and it consists of talks and outside visits. Total time allocated is one and a half days. Custody officer training has a similar input."* [9]

When upon arrival at the 'Place of Safety', in this case it was the University Hospital of North Staffordshire (UHNS), PC Finlayson should have handed the completed Section 136 documentation to the Bleep Holder or nurse in charge, or another appropriate police officer failing he couldn't personally attend the hospital himself. The white top copy should have been retained by the police officer. A record of the time of arrival of Sabina and Ursula would also have been made immediately on reaching the hospital. And when Sabina was transferred the Form 434 must also record the time of arrival at the police station. The form must additional record the time of the patient's release from detention under Section 136, whatever the outcome. It's likely this paperwork is available and can be produced as evidence and why in July 2012 I made a Freedom of Information

Act (FOIA) request to Julia Bridgewater, the Chief Executive of the UHNS.

I requested the following;

1. The 'names of those who came to the decision that the patient was fit and well to be released from the hospital after only five hours of being admitted'

2. Copies of the s. 136 paperwork, including: Form 434, record of Sabina Eriksson time of arrival at the hospital and her release from detention under s.136, and the Trust's completed s.136 Audit Form.

3. Julia Bridgewater's 'position on this case'

On the 23rd August 2012, Catherine Warwick the Information Governance Manager, replied; *"Your request has been considered and I regret to inform you that the Trust cannot supply the information you have requested, as we believe to do so would be in breach of the Data Protection Act 1998 and the FOIA. Therefore, in accordance with Section 17 of the FOIA, this letter serves as a Refusal Notice."*

I replied, stating they have left me no other choice than to re-approach the UHNS Trust's Internal FOIA, allowing them to rectify this currently unacceptable position; *"This fact that Sabina Eriksson was "arrested" under Section 136, on the hard shoulder of the M6 motorway on the 17th May 2008, following being sedated alongside her twin sister Ursula Eriksson, has been 'covered up', and that we have direct evidence this was the case. The UHNS Trust is fully aware of these facts, so we can only construe that UHNS Trust has decided to collude with the other*

authoritative body [bodies] involved, and appear to wish
to continue to help cover up these facts four years later
on."

Up until the time of going to print my last contact with them was in October 2012, requesting an update which they assure me they are treating as a 'priority.' I have not yet received a reply. It appears they are doing their utmost to avoid answering our questions.

UK NHS Whistleblower Dr Rita Pal, raised issues of patient neglect on Ward 87 North Staffordshire NHS Trust Stoke-on-Trent. Professor Steve Bolsin's report [9a] and a 2001 Internal Report into the ward is detailed.[9b] Concerns were raised with the General Medical Council UK, but the investigation reversed on the Whistleblower. The GMC raised the spectre of mental illness to discredit the whistle-blowing issues. Dr Pal subsequently sued for libel.[9c] R Pal v General Medical Council, Sarah Bedwell, Peter Lynn and Catherine Green was the first libel case in the history of the GMC, and Dr Pal won on a strike out. The GNC made a financial settlement with the Whistleblower.

The police, AMHPs and doctors could have argued 'that indeed the Eriksson twins were first admitted under Section 136, but it was the psychologists and psychiatrists who then diagnosed Sabina as being 'normal, fit and a well'.

Though there is the argument that they cannot overlook or ignore; the later diagnosis made by the two forensic psychiatrists who examined Sabina and who both came up with diagnoses of an 'induced delusional disorder' and an 'acute polymorphic psychotic disorder' at Sabina's Crown Court trial hearing in September 2009. This was accepted by the court as being the case. They were both agreeing this was the mental condition of the twins 'at the time of their arrest' on the M6 motorway, - and then following on when Glenn Hollinshead's was murdered, which Sabina wouldn't have been involved in if she was detained under the Section 136 she was first admitted to hospital under and not released within just five hours.

And since the Staffordshire police force's reply on the 31st August 2012, we have to question why was this matter of the Section 136 "arrest", - never again mentioned by PC Finlayson?

For as we say it has never been seen or heard by the millions of people who have watched the BBC's *Madness in the Fast Lane,* [11] and *Dicing with Death* [12] documentaries; simply because this vital evidence was covered-up and edited out.

The Hollinshead family would like to know; why is it that the Staffordshire police's own records have no mentioned of this? For this was also confirmed by Staffordshire police PSD, that they have no record of this section 136 arrest.

According to Jon Hollinshead, the original Mentorn Productions film crew were suddenly changed partway through the original production - and they wondered why? It was thought this is one of reason why the 'uncut' 15 minute edited out 'leaked version' - all of a sudden appeared on the internet as it could only have been done so by someone who had access to the original film footage. Even in the uncut version it appears PC Finlayson was probably readdressed about what he'd said in regards to the Section 136 in this film and possibly pre-prepared as to what to say next. They were likely going to keep this 'Section136' in the original film and why the following statement below was first filmed. It's unclear

101

the exact reasons why this was not shown, perhaps the 'legal' department acting in the interest of the police and the hospital trust or covering any other legal issues decided to have it edited out.

You can immediately see following on from that mentioned; *"Well 136 and she is..."* comment in the film, that it then cuts back to PC Finlayson at the police station or wherever it was he was re-interviewed. It was clearly after the M6 incident as he is talking in reflection as to what had happened that day. He's cleaned up and in fresh clothing. Yet oddly enough there is no mention of his comment about the Section 136 he had discussed with his superior in the film just seconds before. Instead, PC Finlayson goes on trying to now justify the twins arrest; *"These women obviously committed an offence, by being pedestrians on the motorway, she also assaulted Tracey, and she needed arresting for that criminal offence, assaulting a police officer and obviously being on a motorway"*.

Was this comment made so as to try and deflect anyone who may have picked up on the 'Section 136' comment? Because isn't it ironic and as mentioned before that according to Jeremy Wright MPs letter of the 24th September 2012, he confirm the 'assault' charge never took place. Though because the reference to the Section 136 was edited out this probably explains why the above comment was also removed from the other original film.

Perhaps why this 'Section 136' has gone unnoticed for so long is that the majority of those who'd seen this 'leaked' film footage wouldn't have even picked up on this point and even if they did, most wouldn't have questioned PC Finlayson's; *"Well 136 and she is..."* comment. Only those 'in the know', such as other health workers and trained police officers etc. would have

102

perhaps understood exactly what PC Finlayson and his superior were referring to.

I only accidently discovered it on the film because I was transcribing some of the text for this book.

Did the hospital staff realise it was a grave error releasing Sabina so prematurely from hospital; because according to Paul Hollinshead a representative from the UHNS and where Paul coincidently also works, tried to get Sabina back from being in police custody and returned to hospital. It has also come to light that the IPCC were originally called in to investigate "something" and by the Staffordshire police force. The IPCC have confirmed this was the case though they wouldn't divulge who first contacted them. They went on to say that they assumed there wasn't a problem so withdrew their services. Though in a response to MP Rob Flello, who had made an enquiry into what had happened that day at the UHNS; it proves it was the Staffordshire police themselves who called in the IPCC.

Det. Supt. P. Bladen, Head of the PSD of Staffordshire Police; stated in his reply dated the 21st August 2012, that: *"Following the initial incident on Saturday 17th May 2008, the matter was referred by the Professional Standards Department of Staffordshire Police to the Independent Police Complaints Commission. This matter was returned for the completion of the road traffic investigation."*

"Following the death of Mr Hollinshead the updated circumstances were further referred by the PSD to the IPCC. That referral was returned to the Head of the PSD at the time, Supt. Popadynec on the 22nd May 2008. It was the view of the IPCC that there was no evidence of any link between the short period of detention and the actions

of Ms Eriksson or of any misconduct by any police officer. The matter was referred back for the force to deal with as appropriate. "

"It was then appointed to Anthony Fellows, as the Investigating Officer within the PSD and he monitored the ongoing investigation being conducted by the Major Investigation Department. On the 18ᵗʰ October 2008 he reported that no complaints had been made in respect of the case and that the matter should be filed as no further action. "

"You will be aware that a thorough investigation into all the circumstances of this case was carried out by members of the forces Major Investigations Department. The investigation was led by Detective Chief Inspector Ken Raper a Senior Investing Officer [for Staffordshire police]. "

This is because, technically speaking there was 'no one' at the time actually 'complaining'. It seems it was done as a precautionary measure were it to arise that the Hollinshead family or someone else was to come forward and complain to the IPCC about why was Sabina released so soon from hospital; among other matters in general.

Along with recommendations, procedures and guidelines to adhere to within the 1983 Mental Health Act; we also have to consider the aforementioned issuing of a "Warning of Arrest". The Holinshead family ask; *'Why - were all the guidelines and procedures completely ignored?'*

Sabina appeared at Fenton Magistrate Court, on the 19ᵗʰ May 2008, and was 'appointed' a local firm of solicitors from the Stoke-on-Trent area to represent her at the magistrate court. This is normally the case with most people who do not have their own solicitor. A "Duty

104

Solicitor" is appointed via the Legal Aid system. The Crown Prosecution Service (CPS) would have given the court the reasons as to why Sabina was in the dock before them; for example - what the charges were. They should have mentioned the "Assault Charge" on a Police Officer", though perhaps they didn't and only the "Trespassing onto the Motorway" charged was discussed.

For as said it appears that's all she was charged with. It's to be expected that the CPS would have given an explanation as to what took place and how she happened to trespass onto the motorway to begin with. They should have described how they put other people's lives in danger, an officer was assaulted, ambulances; including an air-ambulance were employed, among the many other emergency services that attended the scene. Even if she was only charged with 'trespass', the M6 was closed for several hours, thousands of drivers were held-up, hundreds of businesses must have lost thousands of pounds in lost revenue, and the whole operation must have cost hundreds of thousands of pounds to the tax-payer. Yet the magistrate only sentenced Sabina Eriksson to "one day" in prison. Almost anyone else in this very same kind of predicament would have no doubt been remanded in custody or bailed with or without conditions - and until they had had a Pre-Sentencing Report (PSR) carried out.

We understand the magistrate was probably told about the twins being arrested under Section 136, and that the appointed AMHPs found Sabina 'fit and well to attend court'. Though on hearing such activity on the M6 motorway, the magistrate should have questioned and raised the matter that it may also be necessary to obtain a further medical report on the defendant's physical or mental health. Normally, any offender whether they are suspected of being mentally disturbed or not would find their case being adjourned for at least two weeks and not heard and dealt with there and then like it was at Fenton courthouse that day with Sabina.

They were aware her twin sister Ursula was laying serious ill in hospital and why the Hollinshead family ask; *'Why did the magistrate act so differently in this case?'* *'What were the exceptions to the rule?'*

Sabina was regarded as being "mentally ill" during the alleged attack on Glenn and that moment of madness on the M6 motorway. Yet was no longer mentally ill after these incidents and this is apparently why she was not committed to a psychiatric hospital.

So what's really being said here?

Are the "experts" trying to tell us that Sabina and Ursula were suffering from "induced delusional disorder and acute polymorphic psychotic disorder" at the precise time of the M6 motorway incident, then five hours later Sabina was fine, fit and well and no longer suffering from a mental illness?

Then within 70 hours or so of this occurring these illnesses then returned at the precise time she is said to have killed Glenn, not forgetting Ursula wasn't even present, then some hours later the illness had simply disappeared again?

"You can't have it both ways." – "You cannot be 'half pregnant", said Glenn's brother, Jon Hollinshead.

If anything the psychiatrists and doctors should have kept Sabina in a secured environment for at least 24hrs. It's recommended 72 hours in the Section 136 of the 1983 Mental Health Act. It was a Saturday, so what was all the rush? Considering these alleged illnesses are 'extremely rare', then perhaps arose the occasion and opportunity for the medical profession to have learned much more about them from Sabina's and Ursula's alleged conditions as Professor Eastman points out; *"...we really don't know too much about these rare illnesses."*

It's been claimed that the three medical professionals who diagnosed Sabina at the hospital had no access to the original film footage of the sisters on the M6. Yet this is immaterial as what is as plain as day and even to a layperson, is that the twins were sedated on the roadside due to their behaviour. Between the official story and our investigation we can confidently state that an air and road ambulance was deployed and that an advance warning and indication from the emergency crews on the ground would liaise with those back in the A&E department to indicate what to expect from the "patients" they are bringing in.

Doctors and nurses would have beds and an area would be arranged with specialised medical staff waiting and with the appropriate equipment in place - and they would all be awaiting on 'stand-by' and expecting their arrival. Once they did arrive the paramedics would give a running commentary as to what had happened to the staff in A&E. They would have had to explain how the twins sustained their injuries, which was they 'ran out' into the oncoming traffic. Ursula went under a lorry and Sabina got hit by a VW car. These kind of actions were obviously carried out by 'very disturbed' individuals. Unless it was kept from them, then they would have also known PC Finlayson had 'booked/arrested' them under Section 136 of the Mental Health Act. So it's quite unsettling to hear the following in the BBC documentary:

Det. Sup. Dave Mellor; *"Sabina was seen of four separate occasions, by a police surgeon, consultant psychiatrist and a suitably qualified social worker. Those medical professionals, were satisfied there was no obvious sign of psychological or mental illness."*

You will see below that in the same BBC film, Professor Eastman goes on to justify as to why 'the police' might have not been able to make such a good judgement as to the mental condition of Sabina; though he is 'not' referring to the three medical professionals who assessed her before her premature release from hospital which is an important thing to consider. He also gives reasons as to why normally a psychiatrist may not always get it right when diagnosing someone at a police station, though Sabina was not yet even in police custody. She was taken directly to hospital, so what Professor Eastman is explaining is not essentially directed at why Sabina was released so early from A&E.

He said; *"Usually, when a psychiatrist essentially sees a prisoner, when they're in a police station, it is directed at a legal question; 'Is the person fit to be interviewed, is the person fit to charge, is the person fit to take to court'. So it's a very narrow set of questions, and usually the assessment, if you like, is relatively crude, it's not a cine-film assessment, it's a snapshot assessment. If she had a puff of madness, bouffée délirante, then it can come and go in its severity very quickly. So it may have been, by the time she was seen by police officers, she wasn't that mad if you like."*

We are not questioning what police officers may have seen. We're talking about the three medical professionals mentioned by Det. Sup. Dave Mellor.

It's been said that these rather convenient diagnosis were directed to happen so as "they" could get Sabina out of the mainstream medical environment and back onto the streets for reasons we are highlighting; which is the twins had been /under Obbo' prior to this incident.

And if this was the case then the "order" must have come from a much higher level of 'the powers that be' and totally oblivious to those ordinary police officers at the scene, such as PC Finlayson and PC Cope. If this was the likely scenario then it could be further contended that it was probably the very same people who were no doubt glad when the Section 136 incident was edited out of the BBC films.

As mentioned in the *'Introduction'* chapter; I said I'll explain the law in regards to blood tests and hopefully this will now dispel the myth that the twins were 'blood tested' for drugs and alcohol at the hospital.

Even in the *Madness in the Fast Lane* documentary it states that it was only Ursula who had been blood tested. It is illegal to take a blood test without someone's consent. Even if they took a sample test from Sabina when was still unconscious it couldn't have been used or mentioned for its illegal if she hadn't consented. Ursula was quite seriously injured so did have a blood test, though this was to test for blood-type only and in case she needed a blood transfusion.

So bearing this in mind; this statement of "no drugs found" in their blood stream, fits snugly into place for a suspect under police "Obbo" believed to be involved in drug smuggling. For had they not had these legal medications administered to them and a "positive" result did come back, then the police would be obliged to search both the sisters and their luggage thoroughly and which

109

could have revealed any drugs they may have had on concealed them.

In the BBC documentary it was suggested by PC Richard Elliott, that Sabina acted cold towards her sister; meaning she didn't seem to inquire about Ursula - and looked as if she was flirting with him. However, we have to remember only hours before she had been heavily sedated. You can tell by the film footage and by the look of her eyes and face that she was still clearly under the influence of whatever drugs had been administered to her and/or she had taken herself. Her facial skin seemed to have an allergic reaction to the medication. Perhaps this is another reason why it was said by the police that "no drugs" were involved.

As this worked twofold - for had they "suspected" the girls were under the influence of some an illegal substance which the original motorway police officers did and was probably the case and a view shared by many a viewer; but because of Ursula's injuries she would have no doubt been given Morphine as was likely Sabina - and then they were sedated.

Once in hospital - Sabina would have been given a drug such as *Narcan* that would have a reverse effect on the sedative and the same sort of drug given to people who overdose on illegal drugs.

So we have to appreciate the twins would have had a whole cocktail of prescription drugs within their blood systems – null and voiding any "drug test".

From what was soon to follow on from that brief encounter with officers at Keele Services, we most certainly have to say there were a few things that could indicate that the officers had made a serious error of judgement, though perhaps not as bad as others; such as - why was the evidence that proved PC Finlayson first arrested the Eriksson twins under Section 136 of the 1983 Mental Health Act, edited out of the original film?

Why are there anomalies in the Staffordshire police records that show no sign of this event ever taking place?

Why was Sabina released from hospital only five hours after the M6 motorway dash into the oncoming traffic by three AMHPs all specially trained for such circumstances?

In his reply on the 21st August 2012, to Rob Flello MP, D/Supt P Bladen, Head of Professional Standards at Staffordshire Police, states: *"I can confirm that whilst in custody Sabina Eriksson was examined by three separate doctors and underwent one formal assessment under the Mental Health Act. This assessment involved a social worker and a psychiatric consultant. No evidence was found of mental health problems."* This procedure does indeed back up the evidence that the twins were arrested under Section 136.

Let's not forget; it was alleged that it was their "luggage" that caused all the concern to begin with and why *National Express*, their coach driver and Melissa Dutton all raised their concerns.

Yet the police are now trying to simply brush aside the reasons they failed in not searching the twin's luggage. Then following on from the departure of those three police officers at Keele Services the twins probably thought to themselves - that was a close call: *'...why weren't we or our luggage searched?'* - For had they been searched then who knows what could have been discovered at this early stage?

It probably occurred to the twins they'd best stash "it" and collect "it" later or they could have already done this before the arrival of those police officers.

It could be argued that surely they wouldn't have gone in to St Anne Street police station in Liverpool to report that Sabina was concerned about the safety of her "two" children whilst carrying drugs. And I agree; though we don't know the full facts. Or they simply stashed "it" somewhere else whilst dealing with this matter or they didn't collect "it" until 'after' their visit to the station. It wasn't until 11:30am they boarded the coach, it was around 08:40am when they entered the St Anne police station. Again we don't know, but it's possible if there were any drugs they could have been concealed so professionally, i.e. like the other mentioned case in the *Obbo's and Drug Dealers* chapter; *'...hidden in a false base in the vase which had been filled with expanding foam,'* [13] that no one would be that suspicious especially if they had the affront to walk inside a police station with them. They weren't under arrest and went inside under their own accord, so the possibilities are still there. It could have simply been money we know that's what the partner had alleged they had rowed about just before the twins "disappeared" and turned up at St Anne Street police station.

Before we continue with the actual case it has been said certain parts of the film seem to be "acted" by those at the scene, including one of the police officers, PC Finlayson. They suggest that shots of him being filmed first getting out of the car to attend the scene on the hard-shoulder and when he can be heard reporting; *"...two possible fatal's"*, was staged. It's possible it just means PC Cope who can been seen running away from behind PC Finlayson to warn the oncoming drivers to slow down and stop had too

112

been re-enacted as well. The reason some film makers have to do this is because they probably don't have the original version of events, even though we know for sure it happened for real, it wasn't caught on film. Critics say there is more than one cameraman and it can appear that way, but you have to consider the editing and how many cameras were really in situ, which was three at least. There are two cameras mounted inside the *Motorway Cops* vehicle. One is on the centre of the windscreen filming what it sees directly in front and ahead in the road. There is second camera mounted on the driver's side, this can also capture who is sitting directly behind the front passenger seat in the back of the car. They angle the camera so as you cannot see who is sitting in the other backseat behind the driver for here is camera three, though this time it's held by a cameraman. This is why you get a combination of shots that once edited can appear as if there is more than one or two cameraman.

It's quite possible and very likely that the Mentorn film crew was also following the cameraman and the two police officers attending the scene, so could at some stage produce a forth camera. Though none of this would have affected the film footage of the twins running out into the motorway. For it just happened then and there when no one was expecting it. Had they known in advance then surely they would have wanted another camera shot of the oncoming traffic; with the twins running into the vehicles from that angle as well.

At the beginning of the film and seconds before the police officers arrival at the hard shoulder two Highway Agency officers were already standing with the twins; the mounted camera on the driver's side films the officers discussing what it is they are responding to. The view we then see is in the distance and we can notice the twins alongside the highway officers and their vehicle. This

113

shot was captured by the mounted camera on the windscreen; this also would have caught quite a lot of footage, for it would have just filmed what was happening directly in front of it. On their immediate arrival, PC Finlayson would have got straight out of the front of the vehicle and went to the highway's officer. Yet at this very same instance it was likely the cameraman who was sitting in the rear of their vehicle wouldn't have been able to have captured PC Finlayson doing this, even though he just watched it happen from the back of the car he wouldn't have been able to have caught that precise moment in time on film. And this is when it's necessary to re-enact that scene, so as you can translate what had really just happened. It's a regular occurrence and a technique used in all forms of documentary filming. It's not done to deceive, but to help give a clearer storyline to the viewer. Though we're not saying this was the case here for it seems the cameraman would have had more than enough time to have got out the car by that stage for they are clearly filming PC Finlayson talking to the Highway Agency officers at the side of the road and before he can be heard reporting; *"...two possible fatal's"*.

We also noticed a couple of other anomalies in the film; one being that the alleyway that was used in the film where Glenn died was not the actual alleyway behind Glenn's home and what you can see in the Photo Section of this book. They used an old cobbled side street further up the road. Perhaps it's because the gates that are now there were locked at the time of filming and prevented access. Though we had no problem as Frank Booth had the key and we would have thought he would have done the same thing for the Mentorn Productions crew.

The film was made over a series of months and as and when the case had appeared in the courts. It's obvious the hospital staff would not have had access to the film footage as the film was not even edited by that stage. They filmed the twins dashing onto the M6, then being calmed down and treated by the police and paramedics before being taken to hospital. They then filmed Sabina being discharged from there and back into police custody. We see her being processed, photographed and fingerprinted. She's seemed happily enough chatting away to the officers and giving the 'thumbs-up' as she smiles at the camera. At one time she is complaining about her feet smelling and that she would like to retain wearing her jewellery. She is asked by the 'booking in' Sergeant; *"Had you ever tried to harm herself before?"* Then sternly replies: *"No never."*

As mentioned before, we then see PC Richard Elliot being filmed whilst allegedly speaking to Sabina's partner in Ireland and her family back in Sweden. The officers involved that day would have probably finished their exhausting shifts and went home to have a bath and then off to bed. That's about it really in regards to the film though we do look into it again for it does seem to have slightly altered its original normal format of making a series of the *Motorway Cops*, in which this original film footage first appeared and months before the *Madness in the Fast Lane* documentary was even made; with the older footage combined and edited together with the new, thus making this second film.

Reflecting on the twin's bizarre behaviour; it's feasible that something as close to PCP could have been ingested by them. Peter Molly's statement about Sabina snatching the cigarettes from their mouths, saying: *"These ones could be poisonous,"* is what some people would term; textbook MK-Ultra. As I've said it's quite possible they had cigarettes dipped into some form of drug such as this. They could have smoked one whilst on the hard shoulder of the M6, for we can clearly see them smoking seconds before making their mad dash into the road. Sabina could have also smoked another one moments after she fled Glenn's house. You will see further on that we know at least 10 minutes went by before she was spotted fleeing. She must have come to a standstill at some point, probably hid in some of the many bushes around the area and had her last cigarette before deciding to carry on running and then jumping off the bridge-way above the A50, knowing full well it would be totally painless.

PCP is a recreational dissociative drug. Mainly an American thing and origin; it has since moved on to many places in the UK and Europe. Colloquially it's known as "angel dust" among other things. Its proper name is Phencyclidine, the chemical name is Phenylcyclohexyl-piperidine. It may be ingested, smoked or inhaled.[14] Formerly used as an anaesthetic agent, PCP exhibits both hallucinogenic and neurotoxic effects,[15][16] which alters the normal activity of the nervous system. In a liquid form it can be smoked by dipping a cigarette into the PCP. It's commonly known as "getting wet." There's a whole host of street names; *fry stick, dipper, happy stick, wet stick or a KJ'*, an abbreviation for *"Killer Joint."*

The inhalation of such drug induced smoke gives an instant euphoric feeling affecting the mind and body, especially the body, as to the 'user' it now feels to be almost separate from the mind and it is this separation that gives the body a "numbing" effect and feelings of dissociation that are induced by PCP. You cannot feel pain and could stab with a knife or hit yourself with a hammer with no painful effect. Again we do not know for certain why on earth these twins may have wished to have wanted to kill themselves other than perhaps what I've said; they couldn't face the consequences of being caught by those they were fleeing, - with the additional prospects of facing life in prison for their involvement in drugs or whatever they may have been involved in. It may have proved too much for them to endure and that by simply taking a few puffs on a PCP laced cigarette this would enable them to be able to go ahead and take such a drastic action, knowing full well they wouldn't feel a thing if they were to decide to do so.

Perhaps this is a reason why they may have had such doctored cigarettes on them in the first place; as an emergency precautionary measure. It could be said that Sabina's comment of; '...*not these ones*', and actions of snatching back the cigarettes seems to suggest this was likely the case whilst in the company of Peter Molloy and Glenn Hollinshead, - or at the very least that's what she believed to be the case.

Under "Obbo"

As we currently cannot substantiate the following we can only state we have been led to believe that the Eriksson twins were somehow involved in one or more of the "Obbo's" quoted in the *"Obbo's"* & *Drug Dealers* chapter in the *Appendix* section of the book.

Operation Happy Fish and *Operation Junko,* that through the police's own admission and in reference to that latter operation: *"It's fair to say that if someone has snorted cocaine since 2008, they have snorted some of Dale's product."* So what they're saying by this is that virtually all drug gangs operating in the UK around these times from 2008 and over a period of four years in which this operation ran for they would have had to have gone through Jamie Dale, John Cawley and Barry Hartley and who were arrested and jailed for being the main players in Operation Junko.

These men no doubt had many 'runners' and 'go-betweens' that helped them shift their alleged tons of cutting agents totalling a total market place worth £3.5bn. Hundreds of people must have been drawn in and been placed 'under Obbo' as a direct result of this operation alone. The 'powdered' drugs involved in *Operation Happy Fish*, which had connections to the Netherland's would too at some stage require 'cutting agents'. We also can't rule out their involvement with gangs such as the Whitney family from Liverpool, who also needed 'runners' etc. to either handle the 'real' illegal drugs, fetch the cutting agents or just to simply help launder the thousands of pounds cash from such dealings.

In cases such as this a whole array of agencies can be found working in conjunction with each other. Which ones precisely we cannot currently say for certain, though an inquiry could well reveal such information. It could be any of the following or a combination of them all: Interpol, Europol, the Garda, the National Drugs Unit and Revenue's Customs Service, the FBI, MI5, MI6, various British Police forces, the United Kingdom Border Agency [UKBA], Customs & Excise, London's Metropolitan Police and Swedish, Norwegian and Dutch law enforcement agencies in general.

I hope the details provided in the *"Obbo's & Drug Dealers"* chapter will demonstrate that whilst the Eriksson twins may have fled the Irish borders in what could have been for their lives to the UK; they were almost beyond doubt either being pursued by "others" within "their gang", or any number of the just quoted bodies or agencies who probably had these twins 'under Obbo', perhaps for some period of time. Yet as stated throughout certain sections of this book we're convinced they had already fled Ireland before the 'official storyline' date of the 16th May 2008.

The objective of the *"Obbo's & Drug Dealers* chapter is to help show how prevalent drug smuggling is in Ireland-Cork, Liverpool-Merseyside, Newcastle-under-Lyme, Stoke-on-Trent, Sweden and Norway in general. All these places have somehow been mentioned or perhaps are connected to the Eriksson twins. It's also to show you the kind of deals the police may have made with various criminal gang members and how commonplace covert police operations are, with many suspects kept 'under Obbo' and that in certain cases these unaccounted for "Obbo's" can go on for a number of years whilst costing millions of pounds of tax payers money in the process.

We further believe it was because of them being 'under Obbo' that the sisters were given a series of 'green lights' to continue their journeys unhindered. It wasn't really the fault of those police officers they encountered along the way, as in the case when Sabina pleaded for help as she was concerned about the kidnapping of her two children. In this kind of circumstance if two people under police observation walked into a police station and the police officers at the station were informed following a 'name check' that these sisters were 'of interest' to the police, the local police officers would have been indirectly told to "stand-down" or "back off" so-to-speak and probably why the women were allowed to continue on their journey.

According to Gary Hollinshead, he spoke to a friend of his who we won't mention, but is a senior police officer; that a code or details of information would have been covertly communicated between a superior officer following this name check on Sabina Eriksson and that a 'special' telephone number would be given to them to 'check-up' and find out what to do next. They would have alerted the officers that these twins were under surveillance by any of the already mentioned groups or agencies.

It's alleged the police checked with the Garda in Ireland to see if the children were safe and okay and that the Garda then came back and said; '...all was fine'. I am still trying to get the Garda's version of events and up until the time of going to print I have not had a full answer as to what happened in Mallow on those days.

Following on from what happened on the M6 motorway; those connected to the twins, her partner and perhaps other members of "the gang" - would have soon been alerted to the potential of an "Obbo" of their 'foot soldiers', 'mules' or 'runners' as soon as they got wind that the twins escaped arrest and any 'real' prosecution despite what they did on the M6 motorway.

Though as I point-out, we cannot totally rule-out the twins were already working as informants and that the people they were "fleeing" may have become aware of what was going on and were out to harm or kill them or kidnap her children.

Particularly when they must have learnt that Sabina had not only been discharged from hospital after just five hours, she was then only sentenced to 'one day' imprisonment at Fenton magistrate courts. The word would have spread like wildfire. The sisters would have become like lepers. According to Peter Molloy, Sabina had three mobile phones and a laptop when he and Glenn allegedly first encountered her. That's when he noticed she had a large wedge of cash in her possession. She would have been told to *'Stay away at all costs'*, and perhaps advised to go back to Sweden or Norway where we understand she presently resides.

It's alleged that she had been alone in Fenton for hours, so would have likely spoken to who she needed to, including her family who had already been alerted that she was in some kind of trouble and knew about Ursula's condition. Allegedly PC Elliott said he spoke to Sabina's "partner" and members of her "family" on the Saturday night previously. Her son Simon said on one of his social network pages that he had to go 'back-home' and stay with the family, for his mother and aunt had been involved in a 'car accident' in the UK. Let's not forget the 'two children' Sabina had reported as being kidnapped.

It seems as if Simon was in Norway at the time and was talking about going to the "family home" in Sweden.

He also said he lost around two or more mobile phones at this same time. He even set-up a *Facebook* page, *'411New Numbers'*, claiming to have lost yet another phone, four days after Glenn had been killed. We know mobiles phones have caught many criminals out as their GPS signals can be tracked and traced anywhere on the planet. We have to understand that had things turned out differently, meaning Glenn's death never occurred, then Sabina would have had to adjust to her new situation. Her head and thoughts must have been all over the place. Ursula was in hospital and a new plan of attack would have to be put into place. She would have had to contact those she was involved with seeking advice as to what the hell should she do next.

And like those who she was criminally linked to, if of course she was – they would have insisted she keeps well clear of them. Though they probably wanted to help her and would advise her she should contact someone she could trust. They might have said; 'hold on for a while and whilst they make some contacts in the area.' And it's here where it's possible Glenn may have been contacted by a friend of a friend. They may have asked him if he could help them out by looking after Sabina for the night. He then might have arranged to meet Sabina, though she got lost or the wrong directions before encountering Glenn, (and then allegedly again later on with Peter Molloy). Though we have recently discovered new witnesses and evidence that contradicts Peter Molloy's versions of events – despite him insisting it was a 'chance encounter'. So I put this new evidence to Peter; which is that I could see that Glenn had last spoken to a good friend of his who was a well-known local man named Mike, and who was once the landlord of the *Magician* pub opposite the *Royal Oak*.

Following a visit from Glenn's brothers and when they first informed Mike about Glenn's death, he simply broke down in tears. He got on with Glenn and they knew each other well. When I spoke to Mike in early October 2012, he confirmed Glenn had spoken to him and then astonishingly told me Glenn had said to him that he'd met "Sabina" by the church next door to Fenton courthouse and on his way home with his dog.

This was just gone 16:35pm and long before what Peter Molloy proclaims happened in the BBCs *Madness in the Fast Lane* film and when he states he and Glenn had been drinking until 21:30pm. I put this to Peter. He said perhaps the film makers had made a mistake or misunderstood what he'd said. He also pointed out it was common knowledge that he'd always said and what has often been quoted in the press as being between 19:30pm to 20:00pm when they first met Sabina.

Perhaps Glenn might not have told Peter that he had prior knowledge that they were to meet this Sabina and some sort of plan might have been concocted between Glenn and Sabina. For this is now what Peter has had to concede and he agrees with the fact that if Mike's recollection of events are correct then this additional evidence, alongside everything else we have uncovered – completely alters the story and adds further intrigue and mystery as to what may have really been happening here.

Apart from our own investigations very little is/was known about Sabina and Ursula Eriksson. We've already raised doubt about them not departing Ireland on the 16th or 17th May 2008 though it's likely - and particularly for Sabina that these girls may have done this kind of Ireland to the UK journey on other occasions, though not this specific weekend in question. For that's what 'drug-runners' do. It's how they earn their money and in some cases they may have one or more parcels to deliver to their 'punters', or like I've said it could be money they were handling. Nor forgetting that it appears Ursula had come over from the USA to Sweden and Norway to visit her family around this time in May 2008, and that Sabina was down as living with Ursula at the same address in the USA in 2007.

The reason I've included this example is because it seems we are looking at a very similar situation here with that of the Eriksson twin's case;

Silk, [1] is a British television drama series produced by the BBC and first shown in 2011. Written by former barrister, Peter Moffat, the series two, episode 5 [2], screened on the 12th June 2012, shows a prime example of the kind of extremes the police go to in helping to 'cover-up' a murder for they still had a family 'under Obbo' and why they decided not to act or respond earlier following a 999 call that had been received.

I've not the space to include a full explanation but it's about an Asian family whose father and two brothers are unforgiving for the Westernisation of their daughter/sister. When in a sudden argument one of the brother's grabs his sister and starts to force whisky down her throat. She's choking, though somehow manages to get the bottle from him, smashes it and then rams the broken bottle into the neck of her brother penetrating his main artery - and he dies. She's goes to trial for his murder and the police also give evidence against her.

The timings didn't add up - as from the time the police were first contacted and their response to the emergency call when 26 minutes later they receive a second call and then attend the home where the death occurred.

CCTV footage showed the brother leaving the house with a black bag. It turns out he and his family were 'under Obbo'. The police had been watching them and others trying to build up a case against them - when all of a sudden this 'out of the blue' incident happened in their home.

Instead of the police reacting earlier they held back from responding and gave the brother time to move the drugs from the home - and why the family didn't call 999 until sometime later. This came to light and the trial against the daughter/sister collapsed. Action was then taken against the police who helped cover-up the fact that the family had been 'under Obbo' all the time - and that they could have got to the scene much earlier - thus the brother's life may have been saved.

Cover-up: Two Weapons - Two Killers?

The main reason I contacted the coroner's office in Stoke-on-Trent, was to help clear up the uncertainty of how many times Glenn Hollinshead had been stabbed. Many reports and stories often varied from three to five wounds being inflicted.

I needed permission from the Hollinshead family to be able to obtain such sensitive and confidential reports and this was arranged. When I finally received it I was really just expecting to find and confirm the number of stab wounds for the record. Yet when I began to examine what was in front of me – my jaw almost dropped in total disbelief. Was there some kind of error? For what's utterly amazing is the fact that you can clearly see that two weapons were used to carry out Glenn's murder. Yet incredibly the first pathologist, [for the police], Dr Kolar, report in his 'Conclusion': Paragraph 5, states; *"I have examined a photograph of a recovered blade. The sharp force injuries identified are consistent with being caused by this blade."*

The following details and information will prove Dr Kolar is incorrect in his conclusion. If this doctor sincerely believes his above comment is correct then we must bring into question his ability as a pathologist and perhaps this is why the Staffordshire police said what they did on the 31st August 2012 in response to us indicating - that we believe it's quite possibly another person/s were involved in Glenn's murder and when they replied: *"...you challenge the interpretations of the stab wounds independently made by Dr Kolar and Dr Shorrock; that the knife recovered from the scene was capable of causing*

126

the injuries sustained by Mr Hollinshead. They do not raise the 'possibility' of a second weapon."

We assume the Staffordshire Police only had access to Dr Kolar's report, as after all he was "representing" the police and prosecution. For had they studied the second pathologist report carried out by Dr Kenneth Shorrock on the 19th June 2008 and who was "representing" the defence and Sabina, they would have seen that this doctor too could notice there was a major problem staring us straight in the face, albeit his own findings are somewhat contradictory;

On one hand he reports on page 9: 'Opinion' – Paragraph F: *"Only one weapon need have been used to produce all the wounds..."*

However, his next statements appear to recognise there most certainly is an irregularity, - for he goes onto say: *"...although I cannot completely exclude the 'possibility' that 'there was more than one [weapon].' If the identity of the weapon (s) is an issue, I should be able to determine whether any that are exhibited could have been used to inflict the injuries".*

Though he previously stated on page 8, paragraph D: *"...The wounds are all consistent with having been caused by a knife. The 'only one' whose dimensions are likely to accurately correspond to those of the causative weapon is (No2)."* '...the only one' being wound No 2, is the wound to the heart. Dr Shorrock couldn't be much clearer, concluding there was at least the 'possibility' 'two weapons' were involved in Glenn's death and that the last comment above, couldn't be much clearer and the following measurements prove this to be the case.

In Dr Shorrock's report; the blade and knife used is termed as a 'Paring knife'. We know and especially of that of a 'Paring Knife', (also termed a vegetable knife), - its blade typically starts with a pointed end and then widens outwards to its maximum width towards the handle. [See Photo Section]. At its sharpest end it would start with a pointed tip and gradually widen to its respective width. So for example it could be 12cm long in length, then starting at the tip measure; 0.2cm, 0.4cm, 0.6cm etc. and until it gets to its actual blade width of say 2.6cm wide. If that knife was to be thrust all the way into someone then arguably the wound would be 12cm deep and the skin cut 2.6cm wide. It would typically leave a gape, [or gap] perhaps as thick as what the blade was - such as 0.3cm - if the blade was at least that thick. Of course the size and width can be altered according to how the stab wound was made; the knife could be thrust inwards then twisted or wriggled and moved about so the wound could be made even wider.

We strongly believe there was more than 'one' blade used to kill Glenn Hollinshead, though only one blade is mentioned by the police and in the pathology report. As I've said; we don't know the width of the recovered blade, though we can confidently assume it was at least 2.6cm wide. Dr. Kolar says it was a 12cm long blade. The pathology report states:

1. The wound to the neck; was 2.9cm deep. Skin cut 2.1cm wide and made a gape of 0.2cm.

2. The first wound to the chest went straight through the left ventricle of the heart; it was 11cm deep. Skin cut 2.6cm wide and made a gape of 0.8cm

3. The second stab wound to the chest was 4cm deep. Skin cut 1.2cm wide and made a gape of 0.3cm.

4. The third stab wound to the chest was 3cm to 3.5cm deep. Skin cut 1.2cm wide and made a gape 0.3cm. You'll note, wounds, No 3 and 4, are almost identical, one being slightly deeper than the other.

Using a joint of Pork and the same kind of knife indicated by Dr Sharrock, we tried to replicate the size of the wounds stated in the report. Our tests proved you couldn't get two of the smaller entry wounds using the same blade going the depth of the wound like they allegedly did - and particularly in the circumstance how these wounds would have been inflicted. We therefore would argue with Dr Kolars' above comment - and even Dr Shorrocks'; *"Only one weapon need have been used to produce all the wounds..."*, that they are erroneous in their conclusions.

Throughout the report there is no mention of a second weapon - other than the comments stated. According to the first pathology report carried out by Dr Kolar, it states: *"On the kitchen floor a broken kitchen knife was noted. The blade measured around 12cm in length."*

We question; 'Why is there no width measurement included?'

Normally when a knife or blade is recovered the length and width is reported, it's vital for the pathologist to have such information for this is how they can determine the size of the entry wounds and compare them to the weapon/s recovered.

So important is it to know the width of the weapon that I can't help wondering why this has been missed. Whilst we are not in any way suggesting this has happened here; what if this was a deliberate act or indeed a genuine mistake made by Dr Kolar in not mentioning this fact? For it could be strongly argued this omission of the width of the blade could be misconstrued as a way of trying to obscure the true measurement of the weapon so as the wounds entry marks wouldn't be so obviously and blatantly incorrect - when at first glance at and reading such a report.

For a blade to have penetrated the skin and gone deeper as in the case of wounds No3 and No4, then the 'skin cut' width measurement must be as wide as No1, which was 2.1cm wide, but that only penetrated the neck 2.9cm in depth. Yet in this case both No3 and No4 are measuring a smaller entry skin cut of 1.2cm, though they penetrated deeper than wound No1. This reveals that the weapon used in wound No1 to the neck was different than the implement that must have caused wounds No3 and No4.

Wound No2 to the heart could have been caused by the same weapon that caused No1 and vice-versa. However, wounds No3 and No4 couldn't have possibly been done by this same blade, purely because the depth measurements don't match up. (See Photo Section.)

No3 and No4 wounds could nevertheless be achieved with a 'Boning knife' or penknife. Some 'Fillet knifes' are also similar in shape and size to a 'Boning knife'. These blades are typically around 1.2cm wide and continue at that same width for the majority of the length of the entire blade. With this type of knife you would be able to sustain a wound such as No 3 and No 4, 1.2cm wide and 4cm deep - and 3cm to 3.5cm deep respectively; though because the blade is also around 12cm long it's difficult to understand why it didn't penetrate the body deeper, unless of course they were short jabs.

However, there are many penknives that have blades that are 4cm long and just over 1cm wide; this would have been the ideal weapon to have used to achieve these size wounds. On the other hand you wouldn't be able to sustain this same wound at the depth of say 4cm using the same 'Paring knife' said to have caused wounds No1 and No2; - not forgetting this same blade that only went 2.9cm deep - yet made a 2.1cm wide entry mark as our tests proved - and why Dr Shorrock said: *"The 'only one' whose dimensions are likely to accurately correspond to those of the causative weapon is (No2)."*

This is why we conclude there must have been two separate weapons used to have made these sized wounds and therefore it raises the question of the likelihood that there were at least two people involved in causing such wounds or the 'killer' used two separate weapons.

Glenn showed no signs of defence wounds; it seems to side with the fact two people must have killed him with perhaps one restraining him whilst the other did the stabbing - or one stabbed him first and the other one followed.

Additionally, when the pathologist measures he starts from the heel of the foot and measures upwards to where the wound appears. Then working from the midline of the body, [the centre of the chest], they measure outwards.

Stab wound:

1. Measuring 148.5cm from the left heel and 3cm to the left of the midline, a stab wound to left side of the neck was present.

2. 121cm from the left heel and 6.5cm to the left of the midline the wound to the heart was present.
3. 116cm from the left heel and 16.5cm to the left of the midline a stab wound was present.
4. 113cm from the right heel and 3.5cm to the right of the midline a stab wound was present.

All the wounds are on the left side of the body, bar stab wound No4 which was 3.5cm right of the midline. Virtually just off the centre on the lower ribcage area. With the clear distinction between the size of the wounds suggesting 'two' weapons' were used. The one recovered from the scene, the 12cm blade of a 'paring knife' and probably the suggested penknife that has a 4cm long blade and could have caused wounds No 3 and No4.

Were the attacker/s standing directly in front of Glenn - they would most certainly have had to have been right-handed. Yet we can reveal Sabina Eriksson is a left-handed person indicating a further possibility she didn't inflict any of the wounds.

As mentioned before the lack of defence wounds seem to signifying that perhaps someone held Glenn's arms. This could in fact have been some kind of joint enterprise involving two or more people in Glenn's murder. And we look into the possibilities as to what might have happened further on. The report seems to indicate that the main devastating stab to the heart was probably the second strike to the body.

Our hands and arms instantly go to where we have been attacked - it's a natural reflex that "we" do without thinking about it. When I spoke to the coroner, Ian S Smith, he seemed to accept this would be the likely thing most people would do.

Dr Kolar and Dr Kenneth Shorrock come from the 'same stable', so to speak; they come from the same office. Dr Shorrock, is the same pathologist who incorrectly recorded in his report in July 2005; that Jean Charles de Menezes jumped over a barrier before "stumbling" down an escalator in the moments before police officers shot him. This matter came to light when it was proved de Menezes did not jump over the ticket barrier and probably used a *Travelcard* to pass through; this was subsequently confirmed by CCTV recordings shown at the Metropolitan Police trial.

Shorrock said he was 'given' the 'false information' during a "walk-through" with police officers at Stockwell tube station, South London, hours after the shooting. When Dr Shorrock was asked why were there "significant errors" in his initial report, he replied: *"This was what was told to me"*. Shorrock said he was not sure who told him de Menezes had "vaulted" the barrier before he was shot.

Then in September 2005; a General Medical Council hearing, found that Dr Shorrock had been; 'unprofessional, inconsistent, unreasonable and inappropriate'. He was reprimanded over his role in a botched trial which cost taxpayers £5million when he 'changed his report' into the cause of death of a pensioner who died during an operation and which led to her surgeon being 'wrongly' charged with manslaughter. The surgeon involved was Dr Hurais Syed, who was acquitted of manslaughter because of a lack of evidence. Dr Syed said: *"After the report was changed police decided to bring charges. My career and my life have been destroyed."*

Dr Shorrock was also employed to look at the findings of Dr Carey, the pathologist who carried out the second post-mortem on Ian Tomlinson's body, the newsvendor

133

who was assaulted and violently pushed to the ground during a G20 protest in the city of London, by PC Harwood, in which resulted with him dying. In May 2011, the IPCC released three reports into Tomlinson's death, written between April 2010 and May 2011. The third report detailed an allegation from Tomlinson's family that the police had offered misleading information to Dr Shorrock before the third autopsy report was written on the 22nd April 2009. The Metropolitan (Met) Police's 'point of contact' for Tomlinson's death, was Detective Inspector Eddie Hall. He told Dr Shorrock, who was conducting the autopsy for the Met, and Dr Ben Swift who was acting on behalf of PC Simon Harwood, that Tomlinson had fallen to the ground in front of a police van earlier in the evening though there was no evidence to support this claim.

It was later recorded that the IPCC ruled that D. I. Hall had been reckless in making this statement, yet said he hadn't intended to mislead the pathologists. [4]

In most cases you normally have the defence and prosecution teams coming from different camps. This obviously prevents a conflict of interest. This is why many co-defendants have to have separate legal teams despite facing the very same charges. However, in Sabina Eriksson's case it was Christopher Hotten QC who acted for the Crown and Anthony Barker QC who acted for the defence - Sabina. Both these "Silks" are from - No 5 Chambers, 7 Bedford Row, London.

On their shared website it reads; *"Christopher Hotten QC is one of the most sought-after silks on circuit. He has a particular interest in and experience of Munchausen's syndrome by proxy abuse and Asperger's syndrome in the context of serious crime, and was recently involved in the widely publicised case of Sabina Eriksson."* [5] - Anthony

Barker QC *"R -v- Eriksson - Defendant charged with murder following incident where defendant and her sister ran across the M6. Complex issues concerning mental illness and rare psychiatric disorder eventually resulted in the prosecution [CPS] accepting pleas to manslaughter on the grounds of diminished responsibility."*

It's interesting to note the following entry immediately follows the above listing: *Operation Robot - Prosecution of a conspiracy to supply 'class A' drugs for the Organised Crime Division, complex issues over disclosure."* We've made all sorts of searches on this oddly titled: *Operation 'Robot'* that involves 'complex issues of disclosure', though to no avail. We therefore can only assume it's yet another of those too sensitive to publically disclose what this operation entails as it would most probably have jeopardised other ongoing "Obbo's" on gangs supplying class-A drugs. By it being immediately listed under the R-v-Eriksson case seemed to suggest they could be connected.[6]

In May 2012 and approximately two weeks after contacting Mr Barker QC at No5 Chambers, his CV was removed. I was confused, so enquired and was told that Mr Barker had died in March 2012. Yet it was almost as if he didn't exist, for a man with such long and extinguished career, it appears there was no mention of his death in the media, no sign of an obituary from any of his work colleagues or the date of his funeral in *The Lawyer* magazine.

In 1992,[6a] Anthony Barker QC, represented two Birmingham men who'd been accused of shooting a gangster in a trial that was described by Barker as being; *"Riddled with incompetence and dishonesty."* He told the jury how corrupt CID officers offered a deal to witness Ria Maria Nasir, which involved dropping all charges

135

against her including any arising from a large quantity of drugs found at her home on Teesside. Irrespective of this, Miss Nasir refused to give evidence when the two men went on trial at Teesside Crown Court back in 1992, over the shooting of gangster Lee Duffy, who was later on stabbed to death. She obviously feared for her life to turn down such an offer by the police or has very high morals.

They were cleared of conspiracy to cause grievous bodily harm by acting as hit-men and sued Cleveland Chief Constablee Mr Barry Shaw for damages - due to a malicious prosecution. Mr Barker QC, alleged that Miss Nasir was paid £900 by the Cleveland police force and said: *"The video identification evidence against the men was tainted. The whole case was riddled with incompetence, corner-cutting and dishonesty"*. *"The investigation was so shot-through with flaws that there was no reasonable grounds for believing the men were guilty."*

I'm not at all suggesting Mr Hotten QC or Mr Barker QC colluded or shared case papers in Sabina Eriksson's case in any shape or form; though in such a small office as the No5 Chambers it is questionable that to be so close; is it possible for the occasion to arise that some clerk or secretary could accidently place some paperwork onto the wrong desk? The prosecution team could by chance stumble across the defence paperwork and vice versa. I am in no way saying that's what happened in this case though it's certainly a concern as the possibility must surely be present. According to ex-barrister and writer Peter Moffat; *"Chambers are like one big family, you talk to one another and help each other, but you're also in direct competition with each other for the work. It makes for an interesting dynamic."*

Photo Section

College Wood, Mallow, Cork, Ireland. This is
the typical sort of house found there.

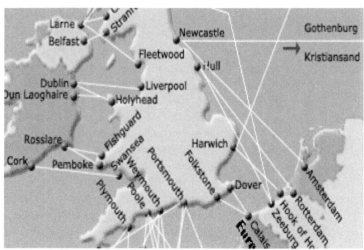

Ferry routes from to UK & Europe via
Newcastle-upon Tyne.

St Anne Street Police Station, Liverpool.

National Express Coach Station, Liverpool.

Keele Services

Another angle of Keele services

This is the bridge-way above the M6, that serves
both sides of Keele services.

The next left is the A500, that leads to Stoke-on-
Trent.

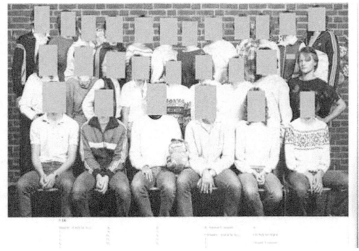

Old school photograph of Sabina.

Glenn's [left] first wedding day, with Jon as best-man. They are both in their RAF uniforms.

Here you can see a young Sabina writing with her left hand.

Glenn Hollinshead at his father's funeral mid 2000's

Fenton Magistrate Court.

The Royal Oak, Fenton.

Christchurch Parish, next to Fenton Magistrates Court.

Glenn's house on far left.

The factory gates, where Sabina was caught on CCTV, cameras mounted in the far back top roof corner.

This is the railway bridge that is at the end of Duke Street. In the far distance under the bridge, is the other side of Duke Street where Peter Molloy lives.

In the very far distance at the end of the road is the above railway bridge. [Excuse quality of photo]

Below is another angle where the CCTV camera is in top left corner.

Frank Booth, looking at the spot where Glenn
died.

The Bridge-way above the A50 at Heron Cross
roundabout, in which Sabina jumped off.

This is looking down from the above shot.

Paul Hollinshead at the top end of the alleyway
behind Glenn's home.

Frank Booth outside his house with another transit van.

The film crew inside Frank Booth's front room.

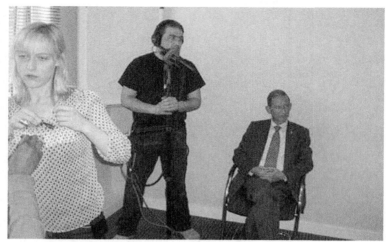

Sharon, Chris the soundman, and Jon Hollinshead.

Crew member Tom talking to Paul Hollinshead shortly before Sharon interviewed him.

Filming outside the offices of Rob Flello MP for
Stoke-on-Trent.

The film crew, the author in the shirt, and Peter
Molloy by his side looking away from the
camera.

Thor, Chris, Sharon, Peter and Dean-
Cameraman

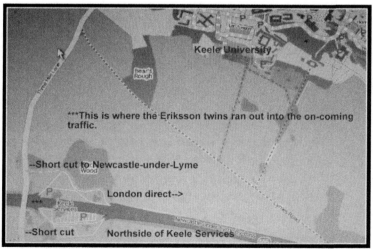

Here you can see the short cuts onto Three Mile
Lane.

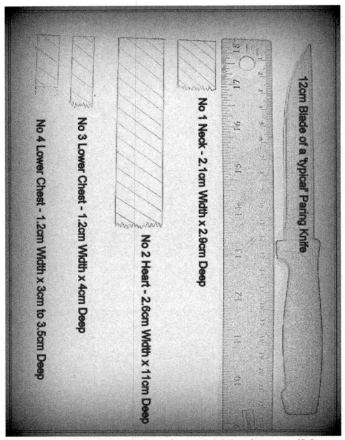

12cm Blade of a 'typical' Paring Knife

No 1 Neck - 2.1cm Width x 2.9cm Deep

No 2 Heart - 2.8cm Width x 11cm Deep

No 3 Lower Chest - 1.2cm Width x 4cm Deep

No 4 Lower Chest - 1.2cm Width x 3cm to 3.5cm Deep

We can clearly see that it would be impossible to cause wounds No3 & No4 with the 'same' sized knife; they are both deeper than No1 yet their entry widths are smaller - being only 1.2cm wide. They should at the very least be as wide as wound No1.

The Killing of Glenn

As a rule people already in police custody are normally the first to be produced and seen by the magistrate. This was very likely the case with Sabina at Fenton Magistrates Court. Its hearsay, though it's been said that Sabina didn't seem to want to leave the courthouse, despite being free to leave. She was allegedly sitting around the reception area and remained there until the court closed around 16:00pm.

I contacted the courthouse, though no member of staff could recall or should I say, the women I spoke to said they didn't remember her case or that day in question. Though according to witnesses, including Peter Molloy, she was seen roaming around a part of Fenton known as *Pit Hill*, on *Glebedale Park*. This is only down the road from the courthouse and near the railway lines and the *Railway Tavern* pub. That's where there is a mud footpath that leads to Glenn's house. It seems as if she was wearing her sister's lime coloured jacket, so must have stood-out-a-mile when sitting or walking about the area and for several hours at that.

It wasn't until our recent discovery reading the text messages on Glenn's mobile phone that Glenn's friend Mike confirmed Glenn had already met a women who he took to be "Sabina" when he spoke to him at 16:35pm that same day. We've always been led to believe it's not until around 19:30pm that she then allegedly first met Glenn and Peter Molloy. This radically changes the "official storyline" and what we've always been led to believe.

It's a very residential area and quite busy where Peter and Glenn are meant to have first met Sabina. *The Royal Oak* is opposite two other pubs and around the corner there are parades of shops and other local businesses. It's where Glenn and Peter Molloy had been drinking. Peter said he had arrived about 17.00pm and they'd been sitting in the Beer Garden that overlooks Christchurch Street which is on the other side of the road opposite Fenton Magistrate Court, next door to Christchurch Parish where it's said they first encountered Sabina.

It means Sabina must have gone back on herself for Pit Hill on Glebedale Park is leftwards away from the courthouse and the *Royal Oak*. It's in the direction of Glenn's home. She must have then turned back around and in the direction of Christchurch Street, the courthouse and *Royal Oak* pub. It was then meant to me much later that evening when Peter Molloy claims he first noticed Sabina praying outside Christchurch parish. It appears he struck-up a conversation with her first and before Glenn did - as he proclaimed at the time to be a "Godly-man" - though no longer is.

According to Peter's own words - when he has written about this case before in 2008 and 2009 on his *MySpace* page it appears he was a rather religiously minded person. On what I can take from his writings is that it seems he lost his faith "in God", previously to encountering Sabina and following the death of Glenn for he refers to having lost his faith earlier in that year and before May 2008. Yet oddly he has also proclaimed it was these events that were the reasons that made him lose his faith and become an atheist.

If Glenn was with another woman prior to meeting Sabina, then who else could Mike be referring to? If it was a local person or someone they both knew then Glenn would have probably said something like; *"Oh, I just met Mary by the church"*, but he didn't, he just referred to;

155

"...some woman". So I'd put my money on it being Sabina who Glenn was referring to.

Peter says Glenn had his dog Troy with him and that Sabina allegedly called out: *"What a nice dog."* And it was at this point Glen joined-in with the conversation and the *'Good Samaritan'* storyline began its play. Mr Molloy said she then enquired if they knew of a Bed & Breakfast in the area. And as mentioned before when Peter Molloy appears on the *Madness in the Fast Lane* documentary, he scoffs at the idea and gives the impression that – 'of course there isn't such a thing as a Bed and Breakfast within the Fenton area.' Despite there being the *Crown Hotel*, the *Crown & Anchor* B&B's and the *Holiday Express* hotel, built in 2001, less than a mile away,[1a] with many more in the locality and all under and around the two mile mark away. Mr Molloy says he couldn't think of anywhere she could have gone and added; *'...for Sabina had nowhere else to go'.* He then turned to Glenn to see if he had any suggestions and it was then when Glenn is said to have invited her back to his home offering her some food, saying they could look into finding a B&B for her back at his place - and she agreed and then went off with two strange men.

Is it possible as has been alleged, though never confirmed, that Sabina just sat inside Fenton courthouse all day long then walked the half mile down to the Glebedale Park area, then after that returned to the same vicinity of where the courthouse is and stood outside the Christchurch parish where there's no seating and praying in that bright lime jacket just before being noticed by Peter Molloy. This means it was the exact same place Glenn told Mike he had previously met 'some woman' and just hours before. Or is outside the Christchurch parish a place to go to pick-up loose women?

156

We're being led to believe a further three hours had gone-by without anyone else encountering her. Her following actions seem to suggest she would have spoken to other people and enquired about a Bed & Breakfast much earlier if that's what she wanted to know and surely she would have done this in the courthouse earlier if that's where she was for so long.

We can't understand why she wasn't assisted long before it's said she first met Glenn and Peter Molloy. It's possible due to her and 'her people' perhaps realising she was 'under Obbo' that she didn't want a taxi to take her from the court to a B&B or ask someone in the courthouse such information because she would probably not have wanted them to know where she was staying - or to be easily able to trace her by asking the taxi where they went - or perhaps worse - they could have followed her to the new location.

In the Staffordshire Police Force Annual Report 2009/10, it reads; *'On 20 May 2008, Glen Hollinshead had been drinking with Sabina Eriksson and had offered her accommodation for the night'*, that seems to suggest they had already been drinking together. Though we must admit this statement is difficult to deduce for on one hand we could construe it means they were in the pub drinking earlier and he then offered her accommodation for the night. Then on the other hand it could be read that it's referring to them drinking back at Glenn's home - when it was then he offered her to stay for the night.

Though this comment made by the police could also imply that they knew Glenn had already been drinking with Sabina and like what Mike now confirms when he last spoke to Glenn that same day and that he was; 'meeting 'some woman' by the church.' Mike said the police came to see him soon after Glenn's murder, they already knew he was close friends with Glenn and asked him had he seen Glenn that day or the day after when he was killed. Though at the time Mike never told the police anything, he didn't think there was anything of importance to tell them – he simply didn't want to get involved with the police. The BBC *Madness in the Fast Lane* film wasn't made and aired until about 12 to 16 months after Glenn had been killed. Mike never knew about the documentary until it was on TV, neither was he aware who Peter Molloy was. He said he didn't really pay too much attention to Peter's statement on the film in regards to when they first met Sabina. Though given he is convinced it was in the afternoon when Glenn said he first met her he was shocked to hear that Peter says Glenn and he 'first' met Sabina around 19:30pm or later.

We simply don't believe it was a "chance encounter". Sabina's "people" would have soon realised - as would of Sabina herself - that she was very likely 'under Obbo'. She very likely would had been told to stay well away from them fearing she could lead the police back to them. They may have telephoned a friend-of-a-friend and someone said they knew a 'safe man' in Fenton and they would see if he could help her - and we believe that person could have been Glenn who may have agreed she could come back to his house until they sorted out whatever needed to be done.

Let us not question - why would two men take back a stranger to their home? When we really ought to question – why would a lone woman go back to a house with two strange men that she has only moments before met on the street? "She mad that's why" – no doubt someone would like to point out. Though were not convinced with that observation. She was not destitute and unable to fend for herself - and will explain in a minute, but we know she had a large sum of money on her person, believed to have been at least a £1,000 in cash - so getting a room at a B&B was not out of the question.

She had a "partner" she had accused of 'kidnapping' 'her' children and must have been desperate to contact them and besides there was her son Simon and her brother Björn who too must have been fraught with worry and awaiting on her to call them. She had been smashed into the air by a car, taken to hospital and then released and kept in a police cell until Monday the morning 19 May 2008. She must have felt awful and we would have thought the first thing anyone would have probably wanted to do was to find a hotel/bed & breakfast, contact your loved ones, get cleaned-up, eat and then perhaps some sleep.

Its true Sabina had nowhere to go until she had found a bed and breakfast for the night. Though on saying that her "people" or those she asked for help would have probably felt safer if she was at a place like Glenn's; out of the public-eye, no CCTV camera's on the reception desk and a 'safe place' where they could meet up with her if they so wished. Glenn may or may not have ever met Sabina before, though he may have been briefed on the phone, as to what she looked like and where she is; *"Blonde hair, lime jacket – outside church next to courthouse"* He may have agreed to go to the *Royal Oak* pub and that directions where to exactly meet-up might have got confused. This could be why Sabina first walked down to Pit Hill, near Glebedale Park and where's there's that short-cut that goes straight to Glenn's road and house and indeed where Sabina was seen hanging around that same day.

This is why I propose Glenn might not have wanted Peter to know what was going on, of course there is always the possibility he did tell him, but it appears something else was devised; perhaps Glenn and Sabina made it look like a 'chance encounter' to Peter. Sabina might have parted with Glenn for a while, perhaps just before Peter turned up. She may have needed to talk to other people, her brother and son for instance and others she knew - and who were probably trying to arrange some further help for her. Apart from her own "people" likely knowing about her being 'under Obbo', they also would have understood she was in rather a desperate state and predicament.

It was in 'their own interests' to see she was looked after. It was Simon's mother who he dearly loves, Björn's younger twin sisters – with one laying seriously ill in hospital and the other now stranded in town in the middle of the UK. This is why Simon said he had to go to Sweden to be with 'the family' after someone in the family obviously contacted him. Besides her family and friends anyone with an ounce of compassion, especially those friends she must know and would have contacted - would have no doubt rallied around and assured her they would do their utmost to help her out and they most probably did - as why wouldn't they?

I doubt any of them would have advised her to go back to a house with two totally unknown men. They would have probably arranged something even if it meant doing a Google search and finding her a B&B to stay.

That is why she may have been reassured Glenn was okay and could be trusted and he could help her out until her 'own people' arrived. Glenn may have advised Sabina or she might have done so under her own accord, perhaps not wanting to go to the beer garden where he was now sitting with Peter and may have suggested she hung around and waited for him to depart the pub at an agreed time. By her standing outside the church, she would have been able to see Glenn, Peter and Troy leaving the beer garden just off Christchurch Street and start to head towards her.

Simon's comments come to mind when he replied to an article in the: *This is Staffordshire* on 27th November 2009: *"I don't know who Mr Hollingshead actually was. I never got to meet the man. I don't know what happened that night. I do know that my Mother Sabina, was a victim. I know that for whatever reason she was scared. I know that my Mom isn't a Murderer. I know that my mom, is loving, kind and caring, and has always been for as long as I can remember. I see this sentencing as an end to a bad chapter in not just my but many people's life. Sometimes... the victim gets the blame..."* -Simon Eriksson.

This comment seems to indicate he knew his mother was with Glenn beforehand and that he was even suggesting that he "knew of Glenn", though never 'knew him'. It's almost as if someone may have told Simon following the accident with Ursula still in hospital and the subsequent court case: *'...no worries, we've got a friend who is going to help us and your mum out for a night or two.'* You'll see he states: *"I never got to meet the man..."* Why would he say that? For it reads even though he might of not known the man, his mother did, though he never 'got to meet him'.

Rumours were rife as to why two men and a strange woman would go back to Glenn's house after just bumping into each other on the street. Though Peter, 27 at the time, has indicated had Sabina who was 40 at this time, been nearer his age then perhaps he might have offered her to stay at his place for the night.

According to Peter, he said: *"I do not believe Glenn knew Sabina before nor do I think she was there to meet him. This was a pure chance encounter. It was myself who had picked the route, it was myself who turned back and spoke to her first. Glenn only came over on my instruction so to speak. Maybe it's possible, I don't know, but with being there I strongly believe it was not the case and this was a chance encounter. Through conversation and the interaction between all three of us there was nothing to suggest Glenn and Sabina knew each other, had met before or had planned to meet. If I'm honest this line of question when you first asked took me back a bit, and it was certainly not a line of question in the interview with the police to my best recollection. If Sabina was meant to meet someone in Stoke on Trent or Newcastle it wasn't Glenn. Why did she never venture far from the court, my best guess she hadn't got a clue where to go. I can't say for certain that this wasn't the case, and it got my little old brain ticking over, but it hasn't made me doubt the facts of how we met her. I guess that's for you to decide or piece together, but in my heart 'I truly believe it was Glenn she was there to meet if anyone at all'* (Was that a Freudian-slip? Was he meant to have said; *'I truly believe it was 'not' Glenn...'*), *there will always be a part of me that's wishes we'd carried on walking home and gone our separate ways.*

I had told Peter I was in communication with the IPCC and the Staffordshire Police and that we had evidence that has never been revealed before.

Peter said; *"Looking back now, she was all over the place, saying her sister was in hospital. She was clearly getting upset and that was the point when Glenn said she could go back to his house".*

Yet we've been led to believe, and especially inside the police station, that she showed no emotions.

"He offered to make her some food because she hadn't eaten all day. I carried her plastic bag which had a red coat, a laptop and her phones."

Was it possible he noticed something else in the clear plastic bag, such as a large quantity of cash? He obviously said he didn't. He told us he could see she was holding a roll of cash in her hand. Her situation about having a large wedge of money was never mentioned by the police or in the BBC documentary.

"That should have sparked some suspicion on my part because people don't usually carry things like that in a plastic bag." "We went into Glenn's house and he made ham sandwiches for all three of us. That's when it all started to get a bit strange."

Once at Glenn's house, they started drinking alcohol.

"She kept looking out the window and I thought she must have had an argument with a boyfriend and was running away." "When I asked her, she said 'I wish.' I should have realised she was really disturbed." "She handed out cigarettes and snatched them back saying they might be poisoned." "There were a million and one signs that something wasn't right but there was absolutely no way I could have imagined what was going to happen to Glenn." "Sabina was friendly but I felt nervous about her and I should have trusted my feelings."

We now know - that according to Jon Hollinshead; the family had informed DC Christopher Short, the Family Liaison Officer that they knew Sabina had left Glenn's house for around 10 minutes and on the evening they first met. - At first I assumed it was the police who may have told Jon Hollinshead this information and further thought it must have come from Peter Molloy who in turn told the police. Though Peter said he didn't even know about this until I recently told him.

Peter Molloy lives in the very same Duke Street as Glenn, (see Photo Section), though on the other side of the A50; a five minute walk away. It's long been known that Peter had said he departed the property at approximately 23:40pm the night before Glenn was killed. Though he has now told us he left the house earlier that same evening, to pop back home and 'get some beers' and then returned to Glenn's again. We wonder; why this too was never mentioned in the BBC documentary? We can't be certain he didn't mentioned it, as Peter can't recall so it could have been edited out as there was of no significance to it at the time. Peter said; *"Sabina was friendly, but I felt nervous about her and I should have trusted my feelings,"* and continued by explaining how he couldn't wait to get out of the house despite his returning, though we can take it these feelings got worse as the night progressed. If the timings are right then in all he was with Sabina and Glenn for at least 4hrs and 40mins, apart from when he nipped back home. It's of course possible he was there even longer.

Jon Hollinshead goes on to say that the police even had the telephone number Sabina had called when she left the house for those 10 minutes. Garry and Paul said Glenn had confirmed this in a conversation with Paul the next day around 12:30pm on the 20th May 2008 in regards to enquiring as to Ursula's condition in hospital, the same hospital where Paul works. It was at this point when Paul offered to drive around and collect both Sabina and Glenn and take them to the hospital to see Ursula. And this is when Sabina was said to have implied she was too tired and wanted to go later on. Paul, who lives with his mother, said that Glenn had offered Sabina the opportunity to use his own mobile phone, though she declined. She also had her own mobiles, though didn't use them, (well not in front of Glenn anyway, though she could have done afterwards and when she returned.)

It appears the police never looked through Glenn's mobile telephone and never did what I did which was to try and contact the people listed within the mobile phone. At that time we don't know whether anything of Sabina's was stolen or went missing. The 'court bundle' would perhaps reveal what was recovered at the scene; e.g. her laptop and three or more mobile telephones etc., if this was the case then the police had the opportunity to scrutinise these details. If they were stolen or went missing, then they couldn't have. They also had the chance to do so when Sabina was in police custody at the weekend. What we do know and mention further on; is that soon after Glenn's murder and Sabina fleeing the home – much of her personal belongings was discovered along a mud path way including the long red coat she was wearing the days before on the M6 motorway.

What's rather compelling is the fact that Sabina's behaviour seems to indicate and suggest that she was convinced she was being followed and watched. If she was still 'under Obbo' at the precise moment then those watching her would have seen her leave the house and go to the phone box. Perhaps they see her call someone and then return to Glenn's home afterwards. "They" would have also noted that they see Peter Molloy leave, return and then leave again later on when he finally went home around 23:40pm, if of course he did. What's even more uncomfortable to contemplate is the likelihood that those who had Sabina under "Obbo", would have seen her flee the house around 19:45pm, the evening Glenn was murdered. "They" may have seen other people come and go prior this tragic event. It's even possible they could have witnessed someone else leave moments before or following Sabina running out of the house with a hammer in her hand and sprinting off down the road – they could have even gone in the opposite direction.

Though because "they" were there purely for "Obbo" reasons "they" could hardly now step forward and blow their cover by declaring who they really were. They would have had to remain hidden in their transit van or whatever vehicle they may have been parked-up in and watched what was about to unfold in front of them. Yet they couldn't have known or seen what had just happened inside the house. It's not as if they had advance time to prepare to 'bug' Glenn's home with sound devices to help pick up their conversations. There's technology that allows the "observer" to be able to point a receiving device at a window, that in turn will return a signal and you might be able to receive some form of conversation being transmitted. Though I reckon they'd have the traditional kit of a camcorder and photographic camera to help record exactly who and when someone turned up at Glenn's home.

Let's not forget, had she been 'under Obbo' then they had her every move covered from the moment she stepped out from Fenton Magistrates Court. To the immediate right of Glenn's house, (if facing the outside of the house), and upwards in the opposite direction of the railway bridge at the bottom of Duke Street, (see Photo Section), then it's quite possible for those who may have been "watching" Sabina - if of course there were – that they could have just seen her from behind - or face on whilst running away. The same could have happened if anyone else was leaving Glenn's house as they could have walked directly towards them - or away - and past their unmarked vehicle. They may have been a little confused as to what they just "observed" for as said they would have been none the wiser until they were made aware that a 'stabbing' had been reported and that Glenn had staggered out to the rear of the property and was now with Frank Booth dying in the alleyway.

So it goes without saying this must have been the most difficult and awkward of situations any "Obbo" officer/s could have possibly found themselves in for they were "blind" as to what had just happened to Glenn. It's also very likely they could tune into the emergency frequency airwaves and soon become aware as to what was beginning to unfold in front of them. Or they heard all the emergency sirens and see the police and ambulance/s arrive.

Glenn's own mobile shows that on the day of his murder the 20th May 2008, he first called his mother at 12:38pm when he spoke to his brother Paul and then again at 14:41pm. Prior to that at 12:55pm, he received another call from his "Mum", as that's what comes up on his phone. At 13:06pm, Glenn received an anonymous call from someone, though as there was "no number" showing we don't know who that person was. The phone reveals he didn't receive any other calls or call anyone else that day.

We can't help wondering - who was the anonymous caller at 13:06pm? Was it someone telling Glenn about Sabina? And who did Sabina contact that first evening when she left the house? If anything this could have been the occasion she told someone else, particularly her family - where she was staying and that she was safe and well. In addition to her going out to phone someone, once arrested the police must have surely checked all her mobile phones and analysed the laptop.

167

According to Peter Molloy, Sabina was talking about her family and wanted to show him some photographs stored in the laptop though she couldn't remember her password so the computer wouldn't open. (The police may too have had this problem - or their 'experts' had already 'studied' the contents after gaining entry to the laptop and not knowing the 'original password' may have accidently compromised the 'password' when finished?) He said this was one of the reasons he thought the laptop might have been stolen and why he wiped his fingerprints off it. Though if this was the case then surely she wouldn't have attempted to turn it on in the first place. Besides what would photographs of her family be doing on a stolen laptop? It's possible that the laptop was Ursula's and that she may have changed the password that Sabina previously knew, perhaps sometime before the M6 incident - on the coach for instance. This was probably the first time Sabina had the chance to turn it back on.

Mr Molloy, said he; '...*regrets missing the 'million and one' warning signs which told him something was wrong the night they met Sabina'*. He goes on to say that as he left Glenn's home that night; *"I checked to see if he was ok with the situation at which point he said come round tomorrow after work, I said my goodbyes telling him to text me tomorrow to let me know how things are."*

Though the Hollinshead brothers can't help wondering that if he was as worried about Sabina's behaviour as he states he was, then why did he return that same evening after 'getting away?'

More importantly they wonder; why didn't he go back around there the following day? Or at the very least telephone or send Glenn a text message to see how he was.

Glenn's mobile telephone shows he didn't do so other than the mentioned call and text message around 33hrs later.

On behalf of the family we put these awkward questions to Peter and he admitted he didn't do any of those things. He went on to say he couldn't explain why either, other than; *'...he's just a bad mate like that.'*

When I relayed to Jon Hollinshead what Peter had told me, Jon indicated that he felt it has nothing to do with being a 'good or bad mate' and would have thought that one's own natural curiosity would have prompted most people to have done at least one of the three just mentioned options. Especially considering how nervous he said he felt about Sabina. Whilst we must acknowledge the difficult predicament and cannot pre judge an individual's reaction in such a scenario - most people whether male or female would be curious to know; *"Well did you, or didn't you?"* Had their friend brought back a strange man or woman to their place and they ended up staying the night. You'd at the least be intrigued to know if they'd perhaps 'slept together'. In hindsight it is of course frustrating to Peter and our investigation that he did not find the outcome of the night, such as had Glenn arranged a Bed & Breakfast for her to go to or did she end up staying the night, especially after Sabina had called Peter - 'an angel.'

Around 20 hours had already passed since Peter Molloy says he last left the house at 23:40pm and when he did he said he ran home stopping in his tracks as he thought to himself: *"Bloody hell, this could look like I'm fleeing a crime scene"*. Perhaps rather pre-emptive thing to stop and think about and especially as no crime had yet been committed.

And perhaps there is bit of a dilemma here - a 'bugger if you do or a bugger if you don't' kind of scenario. Had he admitted he'd gone back around there after work it could have put him in the frame or at least as a witness.

In any murder case the police want to speak to those who last see the victim. Had he said; *'Oh yeah, I popped back around to see Glenn the next day to see if everything was okay'*, it could have entirely altered the picture.

As stated, Glenn's mobile shows Peter did call him 33hrs after he'd last left Glenn's home and sent a text message - two hours after that call.

This is of course only a 'what if' line of thought, though what if Sabina made up some kind of excuse and said to Glenn that a friend needed to meet her so she could give them something. What if this someone then turned up at Glenn's house to collect this "something" and Glenn being forever accommodating, willingly invited them inside. Let's surmise that someone was sent by the "boss" to Glenn's home to collect some drugs or cash, if any, - not forgetting that according to Peter, Sabina already had that large wedge of cash in her hand, and by the size he indicated, (the size of the roll inside a toilet roll), we've assume it was at least around a £1000.

It's doubtful that Sabina would've taken the risk in confiding with Glenn that she had drugs or more cash on her or perhaps stashed away at Keele Services. And if this kind of scenario was the case then there's a few things that could have played out, such as the "boss" could have contacted someone in Liverpool, which is less than an hour's drive away or a 'local' Newcastle-under-Lyme or a Stoke-on-Trent gang member or friend; who perhaps reluctantly or more than willingly would have arranged and agreed to have collected the drugs or money from Sabina. They would have probably known of Glenn, for it's come to light that according to some of those who knew him, he was at one time or another involved in drugs. In a small place like Fenton most people know who the main players are in this kind of field. Not forgetting her actions up at the window and appearing to be looking out for someone, the 'kidnapping' she reported about her children in Ireland must surely play a role in all of this, - and why she was reacting the way she was at Glenn's and the fleeing from the highway officers on the M6 motorway.

Over 24hrs had passed since Glenn first met Sabina. It's said he was making something to eat for the pair of them. This information can have only come from the police. Glenn's body was outside the house in the back alleyway and no one else would have been allowed inside the house. Frank Booth said he never entered the house. Though it's what Glenn's brother, Paul, had claimed had happened. Jon Hollinshead, seemed to mock this 'making something to eat' version of events. Meaning that was the story about the night before when he had met her in the street and offered to make her some food - and now again the next evening at the time she's alleged to have then murdered him. He said that was most unlike Glenn, he was far from domesticated and lived on take-away food. Sabina had more than enough money on her to have paid for a takeaway and may well have been likely to do so as a goodwill gesture for his hospitality.

By this time Scenes of Crime Officers (SOCO) had arrived and secured the scene; a tent would have then been erected around Glenn's body. They took away various items for examination, including bedding. DNA samples would have been taken where appropriate, such as semen or pubic hair that might possibly be found. They took a swap of his penis during his post-mortem and there was nothing to suggest Sabina and Glenn had sexual liaisons. And considering the circumstances; as let's not forget the damage caused to that silver VW car that Sabina ran out in front of and was hit by, leaving it with a smashed windscreen and dented roof on the outer hard edged section of the roof - that we can only assume having sex with someone would have been the last thing Sabina would have wanted to do.

It was odd enough that she showed no signs of injury to herself following that impact, but surely at this stage seventy odd hours after that incident most people would be in agony or at the least very sore, as the bruises would have had time to come out. She may have been in possession of powerful painkillers. You can easily buy them in the USA. Ursula might have brought some over. As Peter Molloy had described seeing Sabina sitting cross-legged and with her back to the TV, which suggests her legs couldn't have been causing her much or any pain at all.

Our visits to Stoke-on-Trent led us to meeting and talking to various people who knew Glenn and Peter Molloy. Frank Booth, Glenn's next door neighbour made some startling claims and revelations, both on and off film. Though when being filmed for the documentary and interviewed by Sharon, he altered his tone a little as he became more reluctant to talk openly and wasn't prepared to say what he had told us off camera. According to Frank, Glenn's own house had ironically been under police "Obbo" 18 months to two years prior to Glenn's death. According to Glenn, he told Frank that the police had set up a CCTV device on a business property opposite Glenn's home. Frank had seen it and they had another CCTV 'Street camera' trained on and watching the comings and goings from that address.

We can't corroborate this but Mr Booth said; '...*they were selling drugs from the house*', though when pushed he said it was one of Glenn's sons, who we won't name. He didn't seem to know what sort of drugs, though assumed it was cannabis. According to some locals at the *Royal Oak* pub in Fenton, Glenn was a gentleman and very helpful to others, though he could also be a bit of a hard bloke when required and who at times viewed himself as a lady's man and even bit of a gangster. He apparently knew some very 'heavy handed' people and it was said he could have quite a temper on him when he'd been on the whisky.

We've also learnt that there was a local chap named Gavin, who Glenn was walking home with one evening when all of a sudden they were set-upon and attacked by some gang or group of young men. Gavin was apparently seriously hurt and was in intensive care for a period of time. In addition, his jaw was broken. The police were involved and were looking for the attackers.

It's then said that when some local's heard that Glenn had been murdered, they thought it was connected to this street attack and that members of this "gang" or group of men might have killed Glenn. They seemed to think that because Glenn was the only "witness" they might have attacked him for that reason. Though to date there's never been anything to substantiate this any further. To this day no one has been arrested for the attack on Gavin.

According to Glenn's friend Mike, he said Glenn had asked him an 'odd' question, which was; *"Would you look after my dog if anything was to ever happen to me"*. Though he put this question to Mike only a couple of days before he was killed and before he had even met Sabina.

173

It's as if he suspected something was about to happen to him.

At one time he got involved with a young local lady who had a heroin habit, which apparently Glenn began to share. As their habit developed they were running up quite a bit of debt with dealers in the area. Frank Booth had said she would often come and sit in his home and talk to him about Glenn. Yet I have since spoken to her and will keep her name anonymous, for she seemed to distance herself from Frank, almost struggling to recall who he even was. I was speaking to her via her boyfriend's mobile phone after getting the number from Glenn's phone. Her boyfriend was in the background listening to our conversation and perhaps she didn't want to let on about knowing Mr Booth. She seems to have since beaten addiction and has a young child who will be around four years old now for she had sent Glenn a text the day before he was murdered informing him she was going for an ultrasonic scan as she was pregnant at the time. (Was Glenn the father?)

Many drug addicts run up debts that they can't actually pay back. In small towns like that of Fenton this kind of thing can't be seen to be overlooked and taken lightly for if the drug dealer wasn't to enforce their authority, then every other Tom, Dick or Harry would be doing the same thing. This is sadly why many people are badly hurt or worse still, killed.

It was reported on the 6th August 2009, that two Liverpool drug dealers, who had tortured a man who happened to be one their 'drug runners', using a hot knife and heated saucepan to burn his lips, had been jailed for a total of 27 years. Jamil Hussain and Mobeen Ahmed also used a pair of pliers to squeeze the drug runner's toes until they broke. They then poured bleach and disinfectant

174

over his burns and cuts, hit him with a hammer and stubbed cigarettes out on his tongue following an argument over some drugs that had gone missing. [3] Their catalogue of crime was revealed when they were jailed for trafficking crack cocaine and heroin.

According to Detective Sergeant Bev Hunt, of Staffordshire Police, it was the force's *Operation Cure*, which caught the drug bosses that began with a "tip-off" from a member of the public who noticed a suspicious packet in a Burton-on-Trent garden. This type of scenario is often used. Instead of saying that "someone", perhaps a person in police custody or prison has tipped them off with this information, it's easier to say you received the details some other way. The Staffordshire Police had uncovered a serious organised crime group operating throughout east Staffordshire and south Derbyshire, with contacts in Liverpool and Birmingham. [4] She said: *"They were trafficking vast amounts of heroin and crack cocaine, turning over up to £1,000 a day and keeping control of their street runners by threatening and torturing them to ensure they complied with orders."*

It also appears there were a few neighbours down the street who weren't too happy with the amount of undesirable people turning up at Glenn's doorstep at all times of the night or day. We can't say that's how it was around the time of Glenn's murder, though as we know according to Frank Booth this was the case at one time, probably 18 months or so before and why the police had CCTV cameras trained on the house.

In addition, these kind of accusations tend to back-up the theory that it's possible some rather objectionable characters may well have got wind about Sabina being at Glenn's home and that they knew she was holding a large wad of cash and who in turn decided to pay him a visit

175

and appeared at Glenn's front door on the 20th of May 2008.

What if Glenn or his ex-girlfriend owed some drug dealers money, according to his brother Jon Hollinshead - he ran up a lot of debts and spent thousands of pounds of his parent's money. The brothers were always lending or giving Glenn money. He'd often deceived his parents and accused the brothers of owing him money so his parents would then give him some cash in return. It caused many a rift and row within the family. Had Glenn or his ex-girlfriend got themselves in this position of such debt, then here arose an opportunity for those they owed the money to, to get their hands on some easy cash.

What if those who turned up at Glenn's home had been high on drugs, perhaps throughout the night or the following day? What if cocaine and heroin had been indulged in? Worst still what if they'd been drinking quite heavily and then an argument broke-out or a combination of all the just mentioned drug taking had taken place and happened within those 24hrs or so. We know they had been drinking in the pub first, then with Sabina back at Glenn's and with Peter going home to get some "more beers", and then returning that same evening. It's quite possible sprits such as *Jack Daniels*, that Glenn was partial to or something like whisky and vodka was then consumed and went on until the next day. This is why it's important the toxicology reports are seen in the court bundle, for it could possibly help address and answer some of these questions and why the two coroners also raise this very problem in their reports.

Glenn had apparently kicked his drug habit long before the time of his death and did so with his ex-girlfriend on a Methadone course of treatment. She then left Fenton and moved to another area. The toxicological results are not present in the coroner's report and the Hollinshead family wonder why? Despite both Dr Kolar and Dr Shorrock stressing the importance of these tests at the time of the post-mortem, for they weren't available to them when they first wrote up their reports. They still weren't present in the copy of the report we got four years later. Dr Kolar stated; *"...they may be relevant to the circumstances surrounding this man's death. Results of these investigations should be sought and 'must' be forwarded to me when they are available."* Dr Shorrock states pretty much the same; *"...it could be relevant to the circumstances leading up to the fatal assault."*

To date there are no other witnesses. Peter Molloy was the last person to see both Glenn and Sabina, apart from Frank Booth, who Glenn died in front of. At the murder scene SOCO would have carried out their forensic tests and the police would have made their investigations. Yet we do not know whether Sabina's fingerprints were found on the alleged weapon and another reason why the Hollinshead family would like to see the 'Court Bundle' of evidence. For as we know the recent evidence presented to us suggests that an additional weapon was used and apart from the coroners findings, Frank Booth seems to confirm this by stating that in his opinion the wound to the heart was unlike that of a knife wound. He said the wound was a complete round-hole and that he 'could have pushed his finger inside it' and presumed the weapon used to be a large screwdriver.

It would seem as if the murderer/s would have then fled the scene directly after stabbing Glenn. They would have known Frank was just no more than 20ft away. Sabina would have seen Glenn stagger out of the kitchen door that leads onto the garden and alleyway where Frank was.

There's a large kitchen window and windowed door that must have been wide open and looks straight out to the alleyway (see Photo Section). Then there's a wooden gate, though you can clearly see into Glenn's house and kitchen. I have personally been inside Glenn's house and around to the alleyway, so could see how close Mr Booth's transit van would have been outside Glenn's back garden. You can easily see where Glenn went to.

The house is a two bedroom semi-detached end of terrace property. As you walk through the front door you go straight into the front room and then the kitchen. There are no other rooms downstairs. The stairs upwards are on the kitchen side and in between these two downstairs rooms. It's unlikely the murderer would have wasted any time hanging about in fear of being seen and recognised.

Duke Street, where Glenn's house is situated, is at the lower end. If you come out of the front door and turn right there's about a further 15 houses or so, before you come to the end of that section of the road where a railway bridge sits. In fact there are actually 9 houses, as the other gap is now two industrial plots of land and companies that would make up at least 6 houses were they still there. If you had turned left then that would take you towards the main longer part of Duke Street and in the direction of where the majority of the houses and shops are. Had a third party walked out and turned left they could have done so without being captured by the CCTV. Had they turned right, like Sabina did they would have been captured on CCTV, as Sabina was. The CCTV camera is attached to the wall of one of those local companies, just yards from Glenn's home. It's positioned so it faces the pavement and the rolling barred gates (seen in the photo) were closed at the time.

The post-mortem report; states Glenn was 164cm [5'-5"] in height, and weighed 68kg [10st 10lb]. Glenn's brother Jon said he was taller, more like 5'-7", and much heavier. From past photographs you can clearly see he was a lot heavier in weight and well in excess of 12st. Perhaps this weight-loss reveals he might have relapsed, though heavy and regular alcohol consumption which Glenn did do can also cause drastic weight loss. Though had he relapsed this could then probably account for him having a slow reaction and perhaps why no defence marks were found on his body for this is the hard bit to understand. Despite the details of Glenn's past for we have to cover this ground to truly examine the facts, we don't believe he had taken heroin. If he was that stoned and that was the reason he couldn't defend himself, then it's also very unlikely he would have been able to then go out of the back door and on to Frank Booth in the alleyway as he would have probably just collapsed in a heap on the kitchen floor to begin with.

We would have thought there would have been some signs of defence wounds on Glenn's arms or hands for how could someone standing either in front or behind you then be able to get four stabs wounds in without you naturally defending yourself?

For arguments sake, let's say someone came up from behind you, then grabbed you around the neck and then proceeded to stab you in the neck and chest. Well I'd argue that you'd be able to protect yourself easier than if being attacked from the front, for you'd still have both hands free and would struggle and wriggle with all your might and that some signs of defending yourself would be evident to forensic scientists.

Glenn's ex-RAF, granted he was a medic-paramedic, but it highly probable he must have undergone some form

179

of self-defence training. He was known to be able to handle himself if and when the occasion arose. Why didn't he grab her by the hair or punch her in the face? Why weren't there any defence marks on his arms and hands as your reflexes naturally want to cover the parts of your body being attacked?

In almost all cases that involve multiple stab wounds there's always defence marks. The O J Simpson case comes to mind and where Nicole Brown Simpson had been stabbed multiple times in the head and neck; she had defence wounds all over her hands. Normally the only kind of cases where you perhaps wouldn't find defence wounds, is if the person was either on drugs such as heroin and why we've had to consider this, they were fast asleep or simply knocked out unconscious when the attack took place, and or perhaps if the person had been stabbed only once or twice.

But to be stabbed four consecutive times and for your brain and body to not automatically reflex itself is most unusual to say the least. And it is because of these reasons I find it so difficult to comprehend how Sabina could have achieved this alone? The brute force used snapped the handle clean from the blade, though at this stage we don't know for sure whether there was a defect or it was a cheap knife with a loose handle. It seems more like someone had grabbed Glenn from behind and then held his arms back leaving his entire chest area completely exposed to be stabbed like he was, thus he wouldn't have been able to defend himself.

Let's remember, Glenn was stabbed in the neck then the heart and twice more in his chest area with clearly two different weapons, as we've proved it is impossible to achieve all four wounds with the same knife discovered at the scene.

180

As I try to point out in the following chapter; *The weakness of the Sabina Eriksson case*, that despite there being overwhelming circumstantial evidence that Sabina was involved in Glenn's death, in a court of law, a jury has to be convinced; *'...beyond all reasonable doubt'*. Any barrister worth his salt would argue these points of 'reasonable doubt', tooth and nail. He'd also pick up on the points and argue that Frank Booth was more than likely mistaken when he thought he heard Glenn say: *'...she stabbed me'*. For he'd argue Glenn was unable to say anything at all, let alone gurgle his words out as claimed by Mr Booth.

On the instant his heart received that massive stab wound that measured 2.6cm in length and 11cm in depth, leaving a gape of 0.8cm, indicating the blade was thrust into the heart then probably twisted in comparison to the neck wound that had a gape of 0.2cm, which would happen if the stab was just straight in and out. Glenn would have gone into a complete state of shock. The adrenaline rush would have minimised the pain. And it's very likely that he had no idea how severe his injuries were. Adrenaline also makes the heart beat faster, so his cavities around his lungs would soon be filled with blood. The pathologist said they had between 3½ to 4 pints of blood in them. And like that of our bodies reflexes that act accordingly to their own will, so does our brains, they kind of switch off. It's a survival thing that could be described as a kind of pre-traumatic stress symptom, known as a 'dissociative episode', or amnesia.[1f] It's to help us not recall such traumatic and distressing circumstances otherwise if we were to survive such horrific experiences we'd be reliving the horror again and again.

Take the case of British actor Gorden Kaye, best known for playing *René Artois* in the TV comedy series *'Allo 'Allo!*. Kaye suffered serious head injuries in a car accident in the 25th January 1990, which may be a lot different than being stabbed, though his own non-recollection is typical of many seriously traumatised people following a serious accident. He cannot remember a single thing about the incident, and has a large scar on his forehead from a plank of wood that hit him as it smashed through his car windscreen.

The following was claimed by a man who had been seriously wounded following a stabbing attack: *"I have been in the situation before, of being in real fear for my life. The brain does a funny thing. I was terrified for a few seconds and then my brain went into a kind of shut down mode. I was calm, could feel no pain or what was happening to my body. It is called a dissociative episode. It was amazingly peaceful and about a million miles away from the attack I was enduring. I have no idea what happened when I was mentally not there. I remember random memories flashing in my head and an extremely peaceful feeling, like nothing in the world was wrong. Our brain protects us from the horrors of violence."* This would have likely happened to Glenn, and probably at that instance, he wouldn't have been able to recall or even tell who did what to him.

Dr Shorrock concludes: *"The wound to the heart will have caused profuse and rapid bleeding into the chest cavity. Consequently, he will have collapsed and lost consciousness within a short time of infliction of the wound. He could have been capable of walking and undertaking other purposeful activity for a period of up to 'two minutes' before he collapsed."* And if that was the case, then it's debateable whether Glenn had said what Mr

Frank Booth proclaimed he had said to him before he died.

Medical opinion is that following the kind of huge single stab wound that penetrated Glenn's left ventricle of his heart and then his lung, then death would have been within seconds. The comment of; *'...two minutes' before he collapsed"*, seems to explain the anomaly as to why was it reported that; *"74 seconds later Glenn staggered back out of the house holding his chest..."* For as mentioned elsewhere we quizzed Frank Booth about this reported *'74 seconds'*, as he is the only person who could have known approximately how long Glenn had been away just prior to asking him for some teabags. He insists Glenn was at least 5 minutes or more. It appears as if someone wanted to be able to portray and quell the argument that Glenn couldn't have survived his injuries no matter how quick the emergency services had arrived. *'74 seconds later'*. Such a precise time, where this disinformation came from and how was it established backed up in the BBC documentary, - remains a mystery to this day.

The statement from Staffordshire police force which I quote further on, might suggest it came from the emergency services. Though what it indirectly confirms is what we suggest that it was unlikely Glenn was able to have had the alleged following conversation with Mr Booth for we believe by the time he struggled out of the house, down the garden path and into the alleyway where Frank Booth was washing his transit van; he then probably collapsed, unable to speak and died within seconds. He wasn't in the greatest of condition, though pretty much normal for a man in his early 50's, and perhaps worst of all the knife wasn't left in the main wound and as said, it appears it was twisted before being pulled back out again.

An important part of any criminal murder investigation is the human interactions that occurred. After evidence is collected and reviewed the police would interview the people involved in the murder. Sometimes a case is very clear cut; a man was 'witnessed' shooting his wife, for example. In this instance the husband would be interviewed along with witnesses, so that the police could be assured that no details were missed. In other cases the identity of the culprit may not be as clear, as could be argued in the case of Glenn's murder. As acknowledged, I know everything indicates and points the finger of blame at Sabina, her crazed actions on the M6 motorway seems to confirm that surely she was the murderer. But there were 'no witnesses' and the evidence suggests a 'second weapon' was used.

In this instance Peter Molloy was with Glenn when they "first" met Sabina. He was also the last person to see her and one of the last to see Glenn. Frank Booth, said it was around twenty five to twenty minutes before eight o'clock in the evening: *"I was washing the mini-bus when Glenn came to see me."* - *"This was quite normal, he was always asking me for favours and he just wanted some tea bags. I would never have refused him."*-*"Everyone in the neighbourhood has a different view of him. I wasn't a friend of his, but I used to see him with his dog and say hello."*

Frank Booth states that Glenn had told him he'd been stabbed: *"He came out of the house saying he was dying and I thought he was joking."* *"When I saw the blood and the round hole in his chest I rang 999. He was talking normally and asked if he could sit down. He was on the bumper of the bus."* *"Blood was pumping from his chest, then he asked to lie on the floor. I said, if it makes you*

184

comfortable. He told me 'she stabbed me' but he never explained who he meant". [2]

Yet in the *Madness in the Fast Lane* documentary, Frank Booth also says; *"He was gurgling as he spoke..."* I pick up on his words; *'He was talking normally...'* could it be possible he was unknowingly and accidently primed to say what he said when 'they' came and collected Mr Booth in a police car and took him to the local police station to make a statement? No doubt the conversation in the car was about what had happened. Again, we are not suggesting that this happened here, but let's imagine someone inappropriately let slip: *'...that it would need to be clear that there could be no dispute, in hearing Glenn's final words, for we don't want anyone arguing, that you could have made a mistake and heard him say; 'he stabbed me', as opposed to, 'she stabbed me.'* I would have thought a person *"gurgling"* when they spoke, wouldn't therefore be able to *"talk normal"*. This is merely a hypothetical scenario, but conversations like this can change one's perspective on the reality of a situation.

The stab wound to his heart was that massive, so much so his chest cavities were internally filled with almost four pints of blood. That if Glenn could have spoken then it goes without saying his words would have most certainly been "gurgled out", probably with bubbles of blood foaming at the mouth.

It would have been virtually impossible to have understood him. It's most likely Glenn's body and mind would have gone into a complete state of shock and he wouldn't have been able to say anything, especially coherently and even if he wanted to.

It must be noted that Frank Booth also told us that he never even noticed the other three stabbed wounds. It's

185

feasible to understand how he might have missed the smaller stab wounds No 3 and No 4 in the lower part of the chest, for as previously presented it was a much thinner weapon used to make the small 1.2cm wide entry marks and bedsides Glenn was wearing a T-Shirt and jumper. Though it's a bit difficult to comprehend how Mr Booth never noticed the No1 wound to the left side of the neck that was 2.1cm wide, and made a gape of 0.2cm.

It's highly possible most likely even that Frank himself might have gone into a state of shock, whereas he couldn't believe what he was encountering. He also admitted he didn't even know Sabina was in the house. And at some stage, it must have been the police who informed him what was believed to have occurred in Glenn's home.

In the *Madness in the Fast Lane* film, it at first shows the actual CCTV footage of Sabina fleeing Glenn's home, though only for a split second as that's all that was captured, the rest is a reconstruction. If the date and time was set correctly on the CCTV recorder it could provide the precise time which could then be compared to the times logged by the emergency services. It could also show vital other scenes, such as when Peter, Glenn and Sabina first arrived. Had anyone else come and gone to Glenn's home from that same direction the CCTV camera covers, then it's possible it would show us and much more.

According to Frank Booth it was around 19:45pm when he first called 999. Though it was taking so long for the ambulance and police to arrive he had to call the emergency services three times. With our own timings, we have to allow for an error of judgment of about 30 seconds either way for we cannot be 100% precise of the times, - though we can get as close as possible by working around the police's own quoted timings below. We also cannot be 100% certain that the manual times "logged" by the following ambulance crews or police officers are correct, for according to Frank Booth at least 20-25 minutes had elapsed from the time he first called 999 and from the time the police arrived at Duke Street.

On the 31st August 2012, the Staffordshire Police PSD, confirmed the West Midlands Ambulance [WMA] service control room had received a 999 call (from Frank Booth), reporting that a stabbing had occurred at Glenn's home in Duke Street and *'...that the offender was still on the scene'*.

Though this comment is disputed; Frank Booth was the only person who could have said such a thing, though he maintains he didn't or in fact say anything remotely like it. As just said he also told us it was the police who told him after the murder that Sabina had been in the house - he never saw Sabina and imagined after the all this had taken place and the police had arrived that she would have run out the house straight away and he confirmed this to be the case on the 5th September 2012, when I last spoke to him.

We have to wonder - did anyone else call 999, reporting the stabbing incident? For if they did then they would have course had to have been in the house as well. Someone involved in "the robbery" I discuss further on, - may not have wanted to be involved in a murder and could also have called 999; by saying the person was still at the scene this would also give them that edge to get away locally. We haven't got a precise time confirming when Frank Booth first called 999, though it's said the WMA service in turn then contacted Staffordshire Police, and this call was logged by the police STORM (incident log) unit at 19:51:40secs on the 20/05/2008.

We wonder what caused the delay before the WMA service contacted the police and why didn't the police's Automated Crime Recording (ACR) unit pick up on Mr Booth's 999 call for the ambulance at around 19:45pm? This means almost 7 minutes had elapsed before the WMA service got onto the police. Then 2 minutes and 20 seconds after that initial 19:51:40 call from WMA service to the police, it's reported the ambulance crew arrived "at the scene" of where Sabina was spotted near to the bridge-way on Heron Cross roundabout over the A50 dual carriageway at 19:54:53secs.

This first crew must have been dispatched by the WMA as close to Frank Booth's 19:45pm call as possible. The Ambulance Station that serves Fenton is in Hilton Road, which is just across the road from the UHNS. According to *Google Maps*, it is 5.5 km - about 10 min drive away. So they were on the scene of the bridge-way within 9 minutes, and this sounds about right.

At 19:53:53secs a number of 999 calls started to arrive in ACR unit from the public describing a woman covered in blood and carrying a hammer near the same roundabout and bridge-way over the A50 dual carriageway. Though this seems to contradict British army soldier, Joshua Grattage's version of events; for according to him he had wrestled with Sabina and removed the hammer from her at the end of Duke Street and before she then went up the hill towards the bridge-way above the A50: '*My job's done now and then left it to the professionals.*'

He lives quite locally in Newcastle-under-Lyme, two or three miles up the road from the incident. . He was referring to the ambulance crew who had first arrived. If Joshua Grattage is correct in his statement then how is it possible these other members of the public then also see Sabina with a hammer?

19:54:40secs was the first log time, 19:53:53, around three minutes had passed, that means within this time Sabina was already being noticed running up towards the roundabout and with a hammer in her hand. It therefore backs-up the theory she had almost immediately fled the scene for her to have reached that point in that time.

According to Grattage, his version of events occurred first. There are two "bridges" mentioned in this story. However, the one at the end of Duke Street is a railway bridge. The "bridge" referred to above the A50, isn't a "bridge" as we know one to be, it's 'bridge-way above that carriageway that happens to be part of Heron Cross roundabout. We've been led to believe Joshua Grattage encountered Sabina by the railway bridge at the end of Duke Street, (see Photo Section), and when he then states he sees the "professionals" referring to the paramedics at the scene, so as just said, this means that at least 9 minutes had passed since Frank Booth's first 999 call. Though this seems to suggest Sabina must have remained in Glenn's house (or at the least stayed about near the house), for around 8 minutes or more then ran out approximately 30 seconds prior to this alleged hands on fight with Grattage, but we now know that didn't happen.

Why would Glenn's murderer wait about in his home for all this time before deciding to then flee?

(It's possible if she was innocent and just witnessed Glenn's murder. She could have remained for some moments - if this was the case - though not as long as Grattage's timings suggest, for those other witnesses see her at 19:53:53 up by the Heron Cross roundabout.)

For all she knew an armed posse of neighbours could have started to charge in through the back door and see her. She'd also surely expect the police to be on the scene any minute and why we believe she had to or would have fled almost immediately after Glenn had staggered out of the back kitchen door.

The actual CCTV camera that captured that fleeting moment of Sabina sprinting past the gates of a local business, is approximately 100ft - 30.44 metres from Glenn's front door as are the following measurements give or take six feet either way for error. The railway bridge at the end of Duke Street is where Joshua Grattage claims he wrestled with Sabina. This is approximately 650ft - 198.12 metres from Glenn's front door.

Joshua said he stopped his car, got out and fought with Sabina: *"...just put my hands straight on the hammer and lowered it and I was just completely like zoned-in on the hammer. She was making crazy grunting noises the whole time, really primitive type of rage. She hit me on the back of the head with something, which I assumed was her fist, but I was told later by the police it was a roof tile that she had in her pocket. My job's done now and then left it to the professionals."*

According to Paul Hollinshead, the paramedics involved in this case, and who know Paul from his work, told him that Sabina ran up the short hill and then entered the Heron Cross roundabout at a 3:30 [clock] position and going anticlockwise, passing one 'bridge-way' on her right hand side, which is also above the A50. She then continued to run anticlockwise around the roundabout and until she got to the second part of the bridge-way above the A50, which is around the 9:45 position on the outer left hand side of the roundabout. The total measurements of this route from Glenn's front door, is around 2,150 feet - 655.32 metres = 0.407196 of a mile to this bridge-way where it's said Sabina jumped off. It was widely

190

reported that this bridge-way was anything between 30ft to 40ft high. Having now visited and filmed the bridge-way in question, it is more in the region of 30ft in height or just less.

This is why it's difficult to understand the timings - how is it that members of the public reported seeing Sabina with a hammer up by this bridge-way above the A50 and before the arrival of the ambulance crew?

It's also challenging to see how Josh Grattage was able to bring his vehicle to a sudden halt, get out of the car and then begin to run and catch up with the sprinting Sabina. She was at the shortest distance from where it's been portrayed she fought with Mr Grattage, which is within the first 650ft - 198.12 metres from Glenn's house and where the CCTV shows Sabina bolting past. It must have taken a few seconds for him to have worked out what was happening, whilst every passing second Sabina was sprinting further and further away.

According to our experimental re-enactment it took approximately 30 seconds to jog the approximate 650ft in Duke Street; Sabina must have been much quicker. Don't forget, but what's shown on the BBC film is based on a reconstruction of Mr Grattage's version of events. Yet if we consider that brief moment where we can actually see what's alleged to be Sabina running on the CCTV footage, she is clearly bolting and we can't see why she wouldn't have tried to maintain such a pace, and she clearly must have, to have been able to have got to where she did in those 3 minutes or so that had just elapsed. We're led to believe she then suddenly came to a slow walk and noticed Grattage in his vehicle and that is when he jumped out of the car and chased her. Staffordshire police's confirmation as to the timings seem to confirm

Mr Grattage's story couldn't have occurred as we've been led to believe.

You might often see on TV police officers getting out of a car then start chasing a suspect and reaching them, though that's normally because the suspect has just also got out of another vehicle and decided to run. It would be virtually impossible to catch a sprinting person from behind if you had to stop and then get out of a vehicle and start to run after the already sprinting person. Over a long distance you might be able to catch them up. But in this instance we're talking of a relatively short distance 650ft - 198.12 metres. Okay, if he had accelerated and driven well past her, then jumped out and confronted her from front-on, then it could have perhaps been achievable. Also, Sabina would have been vigilant, hammer in hand and waiting to defend herself. She would have had to come to a stop and then completely lost her composure for Grattage to have then been able to have crept up on her. For as said, if this really did happened this way then how did the other members of the public see Sabina with the same hammer up by the bridge-way?

According to Jon Hollinshead, Mr Grattage's statement: '*My job's done now and then left it to the professionals.*' sounds as if it's almost scripted. As does the claim about being hit on the back of the head with a "roof tile", though in no way am I trying to imply he wasn't hit over the head with something even a piece of roof tile. Jon Hollinshead said; 'it sounds like an odd prop to appear in the picture.' We're not saying he never fought with her; we just question his version of events due to the timings we've discussed. By him saying this seems to support the claim that he 'must of come into direct contact with Sabina', thus he's a credible witness that can claim 100% he saw Sabina with the hammer running away yards from the murder scene. The police 'told him' it was a 'roof tile'. Not only did she have a 'lump hammer', we're being told she also had a roof tile in her pocket. Where did that come from? She was sprinting, so it's doubtful she stopped to pick up such an item within the 650ft from Glenn's front door, so when did she stop and pick it up? She had a hammer so why would she stop and pick it up? Surely the police meant it was 'part' of a roof tile as I don't think anyone would be able to fit such an item in their pocket. How did the police know about this roof tile? They didn't arrive long after Grattage's alleged fracas with her when they report saying she had already jumped off the bridge-way above the A50. So she was much further away by then and sprawled out on the A50 carriageway. Is that where they discovered this "roof tile" in her pocket? Which means there we have Sabina fleeing Glenn's home with a hammer in one hand, then somehow gets hold of a roof tile and puts it inside her pocket, when seconds later she produces it and strikes Joshua Grattage on the back of the head with it and then after fighting with him sprints away towards the Heron Cross roundabout. Did she put the roof tile back in her pocket before jumping off the bridge-way? Or did she drop it where this alleged struggle took place with Mr Grattage?

Had that been the case then surely he would have heard or seen her do so or at the least noticed it on the floor as she fled away. We would have thought had he been hit on the head with a whole or part of a roof tile his head would have been cut open or quite badly bruised. Though there was no mention he had to go to hospital for stitches or a check-up. We understand he is a soldier and people can say he'd brush it away and get on with his life. But that's not sensible argument as I'm sure with the police claiming such a thing as being hit over the head with a roof tile, that they'd insist he went to hospital for a check-up. For what if he returned to his barracks and became

193

seriously ill? We would assume this roof tile was retained by the police as evidence and that Mr Grattage's DNA (possibly Sabina's as well) would still be present on the roof tile and that this would prove 100% he did actually come into contact with Sabina. Again, these questions can only be answered if the court bundle was handed over or an inquiry is held.

So to help us clear up and address these anomalies we contacted Joshua Grattage to give him the opportunity to explain exactly what happened that day. We wanted to know if he was prepared to appear in our documentary or at least give us an interview off camera. He declined both our offers. At first he explained that he was away and couldn't see us. So we gave him the option and said whenever it's convenient for him, though he didn't reply. Some weeks later in July 2012, Sharon again contacted him to try and arrange another interview with the objective of quizzing him as to how did he manage to catch-up with Sabina and retrieve the hammer, then about being hit on the head with the roof tile and exactly where were the "professionals" positioned when he first noticed them? We pre-warned him with our list of questions. Though that was it, he has never come back to us. There is still activity on his social network pages and I again contacted him on the 10th September 2012, unfortunately with no result.

The Hollinshead family had hoped that he'd be more than keen to help them and as Jon pointed out his actions were hailed as that of a 'local hero'. He knows the Hollinshead family want to find out the truth as to what really happened to Glenn that day and that they are calling on for a new investigation to be held, so they can't work out why he has remained silent?

Going back to what Jon Hollinshead was saying about this, he went on to say, it raises the question; '...*did this event really happen?* '. He said that Mr Grattage's version of events sound almost 'staged' and he seemed to question if he was trying to assist in demonising Sabina by portraying her as some kind of '...*wild crazed like women, making grunting noises the whole time and in a primitive type of rage* ', whilst at the same time helping to plant a seed into the mind of the public that will then grow into a particular series of events and provide a very specific type of scenario taking place within their minds eye.

Apart from the obvious complaints as to why were the family not told about Sabina's reporting the 'kidnapping' of her children just hours before the M6 incident - and as to why was Sabina released from hospital so early despite us uncovering evidence that the Eriksson twins were first arrested under Section 136 of the 1983 Mental Health Act - and that in addition we can clearly see two weapons were used in Glenn's murder; - it now appears the authorities were worried that the Hollinshead family were going to make an official complaint about the time it took for the police and ambulance crews to arrive at Glenn's house.

Is it possible "they" seem to misinterpret - that the family were suggesting Glenn could have been saved had the paramedics arrived earlier, - for it was revealed that the ambulance crew did arrive before the police though due to "Health and Safety" reasons they could not enter the house following such a 'crime' as there was the "possibility": '...*the offender could still be on the scene.* '

Besides if this was true and had such information been relayed then we would have assumed the police would have wanted to get to the scene as soon as possible, with the hope of apprehending 'the offender still on the scene'. Yet this doesn't seem to be the case as the 'only one' responding police vehicle QA21, seemed more concerned with helping to assist with traffic safety.

Considering the circumstances - why weren't there more than one police patrol car responding to this major incident? Yet, there were - but why weren't these additional patrols mentioned in the report as you'll see that it states; *'patrol cars'*, this is why the police's explanation is far from satisfactory. It's almost as if they are trying to justify why things didn't quite work out accordingly - because there was so much confusion.

The Staffordshire police force continue to state: *"Patrol cars were dispatched to the women now lying on the A50 carriageway and to the reported stabbing"*. Notice the plural, referring to more than one car, - so where were they?

They are talking as if these incidents happened in unison which they obviously didn't.

"They" use the term "parallel incidents" though these incidents clearly took place separately and must have been within a significant timescale for the police to have responded accordingly and to have addressed both emergency matters respectively.

There's the time between Frank Booth calling 999 around 19:45pm and for the WMA service dispatching an ambulance and when they allegedly contacted the Staffordshire police at 19:51:40secs who in turn should have then dispatched their police patrols in response to that first call.

Though it seems there was a delay for at least 3 minutes and 49 seconds from receiving this 19:51:40 call before the police sent their patrol car/s, as the only mention about the police responding to anything in the documentation provided by the Staffordshire PSD, was at 19:55:39secs and when it reads; *'...patrol QA21 said they were making the A50 incident to assist with traffic safety'*.

We know at 19:54:53 it was logged that ambulance staff had arrived at the scene of where Sabina was at the bridge-way and not at Glenn's house where they should have been heading.

At 19:55:31secs it was recorded that Sabina had jumped off the bridge-way.

Then confusing the ongoing situation another ambulance was then dispatched to "the woman" lying on the A50 with serious injuries to her ankles and head. But why wasn't the police already at Glenn's home by then?

Hanley Police Station is 2.5 miles to Duke Street, it's a dead straight line to get there and would assume it would take around 4 to 5 minutes averaging 30 to 40mph to reach Duke Street.

Police records show at 19:55:39secs patrol car QA21 said it was making their way to the A50 incident to assist with traffic safety.

Then at 20:01:17secs QA21 stated they were now making their way to Glenn's house in Duke Street.

At 20:03:35 QA21 stated they has arrived at Glenn's to *"...protect the ambulance and crew and secure the scene"*.

11 minutes and 55 seconds after the police control room allegedly received the first call from the WMA

service at 19:51:'40, and 18 minutes and 35 seconds from when it's said Frank Booth first called 999.

The police go on to say and refer to the 19:51:40secs call from the WMA service that they had responded to and directed their patrols to; *"...parallel incident at the A50. In the circumstances, the time taken in arriving at the scene does not appear to be unreasonable. It is not the case that had they arrived earlier, they would have been able to save Mr Hollinshead's life."*

However, that's not in dispute though what is; is why was it that a police patrol car had not arrived at Glenn's Duke Street address long before they did and other than just the one patrol car QA21?

The police quote one patrol car QA21 as if this was the only patrol vehicle responding to a "stabbing incident." Something clearly isn't right here and something clearly went wrong. We can understand the confusion with the ambulance crew as only one ambulance would have needed to have responded. Though under the circumstances and seriousness of the matter of a man being stabbed and the fact that; *"...the offender was still at on the scene"*, we would have thought at least two or three police patrol cars would have been responding and speeding to the address as from the time of 19:52 onwards.

And that had anyone of those patrols such as QA21 then encountered and come across the parallel incident on the A50 they would have liaised with their fellow responding colleagues and worked out which ones would attend traffic safety and which ones would continue onto Duke Street.

So we obviously can't help questioning; why didn't this happen on this occasion?

In 2008, Staffordshire police force had in excess of 2,000 officers, granted not all working at once. There were 4,392 cases of speeding by Staffordshire Police officers across the county of Staffordshire in 2010/11 and a further 4,543 the previous year. We have no records for 2008, though surmise it's a similar figure. Supt Philip Bladen, head of the professional standards department, said; *"...police officers regularly respond to emergency incidents and therefore it is inevitable that sometimes safety cameras are activated."* So what happened that day the 20th May 2008?

It's not certain what really occurred except that we do know the paramedics stumbled across Sabina and thought it was the person they'd been called out to attend following the 999 call.

Yet surely they knew they were responding to an emergency call that a 'male' had been stabbed for that's what Frank Booth had reported. When they did arrive despite the coroner's report stating the contrary, which was that the paramedics entered the property, the paramedics didn't, they refused to enter the house due to Health and Safety guidelines.

Apparently they cannot enter a property following an attack such as a stabbing, until the police arrive. They ended up going around the side of the house and via the alleyway at the rear (see Photo Section) - there were no gates at that time. It was reported the ambulance crews arrived as Mr Hollinshead had just died. They said the stab wound went straight through his heart and they could not have saved him even if they were on the scene *'two minutes'* after the stabbing. [14]

The emergency services knew that soon after this incident there were criticisms and complaints by the public and family as to why did it take so long for the police or ambulance crews to arrive at Glenn's house.

By saying and thinking; '...*the offender was still on the scene*', perhaps gives reason for the paramedics to have not wanted to enter the property, - hence it's not their fault Glenn died before they could treat him.

Though this is not in contention for we're convinced Glenn wouldn't have survived the fatal stab wound to the heart and died within a couple of minutes from being attacked, therefore the ambulance crew not arriving earlier is really not the issue. Other than this 'fabricated' comment; *"the offender was still on the scene"*, obviously is.

Though it's the failure of the police not arriving at the scene earlier that seems to be the biggest problem for had the 'offender' still been at the scene then who knows how things may have panned out. Perhaps Sabina would have been encountered before she had the time to reach the Heron Cross roundabout.

As already state; one of the biggest drug related "Obbo" operations was being carried out by the Serious Organised Crime Agency [SOCA], the very same time the twins were at large and when Glenn was murdered. "Obbo" on *Operation Happy Fish* started in the summer of 2007 and ran for 18 months ending in December 2008 and after Sabina had already been in custody for over six months (three months in hospital).

"Obbo" on *Operation Junko*, started in 2008 and was already in full swing when Sabina was arrested. It ran for four years as an undercover operation. The value of the drugs involved in Operation Junko was £3.5bn, said by police to be a conservative estimate. Following on from the police failing to respond and arriving at Glenn's home much sooner, it has made us wonder if there is any possibility that a "delay tactic" was employed, which then allowed the police to make one or two minor adjustments - similar to what happened in the already mentioned BBC's *Silk,* series.[2e]

For if what we're saying is correct and the twins were 'under Obbo' then perhaps those officers doing the 'observing' needed that little bit of time to be able to leave the area unhindered and without being accidently discovered and arrested near to the scene by fellow police officers who would have had no knowledge of the "Obbo" taking place to begin with.

Let's not forget as it appears "they" had already let her go giving her and Ursula the green light and on three other occasions (twice in the case of Ursula), and before this tragedy had the opportunity to even arise. The agencies implicated in the "Obbo" must have kicked themselves as who in the world would have thought Sabina would have got involved or gone on to do what it's alleged she'd done? There's no way anyone could have predicted what was going to happen that day, not even Glenn's killers.

Let's recall for a moment when Sabina was facing the assault charge on the police officer and for trespassing on to the M6 motorway. I believe though of course I cannot presently substantiate it - that it's quite possible the magistrate at Fenton was advised how to deal with Sabina due to 'exceptional circumstances'. Though of course the police and courts would deny this and perhaps this was the reason his job was made easier, for as we know it appears Sabina wasn't charged with the assault charge against PC Cope after all. Though I refer to my own experiences and to the *Super-grass* chapter where you can clearly see it was a common practice for the police and District Public Prosecution (DPP) to collude and arrange deals of immunity with "criminals". If the magistrate at Fenton was told that the person before them was embroiled in a case of *"National Security"*, they would of course have dealt with the matter accordingly. They needn't have been told about the actually "Obbo's" and probably weren't. This seems to make sense and the reason why it appears the rulebook was completely ignored and why no 'Pre-Sentence Report' was requested by the magistrate as it seems suggests Sabina was only sentenced to one day imprisonment for "they" wanted her back on the streets to continue their 'Obbo'.

Sabina isn't stupid and nor are the other people we believe she's could have been involved with. She would have soon realised that the police "hadn't discovered" the drugs or cash if of course she had any more on her. We know Sabina had quite a bit of cash on her though exactly how much we obviously can only assume. The twins would have without doubt known something wasn't quite right and like I say they would have been surprised the way the police officers at Keele Services reacted and dealt with them and for all the reasons we've already covered.

And then following on from the M6 incident and being discharged from hospital so soon, she now only receives a one day prison sentence. She would have course smelt a rat. The twins probably realised they were being followed and were 'under Obbo' and why she kept acting so strangely in Glenn's home or is it because she too thought about the kidnapping incident in Ireland, so had a combination of thoughts as to 'who was following her' that would likely cause feelings of paranoia in most people and especially in these circumstances.

Not forgetting Peter Molloy's comments: *"She kept looking out the window, and I thought she must have had an argument with a boyfriend and was running away. When I asked her, she said, 'I wish'"*. Which is quite remarkable; for as far as we're aware Peter has no idea what had took place at Liverpool, as it's being mentioned here for the very first time. He's not that far off the mark in what he is saying for we know she did have an argument with her "partner", 'over money' and sorry to mention it again, a kidnapping was involved. Clearly meaning '...that would have been the least of her worries' and that it was something much more serious she was concerned about. And if that's the case and she had already gone through this 'incident' with her "partner", she must have been referring to the police or of course someone else entirely.

According to the Hollinshead family one of the most upsetting parts out of this whole affair was the shocking way that they got to find out about Glenn's death. Many a time you'll recall when someone's death is reported in the media and they state they will not name the person until members of the family has been informed. Over 24hrs had gone by before the Hollinshead family found out what happened to Glenn. In fact it could have been much longer if it wasn't for the fact that Paul Hollinshead was out walking his dog when he came across a news-billboard just outside his local newsagents that had the murder reported by *The Sentinel* newspaper. There was a photograph showing the rear of Glenn's home and Paul instantly recognised it.

On what's been said by neighbour Frank Booth it would appear the police knew who Glenn and his family were. In addition they had his unlocked mobile phone, with his 'Mum' listed among all his brothers and sons and a whole list of contacts that would have soon helped identify who Glenn was.

It could be argued they didn't want to handle it for forensic reasons. They could have worn gloves and bedsides with the kind of technology and information available to them they should have been able to contact his family within a few hours.

His 82 year old mother, Mary, totally changed on hearing the tragic news about Glenn's murder. It's said by the brothers that this was the catalyst that expedited her dementia.

In the same reply from the Staffordshire police on the 31st August 2012, they said it was apparent during the initial hours of the investigation that they could not identify close members of the family. Records show that at 15:52pm on the 21st May 2008, Paul Hollinshead arrived at Glenn's house. He was told to contact the incident room, which "records" show he did at 15:56pm, when he informed them he was Glenn's brother. He was advised to go home and that an officer would soon contact him. At 08:20am on the 22nd May 2008, a police briefing note states that DC Short, the Family Liaison Officer, said that apart from Glenn having four brothers and two sons, his mother and one brother lived locally and *'that they had been notified.'* Giving the impression it was the police that had achieved this objective, yet as we know this was only after Paul had gone to Glenn's home and spoke to the officers at the scene.

So let's just rehash what we're looking at here: Peter said within half an hour or so – that he started to make his excuses to leave: "*...it was getting late after all and I didn't want to feel too rough at work the next day.*" "*Sabina had said something along the lines of "oh don't* *go ", not in an alarmed fashion, but more like a host of a party would say when it became apparent the night was coming to an end and the guests were leaving. I recall asking her if she'd be alright as I looked in her eyes to make sure her reply wasn't just out of politeness but she gave me a reassuring look and smile as I headed towards the door. Glenn saw me out, through after I had a short embrace goodbye with Sabina who stood behind Glenn has I shook his hand. I checked to see if he was ok with the situation, at which point he said come round tomorrow after work. I said my goodbyes, telling him to text me tomorrow to let me know how things are."* He continues: *"...as I look back to that night, I had no way of truly knowing what would happen, despite her behaviour she never once seemed the violent or overpowering type, even a criminal for that matter. I left with a feeling that she was in some sort of trouble or danger, but they both seemed comfortable enough with the situation."*

Again, he seems to confirm Sabina was comfortable in Glenn's company, suggesting this could be because she had probably been told to go there and why she felt this way.

The following day Peter went to work, though he insists he didn't speak to anyone about meeting Sabina and going back to Glenn's and that she had mobile phones, a laptop and at least £1000 in cash, - in which I suggested might have happened.

I thought it could have been likely he was overheard in a pub or at work or accidently told someone and they in turn told someone else. I was trying to say that some local "hard-nuts" come drug addicts in general, knowing about Glenn's old drug habit and that he still might have owed debts from days gone-by that his ex-girlfriend who we know was too once on drugs, may have run up some debts

205

and they see Glenn as being responsible because it was his "girlfriend" at the time.

Did these "someone" else then turn up at Glenn's home that afternoon or early evening? Did they come in, perhaps might have then been friendly etc. and Glenn probably knew them anyway. They may have had a few drinks and bit of a chat etc. when soon after Glenn might have asked them to leave as he was going to make something to eat for the pair of them. He could have used the prospects of having to soon leave themselves to go and visit Ursula in hospital. He then may have popped out to Frank for some teabags, for he didn't want any more alcohol being consumed and as he came back in he could see "they" were struggling with Sabina whilst trying to rob her. Glenn would have no doubt intervened and tried to stop them. According to his brothers this is how Glenn would typically react in such a situation, that he was the type of man who would step-in and help someone out in such a circumstance and especially so in his own home and her being a women.

And as I've continuously tried to point out and I hope I've been able to achieve this and make clear to you, that it only needed one person to quickly stab Glenn in the neck and then the heart whilst at the same time someone else grabbed hold of him. Meanwhile, Sabina was still in the house though she could handle herself more than most people and perhaps this is why she picked up the hammer by Glenn's front door.

She could have got into a struggle and tried to use it against them with them then pulling back for a minute, giving her the opportunity to have fled, whilst they were still inside the house - or it could have happened the other way around. On what Peter has said it appears as if someone might have grabbed some of Sabina belongings and perhaps the plastic bag before fleeing the scene. For just down the road and near to the mud-track they had walked down the night before and back to Glenn's home, Peter said that on the following Thursday or Friday of the same week though it was highly possible the following week, he came across personal items of Sabina's lying scattered about the area, such as; '...copied CDs and empty packets of cigarettes and her red/jumper top'. He told the police about this when they contacted him to clarify certain details in his statement so they were still in the process of writing up their reports.

Peter further suggests: 'I believe she may have chucked a lot of stuff in the bushes on the bridge round to Heron Cross before we met her.' - '...could have dumped some of her stuff earlier in the day, or someone had moved it about, kicked it around etc., from wherever it was left 'dropped.' This could be the case though why didn't they spot these items that same day and as they walked home to Glenn's?

Surely the police combed the area soon after Glenn's death and if so why didn't they discover these same items? In the BBC film they seem to place a burgundy item, representing the coat she was wearing on M6, into the bag Sabina was supposed to be holding when she met the two men. We can see Peter being portrayed by an actor carrying the transparent plastic bag as he follows Sabina and Glenn back to Duke Street. She might have stashed something away like they could have at Keele Services. Though we believe these items appeared after she fled Glenn's house. For why would she throw away her red jumper/coat the day before? It sounds like the one she was seen wearing on the M6 motorway. We seemed to have established burgundy-red is among her favourite colours for clothing. So I can't see why these items would have been discarded by Sabina previous to going to

Glenn's home and it is more likely they were taken by those fleeing Glenn's home in the hope there was something else more valuable within the bag. No one knows when or what was or wasn't taken or found? She may have had a much larger wad of cash or drugs in her possession and whoever took the bag or those items, was obviously hoping to find it.

The emergency sirens were heard that night by Peter but he said he just put it down to some local crime going off. We know he had been asked by Glenn to go back that evening and in addition Peter had told Glenn he would text him the next day. The following day after the murder Peter went to work yet it was only then he said he first heard about something happening to Glenn and then started to put two and two together and wondered was it to do with Sabina?

We know Glenn's mobile phone reveals it was 33hrs and 20 minutes later when Peter texted a message at 09:16am and then phoned his mobile at 10:53am, almost 35hrs after last seeing Glenn alive and giving each other that parting message.

By this time most of the neighbourhood had known about it. It was headlined the following morning on newsagent's billboards advertising *The Sentinel* local newspaper - and has said this is how Glenn's brother Paul found out about it.

Peter Molly's text read: Wednesday 21/05/08 Peter Molloy - 09:16: *"Heard loads of police were down your street last night. Was it anywhere near yours?"*

To look on a map at Duke Street can be confusing, (see Photo Section), it's quite a long street broken into two parts, the Hollinshead's thought Peter lived at top end of the street and far away. You can see Glenn's side of Duke Street from Peter's side. There's a series of steps you use to gain access to his side. If Peter came out of his home and walked some yards to the bottom part of Duke Street his view overlooks the railway bridge and you can see partly up Glenn's section of the road. You'd easily be able to notice the road cordoned off by the police. You only need to turn and look right and Peter would have seen Sabina running up the short hill of the A50 and up to Heron Cross roundabout and where the bridge-way is where Sabina jumped off, if of course he was standing there at the time.

The following words by Peter Molloy are in response to some last minute questions I put to him. They are extracts from a rather lengthy reply: *"Why didn't she go somewhere else/find a B&B. I suspect she may have not spoken to many people that day, there were reports of her sitting around the Fenton area for some time that day before we met her. My thoughts are she didn't get any help from anyone else and we were the first to at least engage in a full conversation with her. Why did she go back to Glenn's? All of your points and reasoning's make perfect sense, why would you, I know I wouldn't. I know if I was looking for a place to stay and had money then that is what I would do and I wouldn't rest until I found somewhere."*

"Do I agree that Glenn may have spoken to or may have told someone she was there? Yes I do. I know he had called his brother. I also recall that he was going to speak to his mate about fixing the laptop (although I've already established it wasn't broken she just didn't know the password) so maybe he did go to the PC repair shop, maybe he did call someone else or someone called him. It's highly possible. Did it happen? I don't know."

"Do I think your theory has some substance? Yes its probable, and if there is evidence to suggest that, then it needs to be looked into, investigated fully, if not to establish what really happened, at least to close the gaps on the unknowns and rule it out altogether, to make sure once and for all the correct person was caught and sentenced for Glens murder."

"Personally upon the evidence given, [this was said before he had the opportunity to read this book], *I believe Sabina killed him. If the new evidence was confirmed and established a different truth, then yes of course I would have to change my mind about that, any rational thinker would have to. Hence why if there are real doubts that cannot be answered an investigation is needed, not just into why she was released, but into what else may have actually happened that night."* - Peter Molloy 20th September 2012. He seems to have conceded that Mike's new evidence indicates Glenn did met Sabina before him after all.

The weakness of Sabina Eriksson's case

For those who've seen the *Madness in the Fast Lane* documentary they would recall Detective Inspector Dave Mellor saying that Sabina never said a word. Yet according to the Swedish press, they state Sabina said; *"Jag är oskyldig, din nåd"* = *"I'm innocent, your Grace,"* on the 15ᵗʰ January 2009 at Staffordshire Crown Court.

Okay, so he might have been referring to whilst she was in police custody, though by the time she said that in court, eight months had passed. So we can't see why she wouldn't have insisted the same whilst with the police or in prison.

As touched on before, no one could have envisaged such an appalling tragedy was going to occur. So again, this isn't just a case of finger pointing for the sake of it or trying to find a quick fix and proclaim we've solved the case for I/we recognise it's far more complex and much more serious than that. But nor should we forget that a man lost his life and supposedly by a women whom medical professionals have agreed; *'...she could do this again at any given time.'* Dr Carol McDaniel said; *"...there is a significant risk of Eriksson committing further offences."* Which makes you wonder had she done something similar in the past then?

When something devastating like this happens we also need to be big and bold enough to address these kinds of major mistakes that have obviously occurred that resulted in an innocent man losing his life. I/we can even see and in a sense identify as to why these twins were allowed to continue unhindered on their journey. These police "Obbo's" are bigger than "any one man or woman", some lasting for many years and costing millions of pounds. Tracking and observing hundreds of suspected criminals whilst trying to obtain as much evidence as possibly that will help lead them to successful convictions, is crucial in many cases and a most complex and difficult task at that. But at the end of the day something needs to be done to help rectify the situation and that's the objective of doing what it is we have set out to do which is to try and get to the bottom of the truth regarding Glenn's unnecessary death, that clearly could have been prevented.

We can't and the family don't directly blame Glenn's death on the police or medical staff that prematurely released Sabina for hindsight is a great thing and obviously wasn't available to them. Though there were guidelines and procedures in place to help prevent such tragedies from occurring, alongside their own professional training and knowhow of what they were doing that has to be considered. For there is no getting away from it "they" have messed up big time and "they" have to hold their hands up and be accountable as to what had happened. Even if it's behind closed doors and in private the Hollinshead family should be consulted and addressed. It's far too late and there's not really any other way this can be resolved. No one's calling on people to lose their jobs or to be criminally charged, but we are appealing to the authorities involved to sort this mess out once and for all.

By this case not going in front of a jury, Glenn's voice has never been heard and whatever truth there is, it has been suppressed. Justice needs to be seen to be done and it never was in this case.

It could even be argued that Sabina was also a victim here for had she remained in hospital under Section 136 of the 1983 Mental Health Act, in which she was first admitted to hospital then Glenn wouldn't have died the way he did and Sabina wouldn't have been on a murder charge. Both Glenn and Sabina were failed miserably by the many authorities and their related bodies of professionals along the way and that's why it's paramount cases like this must always go in front of a jury for at least the full facts would have had to been revealed.

Perhaps what we have uncovered is verification and reasons why the police couldn't let this case go in front of a jury even if they wanted to for the risk of disclosure of what had really took place was far too great as it would have exposed "the truth". In these particular circumstances it seems obvious this couldn't be allowed to happen.

As we know it's been alleged that Sabina refused to make any statements. This would have been following the advice of her solicitor and barrister anyway and especially so in the case of a murder charge. They would have pointed out the gravity of her position and that she would probably be in danger of incriminating herself if she made any statements. People with "mental" conditions often do. She would have been advised to wait until they had gone to a full trial before deciding whether she wanted to take to the witness-stand and address a jury.

Whether you agree or disagree with this kind of procedure it's immaterial for that's how legal advisors work, they are appointed to act the best they can and in the interest and on behalf of "the client." To act otherwise would leave them wide open to criticism that they failed in their duty to protect their client. In the United Kingdom all suspects of a crime are declared 'innocent, until proven guilty'. It's for the police and the Crown's agents to prove their case. It's possible to incriminate yourself of a crime even though you might be totally innocent. This has happened in numerous occasions over the centuries and why legal advocates advise their clients to remain silent. Because Sabina never made a statement of any kind, this of course made it very difficult for the police and the CPS to present a case.

Though in the case of making a 'deal' with the police and prosecution it's probable she spoke to them 'off-record' and they would of course not admit to this occurring, they simply can't as the case would have to be thrown out of court, so they would of course be more than willing to uphold saying - Sabina made 'no comment'.

Going back to what the Swedish press had reported which was that Sabina had said; *"Jag är oskyldig, din nåd"* = *"I'm innocent, your Grace."*, this could be a translation problem though I doubt it, her English was fine she could clearly understand what was being said to her in the police station and she admitted she read English newspapers besides she was provided an interpreter. In Sabina's position the court ask: *"How do you plead, guilty or not guilty,"* = *"Hur plädera dig skyldig eller icke skyldig."* She would have replied; *"Not Guilty"* = *"Inte skyldig"*. Though perhaps she was wanting to enforce how not guilty she was, and why she said: *"I'm innocent, your Grace,"* either way and in whatever language she told the court she was 'not guilty' and if this was the case then her trial should have gone before a jury, that's how the law works in England, though obviously not 'all the time!'

Sabina had been accused of Glenn's murder for over sixteen months. It wasn't until the 11th hour when it appears her defence team agreed to accept the lesser

214

charge of 'manslaughter' and in which it seems Sabina had accepted. We know now that Judge Saunders let the defence and prosecution team's consultant each other so as to 'strike a deal'. And why the prosecution were happy to accept her "guilty plea", due to her "diminished responsibility". An Advance Indication of Sentence and a 'Plea Bargain' would have been put into place indicating that in this instance he would sentence Sabina to 5 years. She had already served 16 months so only had to serve a further 14 months before she was free again - and as was the case. So she was in bit of a dilemma though her own defence barrister Mr Baxter QC, should have recognised the weakness in the CPS's argument and the evidence they had against her. Then on saying that because we've never been able to examine the 'court bundle' we don't know for certain what forensic evidence the police may have.

In passing judgement, Mr Justice Saunders knew that the punishment may seem lenient to the Hollinshead family when he said what's been mentioned in the 'Official Story' chapter. He stated that he based the sentence on the fact that Sabina was mentally ill and therefore her fault, guilt or responsibility was 'low' and why he passed a sentence designed to 'protect the public'.

By accepting that she was mentally ill - then he must also accept that the probability she is likely to reoffend is fairly high and was also highlighted by one of the doctors to be the case.

His conflicting sentence doesn't seem 'designed to protect the public' in fact it could be argued it's on the contrary for if it was he would have understood that by now treating Sabina as a "normal prisoner" in which he did, she would have entered the "normal" prison system and now wouldn't and didn't receive the kind of

215

psychiatric care or medication the public would have liked to see she had been given.

In his reply to Rob Flello Mp, Jeremy Wright MP, Parliamentary Under-Secretary of State of Justice wrote on the 24th September 2012:

"It is clear that Mr Justice Saunders considered the detailed medical evidence available. The medical evidence from more than one doctor indicated that the twins had suffered from a rare but temporary bout of insanity. The medical assessment concluded that Sabina was no longer suffering from any mental illness. This meant that a hospital order would not be available because, crucially, at the time of sentencing Sabina was no longer suffering from a mental health condition and as such there was nothing to treat as part of the hospital order. That in itself is a very unusual circumstance, but it must be right that people should be detained in secure mental health facilities where the medical evidence makes clear the offender is no longer suffering from a mental health condition.

The judge then had a number of options open to him in sentencing for manslaughter. He considered an indeterminate sentence of imprisonment for public protection (IPP) because he wanted to ensure there was some supervision of the offender, presumably in case the medical condition returned. He felt he could not impose a sentence for public protection because the medical evidence also meant that the offender could not meet the legal "dangerousness" test required for that sentence. This is because the evidence did not suggest that Sabina posed a risk of serious further offending because she was no longer suffering from a mental illness. It would not be possible for a court to impose on an offender an indeterminate sentence when the accepted medical

216

evidence suggests they no longer pose a risk of further offending and as a result do not meet the legal test for that sentence.

After having taken those various sentencing options into account the judge decided that a determinate custodial sentence of five years' imprisonment was appropriate for the offence."

In addition to what we've already mentioned about the Coroner's report, and that Dr Shorrock could obviously see there were inconsistencies, when he wrote; *"Only one weapon need have been used to produce all of the wounds, although I cannot completely exclude the possibility that there was more than one."* On a writers forum [21], read the following question: *"What kitchen knife would be best for stabbing someone to death?"*- *"I have a pseudo-god about to kill his semi-worshiper as a sacrifice using one of the knives in the knife block in the guy's kitchen.* (Glenn had one of these blocks in his kitchen where he was stabbed.) - *I have no knowledge either of the knives that go into a knife block, or which one would be best for stabbing someone to death. Or if there's a significant difference, for that matter".* Here's what someone gave as an answer: *"Where are you going to stab this victim? Through the ribs and into the heart?* (Consistent to Glenn's injuries) - *I'd suggest a filet knife or a boning knife."*

The startling new evidence that two weapons were present would have probably seen the collapse of this case within the first few days of the trial. Besides this evidence a jury would have questioned; 'Why was there were no defence marks on Glenn? Indicating the possibilities of a third person being involved was high. The opportunity would have arisen for them to have known about the reported 'kidnapping' at Liverpool police station. They would have questioned; 'Why weren't they searched at Keele Services?' Not forgetting the real nature of their 136 arrest and as to why the police records show no trace of it? That would highlight the problem as to why was Sabina released from hospital after only five hours? They would have likely questioned how and why Sabina's chance meeting took place and why she would even dream of going back to a house with two strange men? They'd wonder why didn't Glenn or Peter immediately address and sort out her original enquiry about where was the nearest bed and breakfast as that would have been the end to the matter. This is why we don't believe it was a 'chance encounter' and that it was probably arranged for her to meet Glenn.

A tragic murder that no one on this earth could have ever predicted that appears to have brought a sudden halt to a multi-million pound "Obbo" operation or at least placed it on hold for a while. They were probably hoping the twins were going to lead them to Mr Big or for them to have just helped them gather more intelligence. Let's not forget *Operation Junko* started in 2008 and involved £3.5bn worth of cutting agents that dilutes cocaine or heroin. *Operation Happy Fish* had been already running for a year up to the point of Sabina's arrest. It lasted for 18 months. Operation Junko went on 'under Obbo' for four years and it's these kind of "Obbo's" we believe they involved in.

So on the current evidence before us we can only assume there really wasn't a secure enough case against Sabina Eriksson and especially in regards to the murder charge with it being equally as difficult to find her guilty of manslaughter. They needed Sabina to agree to a 'manslaughter' charge and the only way to do this without the need to give a reason is to deal with the matter as a cause of 'diminished responsibility'.

Yes we can place her being at the property and we can confirm her odd behaviour. Yet we cannot precisely say she alone killed Glenn. No matter how obvious on the surface it may seem, no one would be able to currently conclude; 'beyond all reasonable doubt' that she acted alone. If indeed she even did anything untoward to Glenn in the first place.

The evidence we've uncovered seems to suggest she couldn't have done it. Sabina is left-handed, (see Photo Section). All the stab wounds on Glenn's body were on the left hand side, (bar one just off the midline). Of course people can be ambidextrous one in a hundred are, though we don't believe that to be the case of Sabina. Scientific tests seem to suggest twins are more likely to be left-handed than the general population, according to a study published in *"Behaviour Genetics"*, a leading journal concerned with the genetic analysis of complex traits - published in cooperation with the Behaviour Genetics Association.

Plea Bargain

Going back to Sabina's predicament I know it's been said Sabina "pleaded guilty" to manslaughter, though it's possible the case was dealt with without her saying a word after all she was in between a rock and a hard place to begin with.

Let me explain some logical thoughts for it appears a deal, a 'plea bargain' was struck. As said she was no doubt interrogated and told time and again she was in big, big trouble and that at the least she was facing a very long time in prison. They would have pointed out to her that they were going to ask the judge to recommend a minimum sentence of say; 10 to 15 years or to HMP her. To detain someone under Her Majesty's Pleasure (HMP) which is an 'imprisonment for public protection' (IPP), and in a sense where a life sentence start at 8 years and where you can technically keep someone in prison indefinitely. Various doctors, governors and boards of visitors will have to all agree on the prisoner's release. If it's believed they're a danger to the public or not shown any remorse then they will not be released.

A 'plea bargain' is an agreement in a criminal case between the prosecutor and defendant, whereby the defendant agrees to plead guilty to a particular charge in return for some concession from the prosecutor. This may mean that the defendant will plead guilty to a less serious charge or to one of several charges in return for the dismissal of other charges, or it may mean that the defendant will plead guilty to the original criminal charge in return for a more lenient sentence.[1] In England and Wales plea bargaining is permitted only to the extent that the prosecutors and the defence can agree that the defendant will plead guilty to some charges and the prosecutor will drop the remainder. The courts in these jurisdictions have made it plain that they will always decide what the appropriate penalty is to be.

No bargaining takes place over the penalty. However, although this is not conducting a plea bargain in cases before the Crown Court, the defence can request an indication from the judge of the likely maximum sentence that would be imposed should the defendant decide to plead guilty.[2][3].

The promise of a 5 year sentence in which you'd only serve 2 ½ years and which Sabina did would sound like heaven following the threats she probably would have received whilst in police custody.

Unfortunately, I too have been 'under Obbo' and know how the dark-side of the police and legal fraternity work in matters of "national security and interest" and why I believe that the twins were part of an ongoing police operation and had been 'under Obbo' from at least the 16th May to the 20th May 2008. At this time a particular police operation was still active and ongoing during these dates and beyond.

It goes without saying that the agencies involved would have too wanted to have prevented this case going to an open trial and why I/we further believe a deal - call it a "plea bargain" if you wish was struck between the defence and prosecution teams. As in the case of 'Bertie Small's' and Michael Michael's in the *'Super-grasses'* chapter in the *Appendix* part of the book it explains the kind of 'deals' that can be negotiated with the Crown and police.

As you know I've also been in this same kind of situation. If I'm right then the deal would have been simple in this case. Sabina would have to remain silent and make a 'no-comment' statement, like she did. In return and in time she would have her charges dropped from murder to manslaughter and like they were. And that if she pleads guilty to that she'd get a much more lenient sentence and that's exactly what happened in this case. It's a lot better getting a fraction of the time for manslaughter, than something like a ten year prison sentence on a trumped-up drugs charge. No embarrassing trials that would probably prove the twins were entwined in an undercover operation was the best possible solution for all, bar the Hollinshead family that is.

On the 5th October 2012, in reply to Rob Flello MP, the Attorney General, Dominic Grieve QC MP, wrote: *"You are concerned about the leniency of the sentence. It should be understood that the nature and severity of the penalties imposed are matters for judicial discretion, subject to any guidelines laid down by the Court of Appeal. In doing so it is not unusual for the sentencing Judge to invite both prosecution and defence counsel to make representations in regard to the relevant guidelines and sentencing law. That occurred in this case."*

Conclusion

So here we are having travelled a full ring of fire to get to this point of our conclusion. What appeared on the surface to be the crazed actions by a pair of twins on the M6 motorway in May 2008, which at first many thought we were looking into the case of something like escaped super strength soldiers, alien hybrids or even clones; seems to have turned out to be that of a sad and tragic "normal" human story that has affected and blighted the lives of many people and particularly that of the Hollinshead family.

Taking into consideration the evidence presented it most certainly seems to appear that Sabina and Ursula were indeed embroiled in some kind of "Obbo" at the time of the M6 incident and probably had been for some period of time. We know they had concerns about the safety of Sabina's two step-children and went to St. Anne Street police station to report they had been kidnapped by her partner Michael Dossou. They may have perhaps stolen some drugs or money etc. and why her partner said they had a row 'over money'. Money that perhaps wasn't even his and they were perhaps now fleeing from this partner's associates as had been suggested by her brother Bjorn and thought the children might be in danger by "those" they had just robbed or for some other reason like we've already covered.

Had the twins been 'under Obbo' then we can only assume the Merseyside police did a 'name-check' on them and that it soon become apparent they were of 'Police Interest', and under 'Police Observation'.

What if we are right and Sabina didn't kill Glenn and it was another person or persons who had stabbed him instead?

What if this person/s had known or thought Sabina had drugs or cash in her possession and that "they" were to kill Glenn then it would be Sabina who was the obvious suspect. Though on saying that I don't believe it was a premeditated murder and happened as a spontaneous incident arose and in which I'll explain. Even if the alleged "boss" or people who may have contacted them to go to Glenn's house to collect "the stash", (if of course this was the scenario and including what I've already mentioned, and we'll look at others further on in the *Appendix*) they could easily say it wasn't there when they arrived. They could basically say what they like. Sabina was probably attacked inside the house by some others who tried to rob her when Glenn then intervened and paid the ultimate price.

Sabina witnessing this surprise attack or set-up would instantly understand the predicament she was in and thought; *'I'm going to be accused of killing Glenn'*, so panicked and run out the front door fleeing for her life and picking up Glenn's lump hammer he kept by it. She could have been struck by the hammer and retrieved it from her attacker/s? She could've fought them off and they fled first? In her current state of mind she might have hit herself over the head with it, as perhaps she was hoping she would be able to say it was "the attackers" or Glenn who did it to her and could explain why she stabbed him out of self-defence. Even knowing she might not have stabbed him - who was going to believe her?

Sabina would have felt powerless, she knows no one will believe her story and like that period on the M6 motorway their first suicidal attempt, perhaps she was petrified and felt she'd rather kill herself than face whatever circumstances were awaiting her. She may have had one of her pre-prepared "poisoned" cigarettes (if of course they ever were), laced with something like PCP so she had no pain threshold and went into some trance like state. After a bit of cat and mouse games with the paramedics she then decided to jump off the bridge-way over the A50 in fact she probably thought she could fly!

We understand that what we are saying might seem wide off the mark and too fanciful a thought to consider, though if we go on the evidence we now have in front of us then it's highly likely we are right. This is what happens when justice isn't permitted to play it due course, had this case gone in front of a jury then many of the unanswered questions could have been addressed and perhaps answered. Had the Hollinshead family been furnished with the 'court bundle' of evidence as promised then perhaps it would have shown it wasn't anyone else but Sabina who killed Glenn. Though this is unlikely given the facts that a jury would have also seen this further evidence they would have been able to see that someone else was very likely involved in Glenn's death.

They'd also question; why would Sabina suddenly wish to kill Glenn who was allegedly just about to make something to eat and drink for them?

Addressing those who have raised such matters in the past suggesting something may have 'triggered' Sabina to react the way she did, then I'd reply the following: Even if she had been hypnotised, micro-chipped or brainwashed to react to trigger words etc. then why on earth would you hypnotise or program anyone this kind of way unless you were present with them?

For if you were then at least you'd be able to trigger them off in some way, but if you weren't then surely such an idea would be rendered useless. For a person to react like this without their 'handler' present isn't sensible or even feasible for why would you want to have someone roaming the planet who'd "deliberately" react this way whenever anyone said the wrong thing to them or at any time they could be triggered off?

We're not disagreeing such a thing isn't impossible and even via remote control it could be achieved, though it's highly unlikely nor credible in such circumstances. In fact quite the opposite how could you rely on waiting for someone to say the wrong or right word that would then be the key so they would react to it, the whole notion is crazy and surely isn't the case here.

Even if Glenn wasn't with Peter, Glenn would still have walked home the way they did for it's the quickest route to Glenn's home. Glenn might have been reluctant about what was being asked from him – if of course it was. He might not have liked the idea of being imposed on him at such a short notice. He might not have wanted to get involved with the people contacting him to help them out knowing that it's probably drug related and was worried about getting involved. He may have said he might know of someone else who could help and put her up for the night and if they can't he will take her back to his. He might have been adamant that he didn't want Peter to get the slightest idea that he was involved with Sabina. He might have viewed Peter Molloy as a straightforward honest, hardworking bloke who worked as a 'Customer Advisor' at a national electricity company and didn't want to let him know about his private life.

Contrary to how it was portrayed in the BBC *Madness in the Fast Lane* documentary; Peter hardly knew Glenn and only got to know him from a friend's boyfriend who had known Glenn for some years. He'd only known Glenn for about three or four months. So Glenn had to tread carefully, it's likely he was told by those asking him to help Sabina not to tell anyone else what was going on. So it's quite possible Peter Molloy could have unwittingly got himself in the middle of this strange encounter that on the surface looked like it was a chance meeting.

Sabina and Glenn might have been told to behave as if they were strangers in front of Peter, as we now know Glenn had encountered Sabina before Peter. Sabina may have been told the way to start the conversation and of course we haven't a clue how that would have worked out, but let's say she was to use the following opening line; 'Do you know where I can find a Bed and Breakfast?' As been suggested by Peter Molloy, Glenn wouldn't have likely wanted his family to know he was putting up some 'strange' women for the night and who was connected to some undesirable people he knew. They were aware of Glenn's trouble in the past with drugs, so it would be far more convenient and easier if Glenn was to pretend to Paul when he spoke to him about Sabina that he told him they met the way they did for it makes it a lot less complicated to explain himself.

It would look at bit suspect if Sabina asked Peter does he know where a B&B was and then Peter turns to Glenn and asks does he know one - and Glenn was to then turn around and say; *"Why not come back to my place for a bite to eat and were sort you out there"*. And then Sabina replies; *"Okay, that sounds like a great idea let's go"*, and off she walks down the road with two complete strangers. So there had to be some foreplay and make it look like a chance encounter.

As I've pointed out before because I think it's a crucial part that has to be considered for we don't believe Sabina to be the travelling, gypsy type of person she has been portrayed as, nor do we think she is a cold callous murderer and did what has been alleged she did due to diminished responsibility, for the evidence clearly suggests there was more than one person involved here. They twins actually appear to be 'normal people' with close family ties. Twins, who came from such a small village and town of 1,200 people or so, appeared to have stood out like a sore thumb and were picked on and bullied and when that happened they most probably fought back and rightly so. It's tough for some people being a twin and you only have to read about some of the tragic cases involving other sets. This 'attention' has most probably been with them throughout their lives and it seems they don't particularly like it. But when it comes to hearing how they are as a family, they seem like decent people, perhaps may have had some drink and drug addiction problems and whom now appear to be deeply religious. And that's why we are certain had it been another set of circumstances then these twins would have no doubt come forward by now as would perhaps other members of their family.

Though what is failing them as being decent people is that you'd expect they would want to explain what happened to them on those crazed days in May 2008 and to help set the record straight for the Hollinshead family. They should want to explain to the family what led up to Glenn's death and why it was perhaps manslaughter as opposed to murder - that perhaps warranted the way she had to defend herself that way. And if of course I'm right, explain her totally innocence.

Even if she (they) went 'insane' for those brief moments in time as has been said was the case and she haven't the slightest memory as to what had happened, you'd think she would still like to explain herself.

This is why the invitation is still open to the Eriksson twins and other members of their family to talk to me, for if I am wrong in what we are saying then I would love to be corrected.

The same applies to any other witnesses in this case, if you are ready to talk you can do so with me in confidence.

Though it must be difficult for Sabina for even if she didn't kill Glenn, she wouldn't easily be able to deny such a claim without explaining what really had happened to her and what she was really involved in.

We can further see the twins were bonded to a loving family unit, a mother with children such as Simon who speaks highly of her and for all the reasons I have pointed out. We cannot accept this type of women would have gone back to a house with two utter strangers she had only just met in the street and spoke to for a few moments walking along a remote railway-side mud track with them and back to Glenn's home. But it seems to have worked with Peter Molloy if of course what we're saying is correct. He was quite convinced it was a chance encounter and we're convinced it was likely Glenn who led Peter to actually think he was taking the initiative and played it out that way.

Peter said Glenn ushered him slightly to one side and: '...*suggested or at least hinted that he* (Peter) *could put her up for the night, but he didn't feel too conformable about the idea and discreetly ruled out the possibility to Glenn before he took it upon himself to invite her back to his for some food whilst they sorted out accommodation and checked to see if Sabina's sister was at North Staffs*

Hospital.' Peter continue to state: *'...they walked off down Christchurch Street towards Pit Hill, with him being lumbered with the gentlemanly task of carrying her bags'.*

Again Glenn tried to suggest to Peter about the idea of offering to put her-up for the night at his house - and again Peter declined. He gives a number of reasons as to why he wouldn't think it would be such a good idea after all. So it seems Glenn was lumbered with Sabina and because they probably both felt awkward it was good to have Peter along to help break the ice. Peter described the short walk as; *'...pleasant and Sabina's interactions had been nothing but gracious and friendly'.*

They arrived at Glenn's home and the night went on as it should have, they had a chat, bite to eat and a drink etc. Peter knew she had a large wad of money and other valuable items. He even thought they could have been stolen. He then decided to nip back home to get some beers and popped back to Glenn's, that's how close he lives. As mentioned previously, even though Peter lives on the other side of Glenn's street they still both live in 'Duke Street', that's since been divided by a slip road off the A50. You can walk to his house in five minutes and jog it in half that time.

Peter said he saw his housemate when he briefly returned home, though never mentioned Sabina or Glenn to anyone until the day after Glenn was killed and when he was in work. Peter's brief visit home would have given Sabina and Glenn enough time to have a quick chat and make sure Peter had no idea who she was and that she was told to meet up with Glenn. She would have probably said fair enough as they were as good as strangers anyway. It's not too difficult to put on a pretence in front of a person you genuinely know nothing about.

Peter returned for a couple of hours (or so he says) and said: '...*the atmosphere remained relaxed, it was more like a get to know everyone situation like the first day of college or work, more like camp fire story telling as they'd listen to Sabina's replies, though any questions in regards to what was wrong with her sister or why she was it Stoke-on-Trent were often met by an awkward silence or a quick question thrown back in my direction to suggest I don't want to talk about that.'*

This kind of conversation adds up, for it must have been difficult for Sabina to come up with a cover story knowing she was now as good as being watched by the police, or still being pursued by those who they were probably fleeing from.

Peter says: '*There wasn't anything overly unusual about the second half of the evening at least up to this point, Sabina at times in my opinion remained wary of the front door and on occasion would continue to look out the window sort of trying to mask her presence whilst doing so once she had moved back up towards the chair. I do recall one strange request when she wanted to change the lighting which I believe after Glenn agreed to her request she made the lighting alterations herself trying different lights on and off, I couldn't help but think after the window incidents that she wanted to either disguise or remove the shadow she was casting across the curtains. I was a little unsettled at her behaviour but I accept others might just put it down to quirkiness or my own over reacting imagination.*"

Peter could clearly see Sabina was concerned about who was on the other side of that front door. For she would have probably realised she was being watched in Fenton and before Glenn and Peter arrived. She may have wondered if they had traced her back to Glenn's house and hoping she had evaded those watching her. By going down the mud-track to Glenn's home it would have been difficult to have followed them without being noticed and why it's very likely they got back to Glenn's home without being seen by the "Obbo team" and at this point they probably lost her.

Which means it was unlikely they were outside Glenn's home, though there is a possibility they may have seen her go to Glenn's earlier in the day or somewhere nearby and they only arrived outside Glenn's home later that evening. They could have had undercover officers watching Glenn's home at the end of the mud path so could have then seen them emerge from that area, (see Photo Section).

Peter continued: *"...at the time I felt uncomfortable and I guess had got a little over paranoid about her actions, maybe even reading far too deep into their meanings, including whilst talking about Glenn's dog, she asked questions like is he protective, does he make you feel safe".* *"...that's when Glenn made Troy bark on command."* *"I just had a nagging feeling in the back of my head that she was hiding or running from someone, in no way did I ever get a feeling that she would be a danger to Glenn, but that's not to say I believe in anyway there was anyone else involved in Glenn's murder."*

This statement was made after we had told Peter we had obtained evidence that indicates a second weapon was used and that a third party could be involved. So yet again he indicates he agrees that 'someone' else could be involved and that something was wrong the night they met and that she acted like she was hiding from someone. Yet he is equally satisfied to accept Sabina simply killed Glenn for no reason whatsoever other than she got paranoid about the conversation Glenn had with his neighbour Frank, moments before Glenn was attacked and killed.

Though let's not forget this is my hypothetical account and therefore it's also possible Peter Molloy knows a lot more than he is letting on. My gut feeling is that he does and I really wouldn't be surprised that he knows who the 'real' killer/s are. Like that of Glenn's brothers, we can't quite believe his story or events and why he didn't allegedly go back around there the next day.

With the Section 136 being edited out of the original Madness in the Fast Lane film and the police records appearing to have no mention of it in their files alongside the UHNS refusing to help in anyway, whose own records should further prove the twins were indeed first arrested and admitted into hospital under Section 136, - it seems suggests they have closed ranks, for they know it will expose this cover-up in its entirety.

Not only is it surprising it's beyond comprehension to hear how the police dealt with Sabina after the affair. They had had her in police custody and they knew what she had been through on the M6 motorway with her sister. They were aware Ursula lay critically ill in bed and only a couple of miles away in the University Hospital of North Staffordshire, yet they didn't take her there or assist her to make sure she had somewhere to go.

Can you imagine being treated like this whilst you were on travelling abroad or holiday in somewhere like Spain or Sweden? It would likely be all over the British media was that the case. This is most unlike our police to behave in such a way. They knew she was not an English/British national and was in a strange country all "alone". This is why I'm very surprised to hear the police wouldn't at least have reunited her with her sister Ursula.

233

At this stage no psychiatric reports had been made suggesting 'a madness shared by two' had not yet come into the equation. The way this situation was handled seems act as a further indicator that the police were told to keep their distance from Sabina and to leave her to her own devices.

It's equally surprising to see that Mentorn Productions didn't cover this part of Sabina's story. Normally when they are filming a story about someone on the *Motorway Cops* series, they follow the development of the persons involved in the programme. What happened at the roadside, the arrest, back at the police station or hospital if involved and then normally what happens to them afterwards. I wouldn't be surprised if this was the case though to date we haven't had a reply to our questions enquiring if they did they actually film more than what was shown on the TV? For we're surprised as to why the cameras didn't follow Sabina up unto the point of her appearance at Fenton Magistrate Court.

They were in the position to interview Sabina as she came out of the courthouse and could have asked her to explain what had happened on the M6? Was she worried about Ursula and her children and the rest of her family? Were her family not concerned to hear about what has happened? What was she going to do next? Yet the film seems to stop with Sabina being taken from the hospital and then at the police station. I'm referring to the original *Dicing with Death* film footage as opposed to the *Madness in the Fast Lane* film that came much later. This sort of non-action seems again to back up the theory "they" wanted Sabina out of the hospital and into police custody and with the film crew in tow, so as "they" could then get Sabina back on the streets and back 'under Obbo.'

They knew her situation was desperate and that she would have to call on someone to help her. She now had to go 'somewhere' after the courthouse. "They" didn't stop "observing" her just because of what happened on the M6 motorway, not forgetting they had already been given so many previous green lights.

When the local Staffordshire police arrived at Glenn's house, to them it looked like a cut a dried case. Sabina had stabbed Glenn and an easy open and shut case - and that was the end of it. Though if the evidence of two weapons had been pursued and the murder investigation was carried out perhaps in a better way than it was, such as Sabina's personal items spotted by Peter Molloy some days after Glenn's murder, then the outcome would have no doubt been different.

Had they gone out and collected these items for it doesn't seem to have been the case, they would have found evidence that could have proved there was an attempted robbery. Meanwhile, whilst under police guard in hospital - for three months and most likely after many visits by the police she was probably told about the "Obbo's" and that they had certain compelling evidence against her and others, i.e. camcorder footage and photographs of the twins at various places coming and going etc. and again that they had enough evidence on her, and that she was going to jail for a very long time if she didn't cooperate with them. As I've said; she could have been looking at 8 to 10 years inside prison, even more. Though if she was to plead guilty to manslaughter and not murder she'd get 5 years and serve just 2½ years in prison instead.

Like all 'deals', there was something to give in return and like most people in this situation she would be expected to assist the police to make up for all the lost time, effort and money wasted having to stop the "Obbo" on her and those she was involved with. They would have probably wanted her to supply enough details that gave the police the evidence they needed to bring something like one of the police operations I suggest to an end. In fact one did, six months after Sabina's arrest and whilst still on remand in Bronzefield prison. This was another reason why I believe her case kept going from one courthouse to another. It's often a tactic used by the police to prevent those who may have had an active interest in Sabina's case from knowing what Crown Court would be used next. She actually ended up getting her final five year sentence at Luton Crown Court in November 2009. She served half that time whilst many others related to the "Obbo" are probably still in prison.

Following our submission to the Independent Police Complaints Commission (IPCC), they informed us they handed the complaint over to the Staffordshire and Merseyside Police Forces despite our request they should be involved with the investigation from the beginning. As mentioned we also contacted the Staffordshire police force requesting a copy of the 'court bundle', though we were informed the Hollinshead's were to make their request via a solicitor and that certain details and evidence will not be given to us due to the Data Protection Act when it comes to Sabina's details.

This is currently a task still in progress though as confirmed the Staffordshire's PSD has refused to hand over a copy of the 'court bundle' as on the 31st August 2012. We also contacted the coroner's office - and Mr Ian S Smith the coroner was at first most helpful. I contacted him again after studying the reports in June 2012, and asked him to put forward my letters addressed to both Dr Kolar and Dr Shorrock, asking them; *"How did they come to their conclusions?"*, considering Mr Kolar only seems to think the one weapon was used. And why didn't he include the width of the blade, instead of just its length? The coroner point blank refused to do so. I was rather perplexed and asked him, - why not? After all he was just to forward my letters. Why did he feel the need to intervene in such an action? After some irate dialogue he agreed to forward my letter to Dr Kolar, though still refused to send one to Dr Shorrock, as he said he was 'very ill'. I questioned what was that to do with it? I asked him, was it anything to do with the fact that Dr Shorrock may be called as a witness in PC Simon Harwood's trial over the death of Ian Tomlinson that was taking place the very instance we were having our telephone conversation?

Considering Dr Kenneth Shorrock was one of the pathologists in that case and that he would probably be asked again about Detective Inspector Eddie Hall who told Dr Shorrock who was conducting the autopsy for the Metropolitan Police Force that Tomlinson had fallen to the ground in front of a police van earlier in the evening, though there was no evidence to support this and that the IPCC ruled that Detective Inspector Hall had been reckless in making this claim.

Then as I say it's highly probable he was to be called as a witness to PC Harwood's trial, but by stating he was very 'ill' he obviously wouldn't have been able to attend that trial to give his evidence. I'm not accusing Dr Shorrock of making up his illness so as to avoid giving evidence at PC Harwood's trial, but like so many of the coincidences that have cropped up in this case, it seems like yet another barrier has been put in place so as to protect this doctor from having to give any evidence in that case and this or answer any of our questions.

The coroner, Mr Ian S Smith, assured me it had nothing to do with that case, yet still refused to forward my letter to him. To date I have not heard back from Mr Smith nor Dr Kolar. And for obvious reasons, Dr Shorrock, has not had the opportunity to reply to my questions as apparently they have never been forwarded to him.

Normally when someone contacts the IPCC it's because they are complaining about a particular police force. The Hollinsheads' complaint is far more complex. They're complaining - not only about the Merseyside Police Force, but also the Staffordshire Police Force as well. Though in addition there are the three "professionals" who were employed by the University Hospital of North Staffordshire who all agreed that Sabina Eriksson was; *"Fit and well"* to be released from hospital despite being admitted under Section 136 on the 1983 Mental Health Act.

The Magistrate at Fenton, who sentenced Sabina Eriksson to just 'one day' imprisonment without a 'Pre-Sentence Report', also has to be questioned; 'Why did he reach such a decision?' As do the "Judges" involved in the High Court hearings, alongside members of the judiciary on both sides of the defence and prosecution teams. The CPS – Northern Sector, the Coroner's office at Stoke-on-Trent, alongside Dr Kolar the pathologist whose report was far from clear and correct and proved to be as such by Dr Shorrock's own findings. All these bodies and a series of individual "professionals" seem to be implicated and involved in the complete and utter failure to address this travesty of justice properly. This is why we recently contacted the Home Office, Attorney General's Office and the Ministry of Justice, before the release of this book for the Hollinshead family would like to appeal to these establishments to see to it that the IPCC do intervene and reinvestigate this case. All heads of these authoritative bodies have commented about the case and defended the police, the courts and medical professional's actions despite not knowing the full facts of the case and especially about our own recent findings. Will they now alter their stance and course of action?

The Hollinsheads' seek a full and independent investigation and inquiry. They would like the following questions answered:

1. Why did the Staffordshire police ignore what happened in Liverpool and not mention it in the BBC documentary?
2. Why did the police officers in the BBC documentary say what they did, knowing what had really happened at St Anne Street Police Station in Liverpool?
3. Why was this Section 136 film footage edited out of the BBC documentary, and who was responsible for doing this? - Why did they feel the need to do so?
4. Why did the three AMHPs and other professionals agree Sabina was fit and well for release after only 5hrs, when the recommendation is normally 72hrs in such circumstances, and considering her twin sister was still in intensive-care.
5. Why did the Magistrate not ask for a pre-sentence report, before sentencing Sabina? Why was the 'assault' charge against PC Cope dropped?
6. Why is it the Coroner's Report, and the first post-mortem carried out by Dr Kolar, not include the width of the blade of the knife found at the scene? Why doesn't he highlight to obvious presence of a second weapon, like that of Dr Shorrock? Why

is there still no toxicology results included in the report?

7. Why is the Hollinshead family being denied access to the Court Bundle of evidence in this case?

8. Why haven't the UHNS replied, or try to assist the Hollinshead family in the matter?

9. The question of compensation for the Hollinshead family ought to be considered. Glenn left his children with no financial security. Even if there was no 'cover-up' involved, the Hollinshead family still have the legal argument, that serious failings and negligence took place on these days in question, and that these issues alone need to be addressed and rectified.

No doubt there are many other questions that need to be added to the above. If there is anyone who believes they could help shed further light on this subject and might have information they would like to share and help an inquiry or a further investigation into this case then why not contact us and let us know. We shall willing hand it over to the Hollinshead family's legal representatives and if need be the police as well. We will respect your privacy if wanted and you can even contact us anonymously if you so prefer.

As I said much earlier we were beginning to doubt whether anyone would believe our findings for we're as good as saying there is a police and even ambulance services cover-up (though only probably involving one or two members), and it's possible they may have colluded to make sure they marry-up certain 'emergency response' times. This is why we will most certainly come under attack, though even if we are accused of being too 'speculative' with our theories, we cannot ignore or deny the actual evidence that speaks for itself and the questions set above do need to be addressed and answered. Alongside these investigations, all of a sudden the already mentioned Hillsborough cover-up scandal broke news on the 12th September 2012, and in many ways it vindicates our own findings.

We at first questioned whether Sabina Eriksson's own case is subject to 'reporting restrictions' due to there being no mention of her case other than the 'manslaughter' charge. Sabina's release from Bronzefield prison was never reported. We know how the media work on other high profile cases; the press are normally camping outside all night and fighting to get the 'first' ever 'exclusive' photographs of their intended target. Yet Sabina was released in a 'hush-hush' style and shipped on to Sweden or Norway where she presently is.

However, we now fully understand the media's silence for to them it's a closed case for that's what the police have led them to believe. They had no knowledge that the section 136 was edited out of the film. They didn't know about Sabina reporting that her children had been kidnapped. They weren't aware the coroner's report indicates 'two weapons' were involved. In fact they didn't have the slightest inclination about the majority of our findings. Let's hope they do now!

As Jon Hollinshead said, *"...I feel more than justified now than ever, for thinking and believing that there really is more to the events and lives of the Eriksson twins...'*
'...make of this fascinating book what you will, but bear in mind that it could happen to your family. The public demand fair treatment and justice for all." - 23rd September 2012.

And it is that alone that makes our investigation worth all the time and effort involved, for we have almost

241

brought full closure to this family. They can at least move on with their lives knowing they were right, they were deceived and lied too, and that there was something drastically wrong in the investigation into Glenn's murder,.

Before we end I could not find any better words to sum up the situation than those of journalist Stephen Glover; that also helps shine the spotlight on the Hollinshead family who are in a sense on a micro-level in comparison to the Hillsborough tragedy, though find themselves in a very similar boat to all those other families who too have been lied to for so many years.

The following extracts are from an article written by Stephen Glover; published in *The Mail* newspaper on the 14th September 2012, following on from the Hillsborough cover-up scandal. The article was titled: *Masters of cover-up: How the Establishment closes ranks to protect its own and deny the people the truth;* All his life Stephen Glover believed in Britain's great institutions. No more. The sad lesson of Hillsborough is how the Establishment, judges, police chiefs, civil servants closes ranks to protect its own and deny the people the truth: *"Cover-up, lies, obfuscation and incompetence: these are the defects in the police and ambulance service revealed by the damning report into the 1989 Hillsborough disaster in which 96 people died."*

"It has taken 23 long years to establish the shaming truth, which is that senior police officers manipulated evidence to hide police failings while attempting, with great success, to blacken the good name of the innocent people who needlessly perished."

"In fact, it has taken the independent panel, chaired not by a judge but by the Bishop of Liverpool, the Rt Rev James Jones, to get at the truth of what really happened. Among the nine members on the panel there wasn't a single judge and only one lawyer. Most unusually, there were two journalists, one of whom has experience of investigative journalism."

"Evil is a strong word, but some of the things the top brass of South Yorkshire Police are alleged to have done, the doctoring of 116 statements to remove criticisms of the force; the imputation of excessive alcohol consumption where none had taken place, would appear to warrant such a description."

"Prosecutions and civil actions will doubtless follow as some of the guilty are finally brought to justice, and there will surely have to be a new inquest. At last everyone seems to be united in condemning the authorities."

"As a young journalist I believed in the integrity and good sense of most of our institutions. Of course, there were bad apples and stupid mistakes, but there were enough good and honest people in charge to come clean and own up when things went badly wrong." "After a succession of scandals over recent years, it grieves me to say that I no longer believe this is true, and I don't suppose it ever was. One episode after another has revealed a familiar and melancholy pattern of skulduggery and concealment.
"

"The police and ambulance service at Hillsborough were supposed to be serving the best interests of the fans, but as a result of incompetence only let them down."

"There's good cause to be disenchanted by the way the police and so many of our other institutions cover up their mistakes and wrong-doing. I'm certainly not naive enough to believe that the wall-to-wall apologies mean that something like this can't happen again."

One of the most moving responses to the report came from Becky Shah, whose mother died at Hillsborough. She said: *"I have mixed feelings', '...it has taken more than half of my life to get justice is absolutely outrageous in a democratic society.'"* - Stephen Glover. 14th September 2012 [1][2]

Appendix

"Obbo's" & Drug Dealers

The objective of the following information is to help show how prevalent drug smuggling is in Ireland-Cork, Liverpool-Merseyside, Newcastle-under-Lyme, Stoke-on-Trent, Sweden and Norway. I've not included anything on gangs in Newcastle-upon-Tyne purely because we cannot see any connection other than they may have travelled that way as a point of call from Norway to Liverpool/Ireland and wanted to return that way. All places that are somehow connected to the Eriksson twins. It's also to show how commonplace undercover and covert police operations are where the suspects are kept 'under Obbo', which is the slang-term for being under 'Police Observation' and for a set period of time. Some operations and "Obbo's" on certain individuals and members of known gangs can go on for a number of years.

We are taking a look at some of the different and ingenious ways drugs can me smuggled - whether it be in the base of a flower pot and plant, impregnated onto someone's clothing or securely concealed inside tins of fruit or fish.

More importantly we home-in on at least three police "Obbo's" and operations that were taking place when Sabina and Ursula Eriksson first came to the world's attention. We also look at the kinds of deals the police might have made with some of these criminals. In addition and to be able fully appreciate our theory it's therefore vital for us to try and understand what kind of predicament these two women must have been in - that perhaps they at first more than willingly got themselves mixed up in. We say theory for despite being tipped-off about the following, we cannot presently prove this to be the case and why an inquiry is needed. For it seems that the twins were either knowingly or unknowingly under 'police observation', often termed, as being 'under Obbo.' In cases such as this a whole array of agencies can be found working in conjunction with each other. Which ones precisely, we cannot presently say for certain, though an inquiry could well reveal this information as it could be any of the following or a combination of them all; Interpol, Europol, the Garda, the National Drugs Unit and Revenue's Customs Service, the FBI, MI5, MI6, the British Police, the United Kingdom Border Agency (UKBA), Customs & Excise, Metropolitan Police and Dutch law enforcement agencies in general.

We hope we've been able to demonstrate, that whilst the Eriksson twins fled the Irish borders in what could have been for their lives to the UK; that they were almost beyond doubt either being pursued by "others" within "their gang", or any number of the just quoted bodies or agencies who had these twins 'under Obbo' and very likely for some time, perhaps months. Let's not forget the "kidnapping" allegations! Yet as stated throughout certain sections in this book, we are convinced they had already fled Ireland, before the 'official storyline' date of the 16th May 2008, and believe they were already in the Liverpool-Merseyside area. It's been our intention to try and bring to light that these sisters were given the 'green light' to continue their journey unhindered, as they were 'under Obbo' and that it was not really the fault of those lower ranking police officers that they encountered along the way, as was the case when Sabina pleaded for help, as she was concerned for the safety of her two children. If of course this version of events is true.

It's very likely their connections are international, involving the USA, Ireland, the UK and the Netherlands. The drug industry throughout country and of course the world is controlled by a layer-cake of people who many are unwittingly connected to each other in some kind of way. All these kinds of gangs and groups need many 'runners', whether their job is to simply hide and keep drugs, money or even guns safe, these 'fall-guys' are essential to protect those above them. They're not paid large amounts of money and many do it more out of fear than because of the earnings. Quite often they'll be addicts themselves, so do it to fund their addiction. When people are 'under Obbo' it doesn't necessarily mean 'they are the target'. In fact it's very likely they are being observed so as the police, or their related bodies and agencies can gather intelligence.

Like I explain elsewhere in the book, it can quite often involve the taking of someone's photograph or the filming of a person's whereabouts and actions. Where they go, who they meet, at what times and how often they do; then it will soon become apparent if someone was dealing in drugs, or at least connected to such activities. The bigger dealers are of course much more discreet. They're often on the move, use various addresses and front businesses, drive different cars and have to stash and hide their illicit wares in all sorts of places. Money laundering is too part and parcel of drug dealing, as large quantities of cash has to be disguised in some way or another; so many will try and turn such cash into items of jewellery, gold bullion or property and land. Quite often cash is turned into different currencies, as it's easier to smuggle out of the country or re-exchange back to a currency of your choice and preference.

Apart from those involved, no one knows for certain what the Eriksson twins may have, or may not have had

247

on them, or for how long they could have been tangled in this kind of world, though our investigations seem to indicate it's been a number of years. Sharon's research seems to signify that the people the twins are either related, or connected to, some living at the same properties as the twins in the USA, seems to point to a possible connection to money laundering on a grand scale, though involving real estate and property in general. Though we cannot suggest they have any involvement, a person who was registered at the same time and address as Ursula appears to be linked; perhaps by association only, to individuals who repeatedly buy and sell a property. One particular property has been sold, then bought and sold again, and again, to the very same two or three individuals, at times with $100,000's in price difference, either as a loss or a gain. So it's fair to say this kind of activity isn't really your normal 'property investments, or 'buy to let' schemes they appear to be involved in.

Nor can we say for sure the twins were carrying drugs or simply large quantities of cash that day, if of course they had anything on their person at all. Though whatever they might have had on them, and the way they reacted seems to suggest it could have been exceedingly incriminating. Not forgetting what the retail manager Melissa Dutton at Keele Services said, the twins held their bags so close to their chests; '...it was almost as if all that they owned in the world was in them.' Not exactly the way you'd expect someone to be holding a bag that contained a bomb, as she also went on to say she suspected the twins may have had.

Take the following example of a gang that David Farrer QC, told a jury how they ran a 'large-scale' scheme for more than two years importing hundreds of kilos of the drugs and netting the gang more than £4.4 million.

248

The court was told on one occasion the alleged gang leader Mark Green, then 31, and another member of the gang, converted £160,000 in cash at the Bureaux de Change,[5a] in 2003 in Manchester. He was arrested on charges of masterminding an operation involving the importation of cannabis and amphetamines, a Manchester Crown Court heard. Alongside three Stoke-on-Trent men, Francis Sargeant 35, Robert Willis also 35, James Kenny 27, and David Arthington aged 49 from Newcastle-under-Lyme. All pleaded guilty to various charges of conspiracy to supply cannabis and money laundering. The gang had been 'under Obbo' by the National Crime Squad. Green, of Higher Lane, Upholland, arranged for drug sources from Spain, Belgium and the Netherlands to post packages of cannabis resin to mailboxes registered under fake names. All received substantial prison sentences.

Unfortunately, it's sad to say the drug problem is prevalent in both Newcastle-under-Lyme and Stoke-on-Trent, though perhaps not much worse than most other towns and cities in the UK, other than due to these towns being relatively small and compact, that it appears more serious. The town of Crewe is around 10 miles away from Newcastle-under-Lyme. The M6 motorway makes it easy access, and only minutes to get to in a car. It's less than an hour to Liverpool. Like other places in Great Britain, most of these towns in the Midlands are blighted with drug gangs, alongside with serious and dangerous individuals. As just said, the drug world is based on a layer-cake of multiple levels of people in hierarchal positions. So for instance, you might get the 'main players' who will fund the smuggling of perhaps 1.5 tonnes of cocaine to come from South America, to say; the Cork, on the West Coast of Ireland.

Millions of pounds have to be invested for this to happen, battling against all the odds of it being discovered by the numerous law and drug enforcement agencies whose job it is, to gather as much intelligence and evidence as possible. This hopefully ensures that as and when they do decide to strike and make a raid, they can expect to find a hefty bounty. If the smugglers are successful, it then has to be unloaded and securely and unnoticeably distributed on a logistical scale that would put most major dispatch and deliver companies, such UPS or the Royal Mail to shame. Alongside the 'raw' drug, it then requires a cutting agent. So 1.5 ton of cocaine or heroin; requires at least 1.5 tons of a cutting mix, which I explain further on.

Whenever you read about the arrests of certain members of a gang or simply groups of individuals dealing in drugs, arms or human trafficking etc. and that they have been under long term "Obbo" - then of course that's not all that happens. You'll find in-depth surveillance was carried out and much of the evidence was gathered prior to the arrests being made. You'll often hear the police branding someone; as 'Mr Big', for they need 'a body' to top the list of indictments, that's how it normally works in all criminally cases, and why you'll get those at the top of the chain given higher sentences than those lower down it. What makes the drugs world an even more dangerous place to be in, is not so much the criminal side of it, it's the fact that it's riddled with so many informants.

Quite often the police are 'tipped-off' as to what's going on and respond to that information accordingly. Many are 'set-up' by the very same people they have just purchased their drugs from. Of course it's unofficial and even illegal, but there are some unscrupulous undercover police officers who I've encountered, and who can work

250

hand in hand with drug dealers. There are also many drug dealing gangs and families who are technically allowed to blatantly trade in their "Manors", for at least the local police know where the honey-pots are, and quite often they are under constant "Obbo" and used to round-up and arrest the various people who are dealing with each other. The worst kind of informants are the addicts themselves, for when they are taken off the street, they're often clucking for a fix after a few hours in the cell, and it's at that stage they are prepared to sell their own grandmother's soul to the devil, and will inform on whoever they have to, so they can soon be released and get their next hit.

Then you have those who are arrested; caught 'bang to rights' and looking at some lengthy prison sentences, where it might be 10 years or so. Though who the police want is 'Mr Big', so they rely on the small-fry to inform on them for a lighter sentence. They may even let them back out on the streets, whilst the drug dealer either knowingly or unknowingly is then placed 'under Obbo'. Their task is to show the police where the dealers are and what kind of level they are at. That's what makes the drug world so precarious, for there is no one you can trust, no matter what side of the fence they may 'appear' to be on. And why it's often argued, even by some senior police officers, that the legalisation of drugs would stop this kind of activity and save billions of pounds to the tax payer.

In December 2011, the North Wales Police Chief Constable Richard Brunstrom, told his police authority a Royal Commission should examine legalising some or all illegal drugs. Mr Brunstom said that, despite billions of pounds and thousands of officer hours, the number of addicts and "recreational users" of illegal drugs in the UK has multiplied at an alarming rate since the 1970s. It is his belief that the war on drugs has already been lost. [12a]

251

Most people haven't a clue about how drugs are smuggled into various countries around the world, technology and knowhow has leapt boundaries over the recent years. People think of heroin and cocaine as a powdered drug, and of course it is at its final morphed stage; though it can be smuggled in a liquid form, and even be impregnated into, or onto various items, including clothing. In 2005, a case study was presented where it showed a woman travelling from South America to the Republic of Ireland, was detained at Dublin Airport and articles of clothing in her luggage were found to be impregnated with cocaine. The study shows that the amount of powder recovered from the garments was approximately 14% of the total weight of the garments. The cocaine was in the form of cocaine hydrochloride and the purity was approximately 80%. An examination of the garments under filtered light highlighted the areas exposed to cocaine and indicated that the method of impregnation was by pouring liquid containing cocaine onto the clothing.[8] Not forgetting the story from earlier, when it was reported on the 9th January 2011 that a woman was arrested in a cocaine swoop; found hidden in a vase by UK Border Agency (UKBA) officers and police in Belfast, hence they let her travel with the drugs 'under Obbo', after undercover police obviously followed her to that address wondering if she would have led them onto "bigger fish", i.e. those who must have funded this "courier" to begin with.[9]

2006 – Turf Wars

As far back as 2006, there was a 'turf war' gun battle between Liverpool and Newcastle-under-Lyme gangs in Ibiza that left three men seriously injured in hospital. [8a] Spanish police said more than 30 shots were fired in the high-speed car chase through the centre of the late-night resort. Liverpool man Shaun Francis Walker, then 23, had a bullet in his spine and ended up in intensive care. Walker was arrested along with his brother Joseph Walker, 19, and Sean Thomas Ion, 24, also from Liverpool. Newcastle-under-Lyme man, Keith Day, 24, was also arrested by Spanish police, along with John Patrick Murray, 20, of Winston, Darlington. [9a] According to the 2001 census, the Borough of Newcastle-under-Lyme, was recorded as having a population of 122,030, spread out over 24 wards, so in all, it's a relatively low number of people covering rather a vast area of 81.5sq miles. Stoke-on-Trent, known as the Six Towns, is a city almost twelve miles long within an area of 36 square miles. It's made up of the following much older boroughs of Burslem, Longton and Stoke, together with the urban districts of Tunstall and Fenton. In 2001, the population of Fenton was 12,194. It's assumed this figure is pretty much the same in 2012. The University Hospital of North Staffordshire, where the Eriksson twins were taken, is in Stoke-upon-Trent, about a mile from the centre of Newcastle-under-Lyme. It's fair to say most people know one another, and many of the cobbled side streets and terraced houses are like that out of a scene of ITV's *Coronation Street*. If you were into drugs, then it goes without saying, you'd know who is who, and what they are selling.

2007 - 10th biggest haul of cocaine in the world

In a five-year joint "Obbo" and investigation with Southern Ireland's Garda and London's Metropolitan Police, that involved the tracking down of a former Metropolitan police drug squad officer; ex-detective Michael Daly, 49yrs old at the time, and who played a

253

pivotal role in supervising a failed attempt to import 1.5 tonne's of cocaine, worth €500m into the UK via Ireland, and who had been taken into police custody in London in July 2007, it was Daly who used skills and knowledge gained while working as a Metropolitan Police [Met] drug squad detective. The plot failed when one of the boats bringing the drugs ashore capsized in Dunlough Bay in West Cork on 2nd July 2007, dumping 62 bales of cocaine into the sea and floating in a bay near Mizen Head, leading to the biggest drugs seizure in the history of the State. On the 7th July 2007, Gerard Hagan, from Liverpool, Merseyside, was first charged at a 'special sitting' at Clonakilty District Court, when evidence was given of his arrest, charge and caution, it's said he made a 'no comment' statement. Perry Wharrie aged 47 at the time, of Loughton, Essex, was charged with possessing cocaine and for its sale or supply. When charged, Wharrie replied; 'No comment' to both charges. Two other men Martin Wanden 44, also known as Anthony Claude Linden of Swanley, Kent, and Joe Daly 40, of Bexley, Kent, were brought before Skibbereen District Court amid tight security, with up to 20 Garda, including uniformed officers, armed detectives and armed members of the Emergency Response squad.

The Irish police had seized 36 items of CCTV footage from premises in West Cork, and a team of ten detectives examined the footage for the purpose of identifying persons on the tapes. At the same time the Garda were awaiting results of a "technical examination" by Spanish police of a catamaran named; 'Lucky Day', which had been detained at La Coruna in North West Spain on the 5th July 2007, following a request from the Director of Public Prosecutions. They examined the GPS navigational system in the hope of being able to trace its movements, while Spanish police were also examining a "mobile phone" found on board the vessel. Also, Spanish police interviewed two men carrying Lithuanian passports who were arrested on board the catamaran, and Garda liaised closely with their Spanish counterparts to try and progress the investigation as quickly as possible. Four of the gang members arrested in Ireland are serving jail sentences ranging from 10 to 30 years. Another two were jailed for 14 and 30 years in the UK. [1]

2008 – "Sea Bright"

In yet another uncover operation, code-named; *"Sea Bright"*, those involved had been under a long term "Obbo" in what was reported as Ireland's record-breaking 1.5 ton haul on the 7th November 2008 - and not to be confused with what I've already mentioned. This haul was expected to have eclipsed Ireland's record find off Co Cork in 2007. 150 miles off south-west Cork. The yacht: *"Dances with Waves"* had been tracked all the way from the Caribbean, and arrived at Castletownbere, County Cork. Two British men and a man from Dublin, all aged between 44 and 52, were arrested in connection with the find. [2][3] It was further reported on the 23rd July 2008, that the Dunlough bay haul put Ireland on the world cocaine map. Irelands 5,000km-long coastline is largely un-policed. Customs, like police forces around the world, now operate mainly on intelligence, whether from detective work, surveillance, criminal informers or information from other law enforcement agencies like the secret service Europol, and even the likes of M15/M16, for drugs and weaponry; 'gun-running' go hand in hand in many cases.

It's long been known that Ireland's coastline is a potential soft spot, for even the EU's police coordinating body; Europol, had warned in recent years that the British and Irish coastlines were vulnerable. [4] And to counter that threat posed to the west European coast, seven states in the EU, including Ireland set up a co-ordinating body to intercept shipments, mainly of cocaine. The shipments, like of the *Lucky Day* or *Dances with Waves* catamarans, came directly from South America or via West Africa. The EU's Maritime Analysis and Operation Centre-Narcotics is based in Portugal and has at its disposal the naval and air resources of the larger EU states, including Britain and Spain. [4]

2011 - Cocaine, Pineapples & Tuna

Still in County Cork, in a joint "Obbo" operation between the Garda National Drugs Unit, the Revenue's Customs Service, Europol, Interpol, and Dutch law enforcement agencies, it was reported on the 14th October 2011, that Seán O'Donovan 45 from Ballinakilla, and 56-year-old Richard Deutschenbauer, said to be a German national, with an address at Alingas in Sweden, were both charged with two offences in relation to 68 kilos of cocaine seized by the Garda in Bartlemy, Cork. The drugs were "found" stored in a shed with an estimated value of €4.8 million. The drugs, which originated in Bolivia, were shipped to Cork via Rotterdam hidden in a consignment of 28 pallets of tinned pineapples. Two days after their arrival in Cork port, on September 28th, 2011, they were collected by a truck provided by O'Donovan.

The consignment had arrived in Cork's port from Rotterdam in the Netherlands, and was taken to the premises in Bartlemy, Fermoy where the seizure itself took place. Another three people were arrested in follow-up searches; two of whom were Irish, aged 42-years-old and 65-years-old, with the third man being a 46-year-old Hungarian national. Seán O'Donovan and Richard Deutschenbaur both pleaded guilty at Cork Circuit

Criminal Court, in March 2012, and the following could be alleged as being some kind of "deal", for Tim O'Leary, defending O'Donovan, said after the indictment, he wanted sentencing adjourned. *"There will be a background story in relation to the matter..."* (This background story will very likely yield other people being arrested.) James O'Mahony, defending Deutschenbaur, asked the same. Then on the 26th June 2012 each were jailed for eight years for their part in this international drugs smuggling operation after they were caught "red handed" according to the Garda in Ireland. They will only serve four years out of their sentences. Arguably not too bad consider the amounts involved. [6a]

12 days later and following the arrests of Seán O'Donovan and Richard Deutschenbaur, and I'm not saying there's any connection in this world of coincidences, it was also reported on the 26th October 2011, that a gang of Liverpool and London-based drug dealers planned to flood Britain with £4 billion worth of cocaine, arranging the plot from a phone box. It's said they were planning to smuggle 40 tonnes of cocaine from South America by sea, hidden inside tins of Tuna and wooden pallets. Liverpool Crown Court heard that the drug would be bought at a "wholesale price" and then sold to other dealers who would cut it and sell it on. As listed further on, in the case of *Operation Junko*, with Jamie Dale, John Cawley and Barry Hartley; where police had admitted in court; *"It's fair to say that if someone has snorted cocaine since 2008, they have snorted some of Dale's product."* That we can safely assume they had; *"...been found to be a party to an agreement to supply criminals, knowing and intending these chemicals would be used to cut controlled drugs to be supplied to others."* [7]

You'll notice that it is reported as saying; *"...the drug would be bought at a "wholesale price" and then sold to other dealers..."* Which means that 'the word' was/is put about that a consignment is due in town, and who wants a slice of the action? Then you have to imagine, if one of these smaller dealers get such information through the grape-vine, and then all of sudden get arrested, they will then very often trade this knowledge with the objective of making a deal with the police, with the likelihood they'd get granted immunity or at the least their sentenced reduced. Though these kinds of informants are then better-off back on the streets 'under Obbo' so as they can then make a deal with the person/s who told them about the new shipment, and so that the police are now ready to pounce and make their arrests.

The Whitney's of Liverpool – 2009-2011

In December 2011, thirteen members of a notorious drug dealing family from Liverpool, with Irish blood and connections, were jailed at Liverpool Crown Court. Described as one of Britain's most shameless and dangerous families, following a long term "Obbo" that started in 2009. Though they were known to the police long before this and were likely under some kind of "Obbo" before the police 'officially' declared their operation. Undercover police officers were deployed posing as drug addicts, who then made test purchases and filmed their illicit deals. When they raided Carol Whitney's home, the police found carrier bags of cash on the kitchen counter and hidden piles of cash amounting to £4,500, as well as 520 wraps of heroin hanging from a bush in the back garden. Cash deposits totalling £114,619 had passed through her bank account. Police called her 'the banker'.

In 2001, Paul Whitney was found guilty of 18 counts of supplying Class A drugs and was sentenced to five years in jail. Those who lived in the same street as the family's four bedroom semi, had often see and knew about the carrier bags of cash exchanging hands on the Whitney's doorstep, but decided to turn a blind eye for fear of reprisals. Throughout the "Obbo", said to be one of Merseyside police's largest surveillance operations, the Whitney's made hundreds of thousands of pounds from what police have described as a '24-hour drugs cash and carry service'. During the 18 months of "Obbo" officers followed the family - on one occasion they saw an accomplice throw 2kg of heroin with a street value of £120,000 from the window of a speeding Mercedes in a bid to avoid being caught with it.

At the head of the family was Leslie Whitney, a 57-year-old former factory worker known as; 'The Godfather'. The couple's three children, Paul, 33, Lisa, 31, and Anthony, 30, were found guilty of conspiracy to supply Class A drugs, along with Lisa's boyfriend Wayne Hincks and Leslie's girlfriend, Emma Mackenzie, 29. Emma's mother Mary McCabe was also part of the gang. When police searched McCabe's car, they found a stolen SA80 assault rifle, stolen from an Army base, and 1,200 rounds of ammunition, stolen from an Army barracks on Salisbury Plain in 2005 and 12kg of heroin with a street value of £600,000. During the raids a year ago, Anthony fled Merseyside. Police later travelled to Spain, where he had become embroiled in another drug-smuggling plot. [20]

Operation Nemesis

It appears various police forces have what is termed; *'Operation Nemesis'*, where in Hampshire it was set up to tackle burglaries, in Staffordshire, it's about targeting suspected drug dealers. They claim proactive police enforcement activity is only part of the story. As Operation Nemesis, is also about working with partners, to help drug-users access help for their addiction, encouraging them to live drug free lives and play a positive role in society. Drugs search warrants are executed at addresses throughout Staffordshire on a frequent basis - some 400 in Stoke-on-Trent alone during 2009/10 - under the Misuse of Drugs Act. Police officers are regularly arresting suspects in connection with drugs offences. Seizures include Class A drugs, Class B drugs, ecstasy pills and significant amounts of cash.

Latest statistics show 2,705 drug offences [Class A and Class B] have been recorded by Staffordshire Police since the launch of Operation Nemesis in September 2007: Sep 07 – March 08 – 1,054, April 08 – March 09 – 870, April 09 – March 10 – 781. The numbers of people who have been arrested in connection with drugs offences [which include supply of, possession, possession with intent to supply, & production and trafficking] since the launch of Operation Nemesis are: Sep 07 – March 08 – 1,100, April 08 – March 09 -1, 483, April 09 – March 10 – 1, 619. To date £2.7m has been recovered through asset recovery linked to the Operation Nemesis campaign. [2a]

Eleven men, aged 28 to 65, involved in the illegal growing of over 800 cannabis plants, with a further 1,600 empty buckets ready for cultivation, were sentenced to a total of 43 years at Staffordshire Crown Court, in February 2012, following being caught whilst 'under Obbo' by Staffordshire Police, in *Operation Nemesis*, that involved more than 40 officers. [3a] Nine of the men pleaded guilty, while two were convicted by jurors. The men, who were mostly from Staffordshire and the West Midlands, had set up a "farm" costing a total of around £1.4 million, with barns installed with generators, fans, lighting and ventilation. Detective Chief Inspector Jane Hewett, from Staffordshire Police, said: *"These men were part of an organised crime group, with criminal links nationwide, who set up one of the country's biggest cannabis factory set-ups."* [4a]

In another "Obbo" operation, in 2009, 250 grams of cocaine, a hydraulic press and the cutting agent *Benzocaine* was seized from a gang of five young men from the Stoke-on-Trent area as part of *Operation Nemesis.* Plain clothes detectives from Staffordshire Police had been watching a house in Warrington Street in Fenton, where's it's said a class-A drug with a street value of more than £700,000 was found. Prosecutor Robert Price said: *"The Benzocaine, if mixed half and half with cocaine, would produce 32kg of sellable cocaine. This would result in crack cocaine worth £22,000 per kilo, netting a total figure of £704,000."*

All admitted conspiracy to supply controlled drugs. Jake Miller, aged 20, was jailed for four-and-a-half years, and Reuben Garswood-Gayle, 20, also from Stoke-on-Trent, was sentenced to two years. Michael Phillips, 19, from Fenton, got three years and Jahcub Shingler, aged 20, also from Fenton, Stoke-on-Trent, was sentenced to two years in jail. John Walklate was given a 12-month sentence suspended for two years and 150 hours unpaid work. All young men and it's very unlikely they set-up such an outfit working alone and why it's highly probable that older and much more experienced gang members were behind the supplying of the drugs, the cutting agent and the hydraulic press. All claimed they had been addicted to cocaine and were involved to either help feed their own habits or to pay-off their 'drug-debts' to 'others', which seems to confirm that someone higher up the Layer-Cake was indeed involved. [11b]

Back in July 2009, Leeds Crown Court heard about two gangs who worked in unison with each other. Christopher Cobby, 39 from Newcastle-under-Lyme was sentenced to 14 years, John Ryder and Mohammed Nazir, pleaded guilty at the beginning of the trial, and got 24 and 26 years respectively for co-ordinating the importation and distribution of heroin right across the north of England.

They were first arrested in November 2008, after a long term "Obbo" by the Serious Organised Crime Agency [SOCA]. During the trial, Leeds Crown Court watched footage of SOCA investigators dismantling two industrial-scale heroin factories, or "bash houses", [where they 'bash', is adding any old cutting agent into the mix] in residential areas of Birmingham and Bradford. Hydraulic presses, respirators, face masks, an industrial blender, bulk quantities of [cutting agent] caffeine powder, part of a hydraulic lift and metal boxes were all recovered. [7a]

Operation Wamego

On the 1st December 2010, it was reported that 21 people were arrested during a series of dawn drug raids in south Liverpool. Around 200 police officers burst into 27 homes across Toxteth and Dingle. Operation Wamego, which targeted suspected cocaine and heroin suppliers, was the culmination of nine months of work by a team of 40 detectives working from information provided by the community. It resulted in police seizing two cars, a quantity of cash and crack cocaine.[10] I've been informed by someone who wishes to remain anonymous; that there was, and still is, a "local-firm" of gangsters who ran the drug scene in Stoke on Trent and Newcastle Upon-Lyme, though not as much now, because the main "players" have since been jailed. They were jailed in June 2010, less than 3 months before Sabina was sentenced to 5yrs. Gary Wakefield, Gerald Tyler and Michael Kidner helped move 725 blocks of cannabis resin worth £400,000 along the M6, and were jailed for a total of more than 14 years.

This originally took place 22 days after Glenn Hollinshead was killed. Stoke-on-Trent Crown Court heard the gang received the drugs on the 11th June 2008, and held them at an address in Ball Green, then changed cars and handed them over to two other men in the chain. Even though they apprehended a large haul of cannabis, the police also said; that in September 2008, 59.86 grams of cocaine was also seized from Wakefield and Tyler. Let's not forget, every seizure of cocaine, also contains a 'cutting' agent. This Stoke-on-Trent gang, also dealt with other people around the country, and that's why 40-year-old Nouredinne Karmass, from Blackpool, and 29-year-old Dil Pazir, from Worcester, were also arrested alongside this trio from Stoke. [11]

Operation Junko

Now oddly enough there was a four year "Obbo" taking place at the very same time Sabina was given the green light, termed; Operation Junko.[18] I find it rather difficult to accept that it was only the following three men involved as that's what happens in the "Layer-Cake", fall-guys who face the rap.

On the 22nd November 2011, Jamie Dale, 32, from Greater Manchester; John Cawley, 31, from Lancashire and Barry Hartley, 63, also from Lancashire, were found guilty of three counts of 'conspiracy to supply' after a two-month trial at Leeds Crown Court. It's said they imported more than 36 tonnes of cutting agent for cocaine, before selling the powder onto dealers at about £1,000 a barrel. The value of their scam was put at more than £3.5bn! The Serious Organised Crime Agency [SOCA] said this was a conservative estimate! They were caught after being 'under Obbo' as part of "undercover operation" by officers who marked their stocks of chemicals bought by the trio. John Wright, who led this "four-year" police operation resulting to their conviction - said: *"The scale of their operation was remarkable"*. He added; *"It's fair to say that if someone has snorted cocaine since 2008, they have snorted some of Dale's product."*

It's also fair to wonder and ask; 'Why on earth was Operation Junko allowed to run for such a long period of time?'

And that's because you have to understand that this worked like a 'honey-pot'. For all the police needed to do was wait until all those other gangs around the country sent their worker bees to go a collect the cutting agent required to help double or treble their yield. The police in turn would have their uncover teams of officers watching from a distance. Photographs and video footage would be taken, telephone calls recorded, listened to and intercepted and when the time is right the 'target' would be raided and in return the police will be rewarded with the 'real thing' as opposed to only a 'cutting agent'.

It makes sense to let such 'front businesses' continue to operate, that people like Jamie Dale, John Cawley and Barry Hartley were running and this must have been one of the main reason why Operation Junko was allowed to continue unhindered and for at least a four year period.

A cutting agent is a chemical used to "cut" (dilute) illegal drugs with something less expensive than the drug itself. Many drugs that reach the street have been cut at the manufacture/producer stage, though many small time dealers then further cut and dilute what's been passed onto them. Drugs such as heroin and cocaine are often 'cut' to appeal to the consumer as opposed to simple diluting the product. The extent of cutting can vary significantly over time, but for the last 15 years or so statistics show that drugs such as heroin and cocaine are often around the 50% purity level. Heroin purity sitting at 50% does not mean 50% cutting agents have been added. The other 50% could be other opiate by-products. Cocaine can often be found to have such cutting agents like *Benzocaine* or *Novacaine* which is an anaesthetic from the cocaine family and mainly used by dentists.

According to a report by Coomber (1997d) [1b] after having street heroin seizures from the UK re-analysed, it was reported that nearly 50% of the samples had no cutting agents present at all. This means that 50% of street heroin in the UK in 1995-97 had worked its way from producer to user without being cut. It's not necessarily illegal to import certain cutting agents such as Novacaine, as it's legally used in dentistry. As is the drug *Ketamine* legally used in human and veterinary medicine and mainly for horses. Its hydrochloride salt is sold as Ketanest, *Ketaset,* and *Ketalar.* At sufficiently high doses users may experience what is called the *"K-hole",* a state of dissociation whose effects are thought to mimic the symptoms of schizophrenia,[1a] and arguably how the Eriksson twins appeared on the M6 motorway.

Operation Happy Fish

We know the Eriksson twins come from Sweden, and that Sabina currently resides in Norway. We also know that smoking hash, is pretty much an everyday occurrence for certain members of the family. As we know, Simon, Sabina's son, who also lives in Norway, has widely and openly spoken on his *MySpace* account, about his interest and activities with cannabis. On January the 11th 2009, it was reported that "Operation Happy Fish" began in the summer of 2007 by police in Norway, which lasted for 18months. It was stated that in Stockholm, Sweden, that an international drug smuggling ring operating in Norway and Sweden had been broken up. Sweden's TT News Service reported that officials had seized more than three-quarters of a ton of narcotics and detained 30 people in Norway and Sweden.

The drug-ring used legal means, such as flower shipments, sent by ship, ferry and land, to help conceal their drug shipments. Norwegian, Swedish, Dutch and Moroccan citizens were among the suspects arrested. [5][5a] *"We noticed that several people had bought quantities of hash and imported them into the country and we noted that these people had close contacts in Sweden,"* said Reidar Brussgaard at Norway's criminal investigation department to news agency TT. Police in Norway contacted their Swedish colleagues who began surveillance of the suspects on visits to Sweden. Swedish police were therefore able to witness the collection of a large quantity of hash from Solvalla outside of Stockholm. The Norwegian-registered car was later stopped at the ferry port by Norwegian customs and around 170 kilograms of cannabis was seized.

After the seizure, the police operation which Norwegian police had named *"Happy fish"*, continued and expanded to involve police in the Netherlands. Stefan Erlandsson at the Swedish National Investigation Department explained that the international police cooperation had been crucial to cracking the network. Norwegian, Swedish, Dutch and Moroccan citizens are among the suspects detained. Several of them have been in work and have on the surface, appeared to live regular lives. Police now claim to have exposed several links of the network. *"We have got the whole chain and have managed to get at the principal figures,"* Erlandsson said.

According to the police the narcotics have been smuggled from Morocco to Holland and then on to Sweden and Norway. The gang used legal means to transport the goods, such as flower shipments used to conceal the drugs. One drug seizure by Norwegian police also netted a number of weapons and a large sum of money. *"There was around six million Norwegian kronor ($862,000) in cash,"* according to Reidar Bruusgaard. He confirms that in total, the Swedish and Norwegian police have managed to seize around 700 kilograms of cannabis and around 50 kilograms of amphetamine. A quantity of cocaine has also been seized.
[5][5a]

Super-grasses

"Supergrass" is a slang-term for an informer who "grasses" on other members of the gang. Throughout history there's been 'grasses' and the police were able to jail the Kray twins on the evidence given by gang member Leslie Payne.

One of Britain's most active armed robbers Bertie "Smalls" was arrested in 1973 and also one of the first police "grasses" to receive the 'Supergrass' nickname. Bertie Smalls, real name Derek Creighton (1935-2008) was born in the East End of London. I recall seeing him at Elton's nightclub in Tottenham during the 1980's. He had a kind of Bob Hoskins look and sound about him, a short, squat man, who loved to emphasis his Cockney accent.

Despite being involved in many violent crimes in London and the south-east area he negotiated himself a deal with the Director of Public Prosecutions Sir Norman Skelhorn, whereby he would go "QE", which means to give Queen's Evidence in trials of his fellow-robbers in exchange for a lighter sentence or complete immunity from all charges. [1a] Although Smalls was generally described as Britain's first Supergrass the former Flying Squad 'Governor' from Scotland Yard, Detective Superintendent Leonard "Nipper" Read, always maintained it was Leslie Payne adviser to the Kray twins who gave evidence against them in 1969, who should have had the title.[1a]

In October 1967, Reggie Kray is alleged to have been encouraged by Ronnie to kill Jack *"the Hat"* McVitie, an associate of the Kray gang who had failed to fulfil a contract which was to kill Leslie Payne. Ronald Kray gave a gun and £100 to McVitie with instructions to murder Payne and the promise of a further £400 [2a] (some say it was more; £1,500[3a]) when the 'job' had taken place. McVitie was lured to a basement flat in Evering Road, Hackney and not far from where I was born and lived - on the pretence of a party. As he entered Reggie Kray pointed a handgun at his head and pulled the trigger twice, but the gun failed to discharge. Ronnie then held McVitie in a bear-hug whilst Reggie was handed a carving knife and stabbed McVitie in the face and stomach, then driving the knife deep into his neck whilst twisting the blade. [2a][4a]

As we know - according to the pathology report into Glenn Hollinshead's death, there were four stab wounds and no defence marks. If he too was held like that of McVitie though obviously not in bear-hug from the front, but someone held Glenn's arms from behind, this would account for the lack of defence wounds.

It seemed that "Bertie Smalls" had set a precedent as many of his former 'associates' soon followed suit once the taboo of 'grassing on your mates' had been broken and went; "QE" as well. Whereas a few of them were given such favourable deals by the police and Crown, getting only five years as opposed to the 18 or more years they could have normally expected.[1a] In 1972, Sir Robert Mark became Commissioner of the Metropolitan Police. In that year alone the annual total of armed robberies in the London district was 380, partly because the culture was rife with bribe-taking, sharing in the proceeds of crime and *"Verballing-up"* which means the police would say the "suspect" had confessed or said something they never did or fabricating evidence against them. [5a] Sir Robert Mark felt compelled to remind his detectives which side of the law they were supposed to be on and told them in his inaugural address: *"A good police force is one that catches more criminals than it employs."* It could be argued this wasn't an exception and took place all around the country and in other forces, though perhaps not on such as a grand scale as London. [5a]

Take Gary Padgett,[1] who exposed a gang in 2003 and who Stephen Kelsall, then aged 36, from Newcastle-under-Lyme, was part of - after Padgett's mate and drug-dealer Philip Smith was shot dead near Bradford in 2002.

269

Padgett now needs 24/7 police protection just like those people who are part of the 'Witness Protection Programme', they are given new identities if they so wish and place's to move to. However, not all 'Supergrasses' are exposed as being so. Many inform on other people to get a 'lesser sentence' and it's done in such a way the persons they have informed on have no idea they have been 'grassed-up'. They might have an inclination they have been though it's so cleverly done they're always in doubt. The police will make it appear you were caught simply as being part of the "Obbo" - and that's how it works.

Probably Britain's most prolific modern day Supergrass was Michael Michael, whose evidence led to 34 people being jailed for 170 years and the dismantling of 26 different drug gangs. Information about Michael's work as an informer were kept secret until December 2001, when a judge at Woolwich Crown Court sentenced him to six years in jail. Reporting restrictions that had been in place for three years were lifted.[2]

Michael's was a former hairdresser who was 'under Obbo', and who too became a target from customs detectives that on the 25th April 1998, Customs investigators launched an "Obbo" codenamed *Operation Draft*. [3] It uncovered 16kg of cocaine, 2.9 tons of cannabis worth £11.6 million, guns and £800,000 in cash. He had been identified as a member of a drug ring, based at the Lee industrial estate in Hertfordshire.

They were smuggling cannabis and cocaine into the country in cars, a coach, nicknamed the *Fun Bus*, and an oil tanker. When officers arrested him after four months, Michael's was wearing body armour and brandished a gun. Woolwich Crown Court heard that Michael's alleged he was paying his 'police handler' up to £10,000 a week in return for providing information; *"of great value"*. He claimed the officer turned a blind eye to the drug smuggling. Tracey Kirby, 38, a former *Sun* page three model, received three years after admitting being a money courier for Michael's. [4]

Michael's evidence led to drugs worth £49m being recovered from a distribution network that is thought to have smuggled more than 110 kg of cocaine and 19,000 kg of cannabis into Britain. Michael has also alleged that a corrupt police officer took £10,000 cash hand-outs from him. [2][3] Including drug smuggling, money laundering and prostitution, it brought him in an estimated fortune of £107million. Among the people Michael Michael had informed on were his own wife Lynn, given a 24-month jail sentence suspended for two years for her role as a cash courier, his younger brother Xanthos, his lover Sue Richards and Janice Marlborough his business lieutenant who ran his string of brothels were all grassed-up. He admitted one count of conspiracy to import cocaine, a similar charge involving cannabis and three conspiracies charges to launder the proceeds. He has also pleaded guilty to possessing a firearm. [2][3] He is thought to have been given a new identity under the terms of the witness protection programme. [2][3]

In 1981 Christopher Black, after securing assurances that he would be granted immunity he gave statements which led to 38 arrests. On 5 August 1983, 22 members of the Provisional IRA were sentenced to a total of more than 4,000 cumulative years in prison, based on Black's testimonies alone (eighteen of these convictions were overturned on appeal on 17 July 1986). [5] By the end of 1982, 25 more 'Supergrasses' had surfaced contributing to the arrests of over six hundred people. Many convictions based on 'Supergrass' testimony were later overturned and the 'Supergrass' system was discontinued in 1985 and until re-emerging recently in 2011. Though to get around this problem many people are 'grassed on' though no testaments are used against them - though it's normally enough to justify an "Obbo" on those the police now have such information on. The first 'Supergrass' trial in 26 years began on the 8th of September 2011, for the murder of UDA member Tommy English. [5]

Staffordshire Police -Annual Report for 2009/10

SPFAR: On 20 May 2008 Glen Hollinshead had been drinking with Sabina Eriksson and had offered her accommodation for the night. [1] (Does the report seems to suggest, that Sabina and Glenn may had already been in perhaps a pub drinking, or are they referring to what took place back at Glenn's house?)

SPFAR: 'A neighbour later saw Glen stumble out of his back door saying; "she has stabbed me" before collapsing and dying. An ambulance crew found him with three stab wounds which proved fatal'. (Though this is inconsistent to the corners report and what the two post-mortems revealed, carried out by pathologists Dr Kola and Dr Shorrocks respectively, Glenn was stabbed four times.)

SPFAR: 'The crew also found a blonde female who had hit herself on the head with a hammer. The hammer was taken from her but she ran off and jumped off onto the A50 carriageway causing severe injuries to her ankles'. (We are not sure what the police are trying to suggest in regards to what came first in the order of events and why we have raised the problem of the inconsistent timings. See the part about how we question the fact how a fleeing murderer who left all their personal items behind in a blind panic, happened to only get yards from Glenn's house and seconds after Mr Booth the neighbour had time to call 999, yet that the ambulance crew was already on the scene of where Sabina was at the end of Duke street.)

SPFAR: 'Prior to meeting Glen Hollinshead, Sabina and her sister had been travelling by coach from Liverpool to London.' (Like that of the BBC documentary there is no mention they had at first been to St Anne Street Police Station in Liverpool where Sabina reported that she was concerned for the safety of her two children after being kidnapped - and we have to question why is this the case?)

SPFAR: 'When the coach stopped for a 'driver change' at Keele Services the sisters left the coach. Their actions at the services caused concern.' (As we've already stated there are three versions of events as to what had allegedly occurred here. Melissa Dutton's statement of; *"The coach driver explains there were two girls on his coach acting very suspiciously. He wasn't willing to let them back on the coach again, so could I deal with it."* This clearly contradicts the police version of events that there was a 'driver change'.)

SPFAR: 'The sisters were later seen walking up the central reservation of the M6. The Highways Patrol and Central Motorway Police Group (CMPG) attempted to remove the sisters from the motorway, but whilst doing so both sisters ran into the oncoming traffic with Sabina's sister receiving leg injuries.' (It's also not mentioned in the *Madness in the Fast Lane* documentary as to why the Eriksson twins were actually heading back in a Northern direction as opposed to the South if they were wanting to go to London. And why we examined the possible reason as to why they may have decided to head North ways for we believe it was the twins' intention to go to Newcastle-

273

under-Lyme in which is the main bordering town of Keele and Stoke-on-Trent. As you leave Keele Services if you head northwards then less than a mile away it's a bridge-way and road known as Three Mill Lane, the twins were nearer to that road than Keele Services, when they were approached by the Highways Patrol officers. It seems that is what they were heading for, and probably misunderstood the 'locals' cut through which is via Three Mile Lane, though behind Keele services.)

SPFAR: 'Sabina was arrested and subsequently appeared at Fenton Magistrates where she was charged and released'. (Despite the seriousness of the twins actions, particular in the case of Sabina; an assault on a police officer and endangering lives of the general public, they don't mention she was only sentenced to 'one day' imprisonment.)

SPFAR: 'The trial in this matter took a considerable time to come to court. This was due to Sabina's lengthy recuperation from her injuries and difficulties in obtaining psychiatric reports as her classification as a 'Category A' (Cat A), offender meant she was moved out of the county.' (This seems rather a ridiculous claim. Sabina was in hospital for approximately three months. Are we to believe it took the police more than one year and four months to get psychiatric reports? The moving out of the local county wouldn't affect any court timings or dates.)

SPFAR: 'The location of the trial was also moved as the incident on the M6 was televised shortly before the trial commenced'. (We are not sure what this has to do with anything for even though it was televised Sabina had made several court appearances at Staffordshire Magistrate Courts via Court TV, then at Stoke-on-Trent Crown Court, Nottingham Crown Court and finalising in Luton Crown Court. If anything the Hollinshead family thought this procedure was more along the lines that it made it virtually impossible for all the family to have kept going to all the different locations and so as they couldn't really see or hear how the hearings were actually developing.)

SPFAR: 'Sabina Eriksson pleaded guilty to manslaughter with diminished responsibility and was given a five years sentence.' (As covered elsewhere, the weakness of the case against Sabina - and why an 'advance indication of sentence' was probably employed at the beginning of the trial, where the judge would have invited both counsels into his chambers and gave his views about the strength of the prosecution case. And where technically a 'deal' is struck and why it appears Sabina went from a person who never made a single comment following advice from her defence team to a person who accepted the lesser of the two charges. She had been on a murder charge right up until that final moment of when she was then sentenced to five years.) [1d]

IPCC

Another eye-opener and surprise was to learn how the IPCC work. For instance when you initially contact the IPCC complaining about a police force, they request you give them permission to then pass your complaint over to the police force you are complaining about. They say; *'...each police force is responsible for considering complaints made against that force and for recording complaints. If you are not happy with the police's decision on recording this compliant, you have a right to appeal to us.'* So from the very start of your complaint you face a dilemma. For why else would someone wish to go to an "independent" body if it turned out they were not to intervene from the beginning and hand your complaint straight over to the body you are complaining about? Why are people not told from the onset - that this is what will happen to their complaint?

In defence of this procedure we can of course understand the 'level' of complaint. If for instance you may wish to complain about the way you were perhaps treated by a particular police force or officer or complain about the method of arrest or your time in custody etc. then perhaps these matters could be addressed by the actual police force involved. However, in more serious cases such as a murder you'd expect the IPCC to be there from the on-start of the complaint. They say in their; 'Frequently asked questions': *"The severity of the complaint will determine how it should be resolved. In certain circumstances the complaint would be referred to the IPCC who may oversee a police investigation by conducting a supervised or managed investigation, or in the most serious cases handle the complaint using our own team of investigators."*

This is why from the very beginning of our complaint we urged the IPCC to appoint a team of their own investigators. Yet our request was ignored so I contacted the IPCC and raised our concerns, the "Customer Contact Advisor" became somewhat incensed and hardly the way you expect a person who is meant to be "completely independent" of the police to react. He then let slip; *"It doesn't work like that in the force."* I picked up on that straight away and asked; *'...was that a Freudian-slip of the tongue? What did you mean by the force?* He totally ignored my question and tried to defend his line of thought and justify why the IPCC will not intervene as yet. I assume he's an ex-police officer now working for the IPCC.

I was not happy with this response so wrote to Dame Anne Owers, Chair of the IPCC. She didn't reply herself, but I got a reply from an IPCC "Casework Manager". She ironically gave me an address to 'complain' about the Customer Contact Advisor. But I wasn't complaining about that, his comment just confirmed that at the first line of defence at the IPCC the department is probably run by ex-police officers. I was more concerned about the IPCC not appointing a 'team of their own investigators', due to the 'unusualness and severity' of the complaint. So in order for the IPCCs Casework Manager to get around my line of questioning; '...The severity of the complaint will determine how it should be resolved.', and the Hollinshead family's continuous appeal for the IPCC to get involved from the beginning, - they now seemed to have changed the goal posts stating they will only directly get involved in complaints; '...such as police shootings and deaths in custody...' Whereas we argue the IPCC should be involved in all cases that involve a 'murder'. And if that's now the case, then why is this not the answer on their 'Frequently asked questions?'

McKenzie Friend

A McKenzie friend assists a litigant in person in a common law court. This person does not need to be legally qualified. The crucial point is that litigants in person are entitled to have assistance, lay or professional, unless there are exceptional circumstances.

Their role was set out most clearly in the eponymous 1970 case *McKenzie v. McKenzie*.[1] Although this role applies in the jurisdiction of England and Wales, it is regarded as having its origins in common law and hence has been adopted in practice in other common law

277

jurisdictions, such as Australia, Canada, Hong Kong, Ireland, New Zealand and the United States.

McKenzie v. McKenzie was a divorce case in England.[2] Levine McKenzie, who was petitioning for divorce, had been legally aided but the legal aid had been withdrawn prior to the case going to court. Unable to fund legal representation, McKenzie had broken off contact from his solicitors, Geoffrey Gordon & Co. However, one day before the hearing, Geoffrey Gordon & Co. sent the case to an Australian barrister in London, Ian Hanger, whose qualifications in law in Australia did not allow him to practise as a barrister in London. Hanger hoped to sit with his client to prompt him, take notes, and suggest questions in cross-examination, thereby providing what quiet assistance he could from the bar table to a man representing himself. The trial judge ordered Hanger that he must not take any active part in the case except to advise McKenzie during adjournments and must sit in the public gallery of the court. Hanger assumed his limited role was futile, and did not return for the second day of the trial.[2]

The case went against McKenzie, who then appealed to the Court of Appeal, on the basis that he had been denied representation. On 12 June 1970, the Court of Appeal ruled that the Judge's intervention had deprived McKenzie of assistance to which he was entitled, and ordered a retrial.[3]

Ian Hanger AM QC, the original McKenzie friend, is now a Queen's Counsel at the Queensland Bar.[2][4]

May we thank you for reading our findings and story
and look forward to hearing to your comments, opinions
and reviews of the book if you so wish. You can contact
us on our website, *Facebook* page, or *Youtube* channel.

www.amadnesssharedbytwo.com
https://www.facebook.com/AMadnessSharedByTwo
https://www.youtube.com/watch?feature=player_embed
ded&v=VJYb7QnV8nE

Sources:

Our Investigation

[1] http://www.religioustolerance.org/fam_love.htm
[2] □ ^ Huxley J (1992). "Sunday Times: Sex-cult children held – Children of God". The Sunday Times (Sydney) 1992-05-17.
[3] http://www.dailymail.co.uk/news/article-2011655/US-army-test-real-life-Iron-Man-exoskeleton-gives-soldiers-super-strength.html
[4 http://12160.info/profiles/blogs/sabina-erikson
[5] □ ^ Richelson, JT (ed.) (2001-09-10). "Science, Technology and the CIA: A National Security Archive Electronic Briefing Book". George Washington University. Retrieved 2009-06-12.
[6] ^ a b "Senate MKULTRA Hearing: Appendix C--Documents Referring to Subprojects, (page 167, in PDF document page numbering)." (PDF). Senate Select Committee on Intelligence and Committee on Human Resources. August 3, 1977. Archived from the original on 2007-11-28. Retrieved 2007-08-22.

The "Official" Storyline

[1] ^ a b c d e f g h i j k l m "Why was Sabina Eriksson free to kill?". The Sentinel. 3 September 2009. Retrieved 31 August 2010.
[2] ^ "Could M6 film of killer have saved victim?". The Sentinel. 7 September 2009. Retrieved 31 August 2010.
[3] a b Madness In The Fast Lane Retrieved 3 February 2011.
[4] a b c "Kvinnans äldre bror: De guilty to manslaughter". The Sentinel. 2 September 2009. Retrieved 31 August 2010.
[5] a b c d e f g "How killer Sabina Eriksson ended up in Stoke-on-Trent to stab Glenn Hollinshead to death...". The Sentinel. 3 September 2009. Retrieved 1 September 2010.
[6] a b c d e f "M6 dash woman jailed over killing". BBC News. 26 November 2009. Retrieved 31 August 2010.
[7] a b "Motorway dash woman stabbed man". BBC News. 2 September 2009. Retrieved 31 August 2010.
[8] a b c d e f "TV Review: Madness In The Fast Lane – BBC1". The Sentinel. 11 August 2010. Retrieved 31 August 2010.
[9] a b c d e f g "Friend haunted by memories of killer". The Sentinel. 4 September 2009. Retrieved 31 August 2010.
[10] a b "Devastated family call for answers over killing". The Sentinel. 3 September 2009. Retrieved 31 August 2010.
[11] a b c Wilkes, David (3 September 2009). "Woman locked up for making mad dash across M6 stabbed stranger to death the day after she was released from jail". Daily Mail. Retrieved 31 August 2010.
[12] ^ "'I tried to make sure dying man wasn't on his own'". The Sentinel. 5 September 2009. Retrieved 1 September 2010.
[13] ^ Chaytor (4 September 2009). "YouTube motorway chicken stabbed stranger two days later". The Mirror. Retrieved 31 August 2010.
[14] ^ "Stab accused in wheelchair". The Sentinel. 20 September 2008. Retrieved 31 August 2010.

[15] ^ "Woman in court on murder charge". The Sentinel. 23 February 2009. Retrieved 31 August 2010.
[16] ^ "Murder case put on hold". The Sentinel. 24 February 2009. Retrieved 31 August 2010.
[17] ^ "Judge told killer was mentally ill". The Sentinel. 26 November 2009. Retrieved 31 August 2010.
[18] ^ a b "Killer had psychiatric disorder". BBC News. 25 November 2009. Retrieved 31 August 2010.
[19] ^ "Update: Woman pleads guilty to manslaughter". The Sentinel. 2 September 2009. Retrieved 31 August 2010.
[20] ^ "Murder trial set to start". The Sentinel. 1 September 2009. Retrieved 31 August 2010.
[21] ^ "Swede Sabina jailed for five years for fatal stabbing". The Sentinel. 26 November 2009. Retrieved 31 August 2010.
[22] ^ "Short madness sparks tragedy". The Sentinel. 27 November 2009. Retrieved 31 August 2010.
[23] ^ "TV Preview: Madness In The Fast Lane – BBC1, 10.35 pm". The Sentinel. 10 August 2010. Retrieved 31 August 2010.

The Eriksson's

[1] https://www.flashback.org/t760519p59
[2] https://www.flashback.org/t760519p60
[3] https://www.flashback.org/t760519p64
[4] https://www.flashback.org/t760519p67
[5] https://www.flashback.org/t760519p68
[6] http://i34.tinypic.com/335e25h.jpg
[6a] http://www.thisisstaffordshire.co.uk/Swede-Sabina-jailed-years-fatal-stabbing/story-12547528-detail/story.html]
[7] http://www.myspace.com/charger420
[8] magnus.hellberg@expressen.se
[9] http://www.expressen.se/Nyheter/1.1313903/kvinnans-aldre-bror-de-var-jagade-av-galningar
[10] http://www.topix.com/forum/world/T9UCI92MJUH9BVP22/p3
[11] http://www.myspace.com/charger420

Sabina's Mystery Partner

[a]
http://www.spokeo.com/search?q=Michael+v+dossou#Georgia:6441888611
[b]
http://www.spokeo.com/search?q=Michael+v+dossou#Duluth,+GA:32453741 7
[c]
http://www.spokeo.com/search?q=Michael+v+dossou#Duluth,+GA:69263359 11
[d] http://marriagesintexas.com/1993/089864.html
[e]
http://www.spokeo.com/search?q=Michael+v+dossou#Georgia:9780563411

[f]
http://www.spokeo.com/search?q=Michael+v+dossou#Marietta,+GA:978056
5011
[g]http://www.spokeo.com/search?q=Michael+v+dossou#Marietta,+GA:6926
351611
[h]
http://www.spokeo.com/search?q=Michael+v+dossou#Smyrna,+GA:9780557
411
[i]
http://www.spokeo.com/search?q=Michael+v+dossou#Smyrna,+GA:9780556
511
[j]
http://www.spokeo.com/search?q=Michael+v+dossou#Smyrna,+GA:9780556
511
[k] http://www.spokeo.com/search?q=Michael+v+dossou#Texas:6926337911
[L] http://www.spokeo.com/search?q=Michael+v+dossou#Texas:9780559011

The "Ferry" Crossing

[1] http://www.thisisstaffordshire.co.uk/killer-Sabina-Eriksson-ended-Stoke-Trent-stab-Glenn-Hollinshead-death/story-12570387-detail/story.html
[2] http://topdocumentaryfilms.com/madness-in-the-fast-lane/
[3]https://ssl.directferries.com/ferry/secure/multi_price_detail.aspx?stdc=DF1
0&grid=0&rfid=18&psgr=2&curr=1&retn=False
[4] http://travel.usatoday.com/flights/story/2012-05-07/A-business-travel-nightmare-Flying-to-the-wrong-city/54814492/1
[5] http://travellerspace-gypsyroads.blogspot.co.uk/2012/04/city-councils-linehouses-gypsy-and.html
[6]http://webapps.stoke.gov.uk/uploadedfiles/North%20Housing%20Market%20Area%20GTAA%20-%20Final%20Report%20.pdf

The Coach Journey - Why on the M6?

[1] http://sentinel.vlex.co.uk/vid/truth-never-revealed-senseless-killing-65975200
[2] http://www.mirror.co.uk/news/uk-news/m6-terror-alert-driver-david-1135633
[3] http://smugglers.jigsy.com/entries/general/woman-arrested-in-cocaine-swoop---news---warwick-courier
[4] ^ a b c d e f g "How killer Sabina Eriksson ended up in Stoke-on-Trent to stab Glenn Hollinshead to death...". The Sentinel. 3 September 2009. Retrieved 1 September 2010.
[5] http://www.guardian.co.uk/world/2012/jul/05/m6-coach-passengers-evacuated-police
[6] http://smugglers.jigsy.com/entries/general/woman-arrested-in-cocaine-swoop---news---warwick-courier

"Arrested" Under the 1983 Mental Health Act

[1]http://www.cnwl.nhs.uk/uploads/SECTION_136_POLICE_POWER_TO_REMOVE_TO_A_PLACE_OF_SAFETY.pdf
[2] http://www.direct.gov.uk/en/DisabledPeople/RightsAndObligations/Police/DG_4018603
[3] http://www.liveleak.com/view?i=c93_1222391289
[3b]http://www.youtube.com/watch?v=gbusYLYRfiY
[4] ^ a b section 28, Police and Criminal Evidence Act 1984
[5] ^ Police and Criminal Evidence Act 1984, section 28.
[6] ^ Taylor v Thames Valley Police [2004] EWCA Civ 858, [2004] 1 WLR 3155, [2004] 3 All ER 503 (6 July 2004), Court of Appeal
[7] ^ Code C to the Police and Criminal Evidence Act 1984, para. 10.5.
[8] ^ a b section 28, Police and Criminal Evidence Act 1984
[9] ^ Police and Criminal Evidence Act 1984, section 28.
[9a] ^NHSexposed.com
[9b] ^NHS Exposed - The Truth Behind The White Coat - A Killing Field - Ward 87, City General Hospital, Stoke-on-Trent
[9c] ^ NHSexposed.com
[10] http://www.whatdotheyknow.com/request/92307/response/232926/attach/html/3/Section%20136%20Mental%20Health%20Act..doc.html
[11] http://www.youtube.com/watch?feature=player_embedded&v=UHH0bysjkpM
[12] http://www.youtube.com/watch?feature=player_embedded&v=XI2RbVimZK0
[13] http://www.irishexaminer.com/ireland/crime/pair-guilty-over-48m-cocaine-haul-186216.html#ixzz1u9UUPCjQ
[14] Maisto, Stephen A.; Mark Galizio, Gerard Joseph Connors (2004). *Drug Use and Abuse*. Thompson Wadsworth. ISBN 0-15-508517-4.
[15] Development of PCP, 2006 ,CESAR (Center for Substance Abuse Research)
[16] Drugs and Behavior, 4th Edition, McKim, William A., ISBN 0-13-083146-8

Under "Obbo"

[1] a b Silk to return to court in 2012 The Guardian, 30th March 2011
[2] http://www.bbc.co.uk/iplayer/episode/b01jxrjh/Silk_Series_2_Episode_5/

The Killing of Glenn

[1] http://www.thisisstaffordshire.co.uk/killer-Sabina-Eriksson-ended-Stoke-Trent-stab-Glenn-Hollinshead-death/story-12570387-detail/story.html
[2] http://sentinel.vlex.co.uk/vid/die-alone-neighbour-waited-dying-stab-66400110

[3] http://www.thisisderbyshire.co.uk/Drug-dealers-jailed-combined-total-27-years/story-11582921-detail/story.html
[4] http://www.metro.co.uk/news/715071-drug-barons-tortured-their-runners

The weakness of the case against Sabina Eriksson - Plea Bargain

[1] ^ Kennedy, Ludovic (1961). Ten Rillington Place. London: Victor Gollancz Ltd. p. 51
[2]http://www.sense-agency.com/icty/three-months-in-prison-for-false-evidence-and-bribing-witnesses.29.html?cat_id=1&news_id=11614
[3] http://www.guardian.co.uk/environment/2011/jan/10/mark-kennedy-undercover-cop-activist

Conclusion

[1] http://www.dailymail.co.uk/news/article-2203524/Hillsborough-disaster-cover-How-Establishment-closes-ranks-protect-own.html#ixzz26YleqG84
[2] http://www.dailymail.co.uk/news/article-2203524/Hillsborough-disaster-cover-How-Establishment-closes-ranks-protect-own.html#ixzz26YHp5CPx

Appendix

"Obbo's & Drug Dealers

[1]
http://www.thefreelibrary.com/Mailbox+drugs+gang+jailed+for+global+plot.-a0120083767
[2] http://news.bbc.co.uk/1/hi/wales/1709466.stm
[3] http://www.drugsandalcohol.ie/6792/
[4] http://smugglers.jigsy.com/entries/general/woman-arrested-in-cocaine-swoop---news---warwick-courier

Operation Junko

[1] http://www.bbc.co.uk/news/uk-england-15843539
[2] Coomber, R. (1997b) The Adulteration of Drugs: What Dealers Do, What Dealers Think, Addiction Research, Vol 5, No. 4. pp. 297-306
[3] Giannini AJ (1999). Drug Abuse. Los Angeles: Health Information Press. p. 104. ISBN 1-885987-11-0.

Operation Happy Fish

[1] http://www.upi.com/Top_News/2009/01/11/Officials-European-drug-ring-busted/UPI-14811231719243/#ixzz1u45c2bYx
[2] http://www.thelocal.se/16848/20090111/

2006 – Turf Wars

[1] http://banuspuerto.blogspot.co.uk/2008_02_01_archive.html
[2] http://costadelcrime.blogspot.co.uk/2012_05_01_archive.html

2007 - 10th biggest haul of cocaine in the world

[1] http://www.upi.com/Top_News/2009/01/11/Officials-European-drug-ring-busted/UPI-14811231719243/#ixzz1u45c2bYx

2008 – "Sea Bright"

[1] http://news.bbc.co.uk/1/hi/world/europe/7715905.stm
[2] http://www.metro.co.uk/news/392469-403m-of-cocaine-seized-from-luxury-yacht#ixzz1u9MTsIYy
[3] http://www.irishexaminer.com/archives/2008/0723/ireland/dunlough-bay-seizure-among-worlds-largest-68004.html#ixzz1u44nv7Xv

2011 - Cocaine, Pineapples & Tuna

[1]
http://www.irishtimes.com/newspaper/ireland/2012/0626/1224318727420.htm
l
[2] http://www.mirror.co.uk/news/uk-news/4-billion-cocaine-ring-gang-275896

The Whitney's of Liverpool – 2009-2011

[1] http://www.dailymail.co.uk/femail/article-2068358/The-Godmothers-How-matriarchs-respectable-Liverpool-family-built-crime-empire-living-invalidity-benefits.html#ixzz1zJr6JGto

Operation Nemesis

[1]
http://www.staffordshire.police.uk/advice_zone/drugs/op_nemesis/how_does_
it_work/
[2] http://staffslive.co.uk/2012/02/29/gang-sentenced-after-staffordshire-police-operation-nemesis-drug-raid/
[3]http://www.staffordshire.police.uk/local_policing/cannock/cannock_south/l
ocal_news/?view=News&itemKey=1812912
[4] http://www.thisisstaffordshire.co.uk/Jail-man-cocaine-press-gran-s-garage/story-12515527-detail/story.html
[5] http://www.soca.gov.uk/news/430-convicted-drugs-trafficker-to-hand-over-illicit-profits

Operation Wamego

[1] http://www.liverpoolecho.co.uk/liverpool-news/local-news/2010/11/30/south-liverpool-drug-raids-net-21-arrests-100252-27739401/
[2] http://www.thisisstaffordshire.co.uk/Trio-jailed-role-cannabis-supply/story-12499938-detail/story.html

Super-grasses

[1a] http://www.guardian.co.uk/uk/2008/feb/12/ukcrime1
[2a] http://www.met.police.uk/history/krays.htm
[3a] http://en.wikipedia.org/wiki/Kray_twins
[4a] ^ Read, Leonard. Nipper Read, The Man Who Nicked The Krays. Time Warner Paperbacks 2001. p.291-292. ISBN 0-7515-3175-8
[5a]http://www.telegraph.co.uk/opinion/main.jhtml?xml=/opinion/2004/05/19/do1901.xml&sSheet=/opinion/2004/05/19/ixopinion.html
[1] http://britainsunderworld.blogspot.co.uk/2011/06/on-run-in-amsterdam.html
[2] ^ a b c Gangster supergrass jailed | UK news | The Guardian
[3] ^ http://www.thisislondon.co.uk/news/article-811197-britains-biggest-supergrass.do
[4] ^ Supergrass shopped 34 crooks - even his mother | Mail Online
[5] ^ Informers crippling IRA...; The Times; 25 Mar 1982; pg1 col E

Staffordshire Police -Annual Report for 2009/10

[1] http://www.staffordshirepoliceauthority.org.uk/policies/annual_reports/

McKenzie Friend

[1]^ [1971] P 33; [1970] 3 WLR 472; [1970] 3 All ER 1034, CA
[2] ^ a b c Forsyth, John (4 May 2009). "Little help from my friends". The Scotsman. Retrieved 26 April 2010.
[3] ^ "Litigant In Person Has Right To Assistance" (Law report), The Times, 17 June 1970, p. 8.
[4] ^ "Council Members". National Alternative Dispute Resolution Advisory Committee. Retrieved 26 April 2010.